IDEOLOGIES
AND UTOPIAS

IDEOLOGIES
AND UTOPIAS

*The Impact of
the New Deal on
American Thought*

by

ARTHUR A. EKIRCH, Jr.

彡 彡 彡

CHICAGO
QUADRANGLE BOOKS
1969

To
K. L. E.

Preface

THE NEW DEAL came to power in the midst of a profound crisis for the United States. The political beneficiary of the gravest economic collapse in the nation's history, the first Roosevelt administration was able to reverse the psychology of defeat that gripped the country in 1932. In the slow process of social and economic recovery after the Great Crash of 1929, many of the historic postulates of the American dream underwent a drastic shift. Swept aside with the simple mass faith in the idea of inevitable progress were the easy shibboleths of the cult of prosperity set forth by a number of the leading business and political figures of the 1920's. In their place, the regulation and reform of the American economy, through the aegis of the federal government under strong presidential leadership, became the new reigning belief and political philosophy.

The varied ideologies and utopias that were at the intellectual center of the New Deal gradually restored a measure of hope and new life to the American scene. But in this process of revival and rebirth in the 1930's, American history was also changed. And at the close of the decade, Americans were confronted again by the challenge of world war.

Whatever the final verdict of history, it seems likely that the

New Deal will rank, and be remembered, as a revolutionary era in American thinking. Obviously many of its ideas continue to influence and affect our lives today. More than in any other comparable period of the American past, the years from 1929 to 1941 transformed the traditional values and attitudes of the American people, conditioning them to look, as never before, to the national state as the basic arbiter and fundamental factor in their lives. Nationalism, with much of the pomp and circumstance hitherto associated only with European monarchies and ancient empires, became a prominent characteristic of the changed American environment and popular outlook. This nationalism or statism of the New Deal inaugurated the real revolution in modern American life and thought.

Although my book cannot pretend to be a general intellectual history of the thirties, encompassing all the diverse ideas and cultural interests of that decade, it is based on a wide reading of New Deal literature—both primary sources and secondary works. The detailed bibliographical references to these materials may be found in the citations of the notes. Major depositories and collections are listed in the Note on Sources.

In undertaking this study, I have incurred a number of obligations or intellectual debts to persons and institutions, particularly the State University of New York, which granted me a Faculty Fellowship for the summers of 1966 and 1967.

To the many librarians who have satisfied my quest for books, I express my sincere appreciation. At the National Archives, Jane F. Smith and her assistants ably helped me to locate diffuse materials. Director Elizabeth Drewry and the staff of the Franklin D. Roosevelt Library at Hyde Park were similarly efficient. Students in my graduate seminars at the American University in Washington, D.C., and at the State University of New York at Albany have contributed importantly to my knowledge by their essays and dissertations.

Several friends and colleagues have called to my attention, or made available to me, materials that I might otherwise have over-looked. In this regard, I am indebted especially to Belisario Con-treras, Richard Lowitt, Catharine Newbold, and Susan Shafarzek.

Norman Thomas kindly allowed me to use his papers, and Allan Nevins extended the same courtesy for the James Truslow Adams Papers. Unfortunately, Professor Nevins' recent personal memoir of Adams was not published until after I had completed my own research and writing.

For permission to quote from collections in their custody, I am indebted to the Franklin D. Roosevelt Library at Hyde Park (the FDR Papers); the Houghton Library at Cambridge, Massa-chusetts (the Oswald Garrison Villard Papers); and the Yale University Library (the W. L. Cross Papers in the *Yale Review* archive in the Collection of American Literature).

Kendall Birr and William Neumann did me the great favor of reading critically the entire manuscript.

I have dedicated this book to my sister, who shared with me those eventful years of our youth in the 1930's.

A. A. E.

Albany, New York
1969

Contents

IDEOLOGIES
AND UTOPIAS

ONE

The Crisis in the
American Dream

Two YEARS after the fateful stock market crash of October 1929, in the midst of the deepening economic depression, a distinguished American historian published one of the most widely read books of the 1930's. The overriding question posed by James Truslow Adams in his work, to which he gave the title *The Epic of America*, was what the fate of the American dream, as he called it, would be.

Centuries before the birth of the United States, the special deity of the Aztec Indians was a bearded god of white skin who had promised to return and was still awaited. From this primitive hope can be dated, perhaps, the remote antecedents of the American dream, and from 1492, when Columbus and his three tiny ships were sighted off the coast of North America, its first dim realization.

Many decades later, during the American Revolution, a young patriotic poet composed a long epic entitled *The Vision of Columbus*. In his poem Joel Barlow depicted the consequences of Columbus' voyage in the form of a dream in which the ghost of the great explorer was comforted by the knowledge that his discovery had not been in vain. Throughout the vast history of the New World, from the ancient Indian civilizations in Peru and Mexico to the founding of the Spanish and British colonies and later the success of the United States in its revolution, Barlow saw the hand of God guiding the new American republic in the course of its progressive destiny.

> In this extended view,
> Behold the path, thy changing race pursue,
> See, thro' the whole, the same progressive plan,
> That draws for mutual succour, man to man,
> From friends to tribes, from tribes to realms ascend,
> Their powers, their interests and their passions blend;
> . . . .
> Till tribes and states and empires find their place,
> And one wide interest sways the peaceful race.[1]

The concept of the American dream, which many disillusioned and bewildered Americans in the darkest days of the depression were ready to dismiss as beyond recall, played an important role in American history. To the early discoverers, and to the settlers who had fled the political and religious strife of the Old World, the virgin North American continent was a New Eden or El Dorado, rich in the promise of unsurpassed material and spiritual rewards. Building their Bible Commonwealth in the wilderness, the New England Puritans, like the ancient Hebrews, considered themselves to be God's chosen people. And in the Thirteen Colonies this same sense of grandeur and uniqueness was reinforced and fulfilled by the glorious triumph of the American Revolution. Confident of their manifest destiny and of the inevitability of their progress, the American people believed they had a mission to educate the rest of the world in the virtues of republican government and free institutions.

Americans were optimistic because within their own lifetime they could see tangible results: they had spanned a continent and tamed the wilderness. Already by the close of the nineteenth century the United States, despite the trauma of its Civil War, was the premier industrial and agricultural nation of the world. And at the dawn of the new century, American fighting men crossed the oceans to plant the American flag on distant shores, thus adding new worldwide dimensions to the American dream.

If imperialism seemed somehow alien to American traditions, at least the new overseas interests of the United States were not untouched with idealism. A war for democracy, "for the ultimate peace of the world and for the liberation of its peoples," was compatible with the American dream. Indeed, as President Wilson, the author of a popular *History of the American People,* told a hostile Congress in 1920:

> This is the mission upon which democracy came into the world. Democracy is an assertion of the right of the individual to live and to be treated justly as against any attempt on the part of any combination of individuals to make laws which will overburden him. . . . The old world is just now suffering from a wanton rejection of the principle of democracy. . . . This is the time of all others when democracy should prove its purity and its spiritual power to prevail. It is surely the manifest destiny of the United States to lead in the attempt to make this spirit prevail. . . .
>
> The United States is of necessity the sample democracy of the world, and the triumph of democracy depends upon its success.[2]

Woodrow Wilson, President of the United States during the first Great Crusade, was one of the company of political leaders who sought to fulfill the promise of the American dream. But among all the great or near-great American heroes, none was able—though Wilson and others tried—to shape the American dream in his own fixed image. Almost a hundred years before Wilson, President John Quincy Adams had entertained an equally lofty and comprehensive vision of the dream. In his annual message to Congress, he promulgated a startling suggestion that governments had the moral responsibility and power to attain the great goal of "the progressive improvement of the condition of the governed." [3] But the common man seemingly cared little for Adams' grandiose objectives. His concept of social and cultural progress via a national university and other federal projects did not stir the masses as they had been stirred in 1776, or as they were aroused again by Thomas Jefferson and Andrew Jackson.

Jefferson, the apostle of agrarian democracy and the President whose ideas have stood as the most enduring stimulus to the American dream, believed its promise could be realized only in a nation of independent farmers and small landowners. Yet within a generation a successor, Andrew Jackson, was forced to redefine Jefferson's agrarian philosophy in order to meet the needs of the encroaching industrial age. Both Jefferson and Jackson interpreted the American dream in terms of the prevailing ideas and interests of the people in their own time. Moreover, the common man himself, although he apparently did not appreciate John Quincy Adams' kind of lifelong intellectual and moral integrity, nevertheless did have his own idealism. In the view of James Truslow Adams, "He did not seek to plunder the rich. What he asked was what he thought America stood for—opportunity, the chance to grow into something bigger and finer, as bigger and finer appeared to him. He did not envisage America as standing for wealth only, and certainly not as standing for culture; still more certainly not as a reproduction of European classes and conditions. Somewhat vaguely he envisaged it as freedom and opportunity for himself and those like him to rise." This Americanism of the common man was, perhaps, a dream but, Adams wrote, "it was a great dream," and he added:

> If Americanism in the above sense has been a dream, it has also been one of the great realities in American life. It has been a moving force as truly as wheat or gold. It is all that has distinguished America from a mere quantitative comparison in wealth or art or letters or power with the nations of old Europe. It *is*

Americanism, and its shrine has been in the heart of the common man. He may not have done much for American culture in its narrower sense, but in its wider meaning it is he who almost alone has fought to hold fast to the American dream. This is what has made the common man a great figure in the American drama. This is the dominant motif in the American epic.[4]

A mixture of romance and reality, of idealism and practical common sense, the American dream was not a logical idea. "Like every great thought that has stirred and advanced humanity, it was a religious emotion, a great act of faith, a courageous leap into the dark unknown." Yet, until the depression of the thirties, following hard upon the disillusionment over American entrance into the First World War, the American dream stood largely unquestioned in the minds of the American people as a valid philosophy and article of popular belief. In the nineteenth century, for example, Americans, though occupied with the conquest of a continent and the building of a civilization, never lost the vision of something nobler. "If we hastened after the pot of gold, we also saw the rainbow itself, and felt that it promised, as of old, a hope for mankind." In its material achievements alone, Adams believed, America "would have made no distinctive and unique gift to mankind. But there has been also the *American dream*, that dream of a land in which life should be better and richer and fuller for every man, with opportunity for each according to his ability or achievement." [5]

A stockbroker before he turned author and wrote a Pulitzer prize–winning history of the founding of New England, James Truslow Adams passed severe judgment on his own postwar generation. What he called "Our Business Civilization" and "The Tempo of Modern Life" he found equally wanting. The country in its rush to forget Europe and the war had succumbed to the

Red Scare of 1919. "The whole state of mind of the nation, including many elements in it which should have kept their heads, was disgraceful, but tended strongly to alienate us from Europe, with its Bolshevism and what was considered, somewhat vaguely, its sources of infection for Socialism and Communism." The sudden end of the war, Adams suggested, left the American people emotionally unsatisfied. Urged to build up a great fighting machine, and encouraged by propaganda to concentrate all their energies upon the war, the mob element and mass psychology in the population "demanded sacrificial victims and found them in all who differed in any way from the conservative and the stereotyped." [6]

The idealism of the Progressive era largely disappeared in the twenties, a decade which Adams described succinctly by saying that "Harding had to liquidate the war; Coolidge had quietly to liquidate the scandals of the Harding régime; and Hoover is now watching the liquidation of the 'Coolidge prosperity.' . . . The battle cries of [Theodore] Roosevelt and Wilson in the struggle to realize the American dream had been changed into the small-town Chamber of Commerce shouts for 'Coolidge prosperity.'" "Much as I disliked Roosevelt in many ways," Adams confided to a friend in the summer of 1929, "I believe he did much to stir the conscience of the country. The war and the huge prosperity since have swept over all the old ground gained and we need a new leader and a new regeneration." [7]

Even the prosperity of the twenties was, in Adams' eyes, a troubled achievement. It entailed a heavy expense in goods and services which encouraged materialism and standardization and damaged intellectual life and moral values. As compared with England and Europe, Adams argued that America's business civilization exacted a high degree of social conformity with an accompanying decline in the art of living in favor of piling up material goods and "things." With business and money-making

8

and material improvement accepted in themselves as ultimate goals, they took on the qualities of moral virtues, while serious criticism was regarded as obstructive and dangerous. "The one liberty that is still valued is the liberty to exploit and to acquire. That liberty will be defended to the death, but other liberties, such as freedom of thought and speech, have become pale and unreal ghosts, academic questions of no interest to the practical man." Meanwhile, the demand for more money to meet the high cost of postwar living put a premium on speculation at the expense of traditional values of hard work and thrift. "The old desire to control the great corporations in the interests of the American dream became changed into a desire to see their stocks go up. . . . " Eventually, however, the law of diminishing returns was bound to affect even the optimism of Wall Street.[8]

Fortunate in his unusual combination of the talents and insights of financier and historian, Adams was one of the prescient few who were not caught in the collapse of the stock market. His belief "in laws and precedents, and merely following history, declining to believe in a 'new era,' " he later wrote, "enabled me to scuttle out of every stock before the crash." He selfishly welcomed the 1929 panic which, he declared, he "would be glad to see go further." He predicted in November "a long slow decline," noting that it was silly "to say that the slump can't hurt business for there have been only 'paper losses.' " Although the end of the bull market had been foreseen by some of the saner financial heads in Europe and America, "In no case," Adams pointed out, "could the nation, or whatever party might have been in power, have avoided the inevitable, but," he added, "the country need not have been advised to crowd on every rag of extra sail as it headed into the hurricane." Disillusioned by the Great Crusade for peace and democracy, the American people had been urged to place their destiny in the hands of practical businessmen and realistic politicians. " . . . Having surrendered

9

idealism for the sake of prosperity, the 'practical men' bankrupted us on both of them." [9]

Studying the collapse of the American dream from the vantage point of the depression, Adams contended that it had been a mistake to consider man merely as a producer and consumer. Material plenty, though it seemed now to count more than ever, was not the foundation of the dream, and any future restoration would require a greater concern for human and aesthetic values. In the modern industrial state an economic base was essential, and Adams found "no reason why wealth, which is a social product, should not be more equitably controlled and distributed in the interest of society." But, if the American dream was to come true and again be a reality, "those on top, financially, intellectually, or otherwise, have got to devote themselves to the 'Great Society,' and those who are below in the scale have got to rise, not merely economically, but culturally. We cannot become a great democracy by giving ourselves up as individuals to selfishness, physical comfort, and cheap amusements. The very foundation of the American dream of a better and richer life for all is that all, in varying degrees, shall be capable of wanting to share in it." Adams was certain that neither business nor political leaders could guarantee the American people a "good life" in the old Greek sense, and he feared that "just so long as wealth and power are our sole badges of success, so long will ambitious men strive to attain them." The prospect, he concluded, was discouraging but not hopeless.

> We have a long and arduous road to travel if we are to realize our American dream in the life of our nation, but if we fail, there is nothing left but the old eternal round. The alternative is the failure of self-government, the failure of the common man to rise to full stature, the failure of all that the American dream has held of hope and promise for mankind.[10]

A modern conservative, or an old-fashioned classical liberal,

Adams stood somewhere between the New Humanists and the Old Progressives of 1912. Like the Humanists, he feared the implications of mass production and doubted most of the claims of modern science. But he also followed some of the Progressives in questioning the wisdom of tying the economic welfare of the nation to the policies and credo of a businessman's government. In the golden glow of the twenties, the Republican party had staked its claim for political support on the argument of presidential prosperity. Under the leadership and ideas of Secretary of the Treasury Mellon and Secretary of Commerce Hoover, Adams wrote, "we are asked to envisage and experiment with a wholly new conception of the Business-State, a Business-State under Capitalism much as the Soviet government is a Business-State under Communism." Caught in the trap of their own optimistic political and financial philosophy, President Hoover and his associates continued to predict the return of normal business conditions in the months after the stock market crash. Noting the statement of Governor Roy Young of the Federal Reserve Bank in May 1930 that the country was now in "what appears to be a business depression," Adams penned a sarcastic epitaph for the reigning Republican theory of engineering permanent prosperity: "If we were not also in a Republican administration, there would be less doubt among our present leaders as to whether we were in 'what *appears* to be a business depression.' " [11]

The crash and ensuing depression were climactic blows in the series of buffetings which had beset the American dream in the decades before and after the First World War. In his *Epic of America*, Adams put into historical perspective the increasingly troubled concern and sense of malaise shared by so many of the intellectuals of the twenties. At bottom, one sensed, was a disillusionment not only with the late war and the cult of prosperity, but also, and even more importantly, with democracy and the whole philosophy of progressive reform as it had developed in the early 1900's.[12]

One of the first to prepare a formal statement of liberal disenchantment was Harold Stearns, who wrote in the tradition of Randolph Bourne's indictment of the pragmatist-progressives for their support of the war and the administration that had waged it. Stearns in his own career fulfilled the popular stereotype of the sensitive, young literary radical who was part of the postwar Lost Generation. An alumnus of Harvard and Greenwich Village, where he mixed journalism and the gayer side of life, Stearns left the United States after the war to join the growing number of American expatriates in Paris. His *Liberalism in America: Its Origins, Its Temporary Collapse, Its Future*, published in 1919, was his first critical salvo. Three years later he added a postscript, editing a symposium in which some thirty well-known writers analyzed the defects in American civilization.[13] In between these works, Stearns also composed his *America and the Young Intellectual*.

Convinced that a decent respect for the dignity and worth of the individual had vanished since 1914, Stearns noted bitterly: "Everywhere we turn it is the same story—coercion, force, force to the utmost without stint or limit." The war had failed to achieve its liberal ends partly because the leaders themselves were not liberal; they had been content, with the intellectuals, to become the hired dupes of the military machine. The charm of being a big-shot in Washington had occasioned such a flood of eager personnel and energy that the "war itself was forgotten in the intensity of waging it," while President Wilson, the most conspicuous exemplar of "The Technique of Liberal Failure," showed "to what extremes of cruelty and intolerance and injustice the idealist in politics can go." With the intellectuals and educated leaders of the country more hysterical and wrongheaded even than the masses, Stearns concluded that disillusionment was inevitable. The American people no longer believed Wilson's pious phrases.[14]

Among the thousands of young men who came back from France after the Great War, one of the most promising was Walter Lippmann. A youthful Harvard radical and journalist like Stearns, Lippmann had left his post with the *New Republic* magazine to help fight the war in Washington and then had joined the large group of experts who accompanied President Wilson and Colonel House to the Paris Peace Conference. Like his fellow editors on the *New Republic*, Lippmann was affronted by the harsh peace terms he found in the Treaty of Versailles and by the grave weaknesses of the League of Nations. "In my opinion," he declared privately in midsummer of 1919, "the Treaty is not only illiberal and in bad faith, it is in the highest degree imprudent. It is a far worse job, I think, than the Treaty of Vienna a hundred years ago. . . . I am certain that the present League is in structure and function and ideal the enemy of a real League of Nations, and the greatest danger is that its failure, like that of the Holy Alliance before it, will disillusionize a whole generation." [15]

If Lippmann was upset over the Treaty and the League— except as an instrument to preserve the international status quo —he was disturbed, even more, by the dismal prospects for democracy at home. In a frank and anguished correspondence with his old friend and wartime boss, Secretary of War Newton D. Baker, early in 1920, he made clear the bases of his despair: "You know what hopes were put in this administration, how loudly and insistently it proclaimed its loyalty to the cause of freedom. Well it was possible to fail in these hopes. It was credible that the wisdom and the strength to realize them would be lacking. But it is forever incredible," Lippmann continued, "that an administration announcing the most spacious ideals in our history should have done more to endanger fundamental American liberties than any group of men for a hundred years." Citing the political sentences, deportations, censorship, and new sedition legislation advocated by the Justice Department, he concluded: "These are dreadful things and they have dreadful consequences. They have instituted a reign of terror in which honest thought is impossible, in which moderation is discountenanced, in which panic supplants reason." Instead of carrying out its "solemn duty to allay fear and restore sanity," the Wilson administration had "done everything humanly possible to add fresh excitement to an overexcited community." [16]

In reply to his younger correspondent, Baker sadly indicted his own generation. At the same time he tried to explain to Lippmann his deep personal sense of hopes unfulfilled:

> I have no fears about America; the excesses and hysteria to which you refer are clearly passing phases which trouble the surface after a deep disturbance; but I have a grief which time may modify but can not cure, and that is that at the very crossing of the ways, when the supreme moment for America had arrived, we poured our liberal spirit through a sieve, each of us became particularists and formalists and so lost the opportunity to seize and hold the spiritual leadership of the world. [17]

As he looked back upon America's wartime experience from the background of the early twenties, Lippmann wondered whether democratic self-government, in the historic sense of the American dream, was still possible. Continual government propaganda under the Creel Committee on Public Information had created "something that might almost be called one public opinion all over America," but for public opinion in a democracy to function well it had to be spontaneous and well informed. In the simple, more intelligible society of the past this was possible, but in the complex modern world people mistook images for realities, accepted the public façade thrown up before them, and spoke in generalities and stereotypes. "It is idle under such circumstances," Lippmann wrote, "to talk about democracy, or about the refinement of public opinion. With such monstrous complications the public can do little more than at intervals to align itself heavily for or against the régime in power. . . ." [18]

Proponents of democracy, Lippmann made clear, could no longer assume that the truth would prevail if only it were given an opportunity to be heard. Problems of public opinion now transcended such relatively simple issues of civil liberties as free speech or a free press. Under the propaganda of governments and of highly organized and well-financed pressure groups, minorities could sway and control majority opinion. Having thus analyzed the problems of achieving a democratic public opinion, Lippmann turned to a lifetime career as perhaps the most brilliant and influential journalist of his time, constantly seeking as an editor and columnist to guide the thinking of a large number of his fellow citizens.

Very early in his life, as a young man fresh from a brief postgraduate course in government as an assistant to the muckraking Lincoln Steffens, Lippmann had published *A Preface to Politics* (1913). In this precocious work, its author, scorning moral absolutes and traditional values, set forth an ambitious psychological analysis and theory of progressive politics. Years later, on the eve of the Great Depression, Lippmann wrote a companion piece to his earlier work which he entitled *A Preface to Morals* (1929). The first book had celebrated America's coming emancipation from conservative modes of thinking. But now Lippmann, surveying "the dissolution of the ancestral order," in which "whirl is king," sought a principle of authority, some certainty in the midst of "the genius of modernity" to which "the moralist in an unbelieving world" could cling. ". . . The modern man who has ceased to believe, without ceasing to be credulous, hangs, as it were," he wrote, "between heaven and earth, and is at rest nowhere." Coerced no longer by moral authority, but compelled nevertheless by the force of events, the modern man was conquered but unconvinced. "In the old order the compulsions were often painful, but there was sense in the pain inflicted by the will of an all-knowing God. In the new order the compulsions are painful and, as it were, accidental, unnecessary, wanton, and full of mockery." [19]

What Lippmann said with scholarly restraint and a certain piety, H. L. Mencken, whom Lippmann called "the most powerful personal influence on this whole generation of educated people," [20] spread flamboyantly across the pages of the *American Mercury* magazine. More savage than the New Humanists in his indictment of the materialism and conformity of the great mass of his fellows, Mencken joined the growing company of intellectuals who despaired of the future of democracy. More faith than reason, democracy, in Mencken's view, was always in need of elevating new leaders to prevent its degenerating into a mob.

In his *Notes on Democracy*, published in 1926, Mencken argued that fear and envy were the two main characteristics of democracy and "of its twin, Puritanism." Evidence of fear he saw in the United States' tendency to chase monsters, from the time of the British Redcoats to the Bolsheviks in the Red Scare of 1919. In a democracy motivated by such hysteria, "The statesman becomes, in the last analysis, a mere witch-hunter, a glorified smeller and snooper. . . ." The Department of Justice he attacked as misnamed and as the chief violator of the Bill of Rights it was supposed to defend. Nine-tenths of American Presidents, he pointed out, had reached office by making promises that were basically immoral. Yet, after election day, the President was criticized not for making the promises but for his failure to keep them. "No man," he wrote, "would want to be President of the United States in strict accordance with the Constitution. There is no sense of power in merely executing the laws; it comes from evading or augmenting them." [21]

An individualist rather than a Progressive, Mencken's liberalism was personal rather than social in scope. Like so many intellectuals in the twenties, he saw little hope in political action.

The Progressives' old hero, Theodore Roosevelt, he likened to the German Kaiser as an exponent of authoritarian reform from the top, while Woodrow Wilson was "the self-bamboozled Presbyterian, the right-thinker, the great moral statesman, the perfect model of the Christian cad." Mencken denounced the regal concept of the citizen's duty to the state, race, or nation, as a synonym for docile obedience: "For the man who differs from this inert and well-regimented mass, however slightly, there are no duties *per se.* . . . Human progress," he contended, "is furthered, not by conformity, but by aberration. The very concept of duty is thus a function of inferiority; it belongs naturally only to timorous and incompetent men." [22]

Under the new businesslike interpretation of the American dream during the 1920's, the alienation of the intellectuals was perhaps inevitable. The widespread demand for conformity in politics and morals and the all-pervading emphasis on material prosperity seemed accurate measures of the enormous decline from the idealism of the war and the Progressive era. Like certain of the Jacksonian Democrats after the defeat of their party in 1840, many of the older liberals and Progressives of 1912 lost confidence in the virtue and intelligence of the people. Harding's triumph, followed four years later by La Follette's disappointing showing as presidential candidate of a renewed Progressive party, cast doubt on the traditional liberal assumption that the average citizen wanted government to be an instrument of reform and progress. The severe judgments of a Lippmann or a Mencken on the possibility of an informed public opinion or mass democracy appeared to be confirmed all too well by the election returns.

By the mid-1920's old-line progressives were voicing their dismay. Lincoln Steffens, whose *Shame of the Cities* had buttressed the case for sweeping political reforms in the 1900's, now tried to salvage his faltering hopes for democracy by looking expectantly to the communism of Soviet Russia. Like Steffens, Frederic C. Howe was impressed in the twenties by the example of the revolutionary changes occurring in Russia. A Progressive who once saw American cities, purged of their shame and corruption, as the hope of democracy, Howe as Wilson's Commissioner of Immigration had attempted to resist the worst of the postwar alien deportations and antiradical hysteria. Under Tom Johnson, the reforming mayor of Cleveland, he had worked to bring government closer to the people. But after the war, the collapse of idealism and the increasingly vindictive use of governmental power by bureaucrats and politicians disillusioned him, and he wrote in his *Confessions of a Reformer*:

> My attitude toward the state was changed as a result of these experiences. I have never been able to bring it back. I became distrustful of the state. It seemed to want to hurt people; it showed no concern for innocence; it aggrandized itself and protected its power by unscrupulous means. It was not my America, it was something else.[23]

The postwar dilemma of the liberal democrat and reformer was well illustrated in the writings of J. Allen Smith and Vernon L. Parrington. Close friends and colleagues at the University of Washington, both men were scholars who also exercised a wide intellectual influence. Smith's first book, *The Spirit of American Government*, published in 1907, attracted the attention of Progressives—including Theodore Roosevelt and Robert M. La Follette—by anticipating in part Charles Beard's celebrated thesis on the economic origins of the Constitution. Overlooked, however, by most Progressives was Smith's insistence on the need for strengthening local government—the theme of his now almost forgotten work, *The Growth and Decadence of Constitutional Government*, which he completed in the early twenties. The late war, with its encouragement of centralized power, showed Smith the undemocratic, illiberal side of government. There was a wide discrepancy between the theory and practice of democracy, while the growth of the suffrage and the acceptance of majority rule were no guarantees of individual liberty. Such political democracy, by removing the main ground for the people's distrust of governmental authority, merely concealed the steady rise of state supremacy over the citizen under the guise of popular sovereignty. Centralization, accompanied by militarism and imperialism, Smith believed, was a direct threat to popular rule. "Democracy, in any sense of the term," he concluded, "is possible only when there is the largest practicable measure of local self-government." [24]

Smith's book, with an introduction by Parrington, was generally ignored when it was published posthumously at the outset of the depression. In contrast, Parrington's *Main Currents in American Thought* was an outstanding critical and popular success. Yet *Main Currents*, with its rich historical details about American literature, reflected also much of Smith's pessimistic point of view. Reread today for the insight it provides into Parrington's own beliefs, *Main Currents* is an impressive monument to its author's lamentations over a declining liberalism and a failure to realize the American dream. "We must have a political state powerful enough to deal with corporate wealth," he wrote to a friend a few months before his own death in 1929, "but how," he asked, "are we going to keep that state with its augmenting power from being captured by the force we want it to control?" Power, Parrington recognized, resulted always in a struggle to dominate its use.

> When one controls the political state, whatever one wants can be done under cover of the law and with the sanction of the courts. Have you been able to convince yourself that the corporate wealth of America will permit that centralized political state to pass out of its control and become an agent to regulate or thwart its plans? [25]

Parrington's query, posed in the final year of prosperity, on the eve of the stock market crash and his own death, lay at the heart of the liberals' difficulties. Neither Parrington nor most of his contemporaries could foresee, of course, that the depression would go far to destroy the political influence of big business and to restore to the people the political power they appeared to have lost in the twenties. Both Parrington and Smith were pessimistic idealists whose vision of the American dream carried them a century into the past, back to the era of Jeffersonian liberalism and a simpler, agrarian type of society. Neither as sophisticated nor as cynical as Lippmann or Mencken, they were also not as sanguine as, for example, Charles Beard and John Dewey, who retained their belief that the American dream might still be realized through the great vistas being opened up to the common man by science and education.

In *The Rise of American Civilization*, the magisterial historical synthesis which he wrote with his wife and published in the same year as Parrington's volumes, Beard called attention to the coincidence, and even probable causal relationship, between scientific progress and the rise of democracy in the United States as well as in Europe in the second quarter of the nineteenth century. It was science, the Beards wrote, which

> pointed the way to progressive democracy in its warfare against starvation, poverty, disease, and ignorance, indicating how classes and nations long engaged in strife among themselves might unite to wring from nature the secret of security and the good life. It was science, not paper declarations relating to the idea of progress, that at last made patent the practical methods by which democracy could raise the standard of living for the great masses of the people.[26]

That confidence in the efficacy of science which the Beards traced back one hundred years to the age of Jackson they also invoked to resolve some of their own doubts concerning the preemption of industrial society by the conservative political and business forces of their day.

Seeking still an answer to the eternal question, "Whither Mankind," Beard invited a group of scholars and practical men of affairs to contribute to a symposium on the state of modern civilization. As he himself noted in the introduction to this work, despite prosperity there was widespread anxiety about the future and much political uncertainty especially in Europe. "The age of Victorian complacency has closed everywhere; those who are whistling to keep up their courage and deceive their neighbors merely succeed in hoodwinking themselves." America, where the full power of the machine was apotheosized, stood as a challenge to this older European civilization so badly shattered by the late war. And it was the dynamic power of the machine, the true revolutionary element in a changing civilization, that offered salvation to the modern world. The return now in any guise to a pre-machine, agricultural society, "with its low standards of life, its diseases, and its illiteracy," Beard declared, was "beyond the imagination." Of course a machine civilization was open to attack on aesthetic, moral, and humanitarian grounds, but Beard argued that none of these values had to be destroyed. Science or machinery were not to blame, only man's faulty application of their immense powers.[27]

If Beard minimized the adverse effect of machinery upon the individual—a point which at least one of the contributors to his symposium, the philosopher Bertrand Russell, raised—it was perhaps because Beard and Russell, echoing Tocqueville, both agreed that in the future the collective power of man would tend to dwarf his significance as an individual. Noting that the satisfaction of the individual ego had often been associated in the past with the supernatural values of another world, Russell contended:

> In the modern machine-world, owing to democracy and to the achievements of science, other compensations are possible, more especially nationalism, which identifies the individual emotionally with the power of his group. But in order that such compensations

may satisfy, it is necessary to belittle the individual wherever he is not contributing to a totality.[28]

Like Beard and Russell, John Dewey, who had once described democracy as an ethical ideal, now believed it was even more a social experience, "a mode of associated living, of conjoint communicated experience." Not just a form of government or the product of political forces, democracy represented "the convergence of a great number of social movements," and in this sense it had to be born anew in every generation with education serving as its midwife. But the democratic public was "still largely inchoate and unorganized," apathetic to false issues stirred up by the "hired promoters of opinion called publicity agents." [29]

To Dewey the major question was when the Great Society, fashioned in the last century by the discoveries and use of steam and electricity and by technology in general, would become the Great Community. The traditional individuality of the Western European civilization, which was threatened by American mass culture, had been a very limited boon in which the peasantry and proletariat had hardly participated. In America, many of the attributes of rural community life, which had formerly given focus and direction to personality, were being lost, and as a consequence the individual found himself bewildered. Thus insecurity with unemployment was often a feature of modern industrial civilization. But it was also true, Dewey wrote, that "Evils which are uncritically laid at the door of industrialism and democracy might, with greater intelligence, be referred to the dislocation and unsettlement of local communities." American democracy, which had developed out of small community life and been taken over from English political institutions, now was in the process of evolving into a public or democratic socialism. Yet Dewey also believed that "Democracy must begin at home, and its home is the neighborly community." The problem, therefore, was somehow to preserve the individualistic values of the older community and transmit them into the newer social or collective democracy that Dewey called "corporateness." [30]

Convinced of the need for a thorough political and social reformation, and dissatisfied with the business civilization of the twenties, liberal thinkers nevertheless differed widely in their prescriptions for the realization of the American dream. Individualism, socialism, science, education, and democracy were all accordingly subjected to searching analysis and considerable reinterpretation by the scholars and journalists of the postwar decade. Yet few of them discerned any immediate crisis until the detonations in Wall Street heralded the end of an era and the onset of a major economic depression.

However much intellectuals decried its crassness and lack of culture, the economic structure of business enterprise was able to win their general, if grudging, acceptance in the years before its 1929 collapse. Like science and machinery, big business was conceded to be a part of the price of modern civilization, and, at least in an economic sense, the system admittedly seemed to work. "In 1929 business, particularly big business," writes historian Thomas C. Cochran, "enjoyed a degree of public approval unique in American history." Walter Lippmann, for example, found the chief cause of widespread political indifference in the mid-twenties in the rising standard of living under the New Capitalism. The American people simply believed that "the opportunities to make money were so ample that it was a waste of time to think about politics." In an urbanized, industrial society, American business had moved ahead faster than its socialist critics, so that "The more or less unconscious and unplanned activities of businessmen are for once more novel, more daring, and in a sense more revolutionary, than the theories of the progressives." [31]

As Arthur Schlesinger, Jr., has pointed out in *The Crisis of the Old Order*, the suspicion grew by 1929, "even among liberals, that the theorists of the New Era might be right— that business leadership was not only stronger but wiser than ever before, that the next step might really be, as Mr. Hoover had promised, the abolition of poverty." Lincoln Steffens, who at the beginning of the twenties had been impressed by both the Russian Revolution and Benito Mussolini, who "took the method, the spirit, the stuff, of Bolshevism and used it to go—right," was moved to reconsider. Russia and the United States each empha- sized mass production and mass consumption, while the best of American businessmen, like Henry Ford, had a plan. Wasn't it possible, Steffens wondered, "that these two young peoples, the Russians and the Americans, are driving, the one consciously, the other unwittingly, toward the same end?" Perhaps "the un- conscious experiment this country is making in civilization and culture is equal to that of Soviet Russia. The race is saved," he concluded, "one way or the other and, I think, both ways." [32]

Like Steffens and Lippmann, the Beards in the concluding pages of their *Rise of American Civilization*, published in 1927 at the high noon of the Coolidge prosperity, were inclined toward a hopeful appraisal of what they called the Machine Age. The large American middle class, about equal to the total population of the North in 1860, through its investments in stocks and bonds, "had become part owners, usually absentee, of the enterprises managed by captains of finance. Even the industrial multitudes in the United States, like the middle class and in contrast to the proletariat of ancient Rome, "paid for their own diversions and bought their own loaves. . . . No doubt there were dark sides to the picture . . . ," the Beards acknowledged, "but the area of grueling poverty was relatively so limited that revolutionary calls to working people to shed their chains met with no wholesale response." Seeing dangers only in war or in some Malthusian crisis of overpopulation, the Beards concluded that "there was no doubt about the nature of the future in America. The most common note of assurance was belief in unlimited progress. . . . Concretely it meant an invulnerable faith in democracy, . . . a faith in the efficacy of that new and mysterious instrument of the modern mind, 'the invention of invention,' moving from one technological triumph to another, overcoming the exhaustion of crude natural resources and energies, effecting an ever wider distribution of the blessings of civilization—health, security, material goods, knowledge, leisure, and aesthetic appreciation. . . ." [33]

The leading journals of liberal opinion, in their comments on the American business system in the months of its transition from prosperity to depression, shared on the whole the Beards' optimism. The major emphasis of the *Nation* and the *New Republic* at this time was upon foreign affairs. In the *Nation*, for example, its longtime editor Oswald Garrison Villard wrote at length of his 1929 summer tour of Russia, and the magazine continued to advocate disarmament and diplomatic recognition of the Soviet Union. There was space, however, for some analysis of prosperity. Late in July a contributor noted that, on the evidence of the popular novelists of the decade, Americans were unhappy despite the good times. Contending therefore that "It is not enough to have prosperity," and that "It is high time to be done with complacency," the author called for planning and sacrifices to conquer unemployment, to preserve the beauty and resources of nature, and to end national isolation.[34]

Especially interesting in view of his later eminence as a popular writer on economics, and because his articles were obviously written before the Great Crash, was the series in the *Nation* by Stuart Chase entitled "Prosperity—Believe It or Not." On Wednesday, October 23, the first day in a week of catastrophic breaks on the New York Stock Exchange, Chase's initial essay, subtitled "What Is Prosperity?," appeared with ill-fated precision. Through the next three months, into the following January, the series continued with Chase doggedly analyzing the effects of prosperity upon America's different social classes and income groups. In common with the prevailing progressive thought of the twenties, Chase pointed to the many Americans who did not enjoy the prosperity of their fellows. He gave no indication, however, of any premonitions of the crash.[35]

Editorially the *Nation* viewed "Wall Street's Crisis" as a healthy, though costly, reaction to overpriced stocks and excessive speculation. It found fault chiefly with the Federal Reserve Bank's easy money policies, established in 1927 to help resolve the financial difficulties of Europe. Dissenting still at the end of November from the blame being heaped on Wall Street, the *Nation* contended that the stock market was only a reflection of business conditions. Surprisingly, in the light of this comment, the editors responded negatively to their own question: "Is the country headed for calamity, with the stock market carrying the flag?" After some relative stagnation, a slow recovery was expected. And, in tune with most statesmen and financiers, the *Nation* affirmed solemnly: "The great task of the next few months is the restoration of confidence. . . ."[36]

The *New Republic*, like the *Nation*, was cautiously optimistic form of economic planning. Praising President Hoover for calling about economic conditions, although its editors preferred some a conference of leaders from trade and industry, agriculture and labor, the editors nevertheless declared that they did not want merely another report from a conclave of experts. Instead, "We must begin to experiment with a governor for our engine. We must frankly recognize that the wild play of individualistic forces out for private gain does not automatically result in a desirable economic equilibrium. . . . Fortunately," the editors concluded at the end of November, "the present breakdown is not likely to be serious in any case." Two months later, after exploring the connection between automobile production and prosperity, the *New Republic* expressed the view that prospects were not at all bright. "We shall have to look for our stimulus elsewhere. Can it be aviation, television, motor-boating? Or what?" As the decline in key industries continued through the spring of 1930, the editors decided that fundamental readjustments were necessary and that "such a prosperous era as we have recently experienced cannot again arrive without being preceded by a deeper depression than we have yet had—accompanied, of course, by a general increase in the efficiency of production which will make possible a higher average of incomes with a lower average of retail prices." [37]

Prominent contributors to the *New Republic* offered varied advice on the causes of the depression and the magazine's own responsibility to the future. For example, Lewis Corey, later the author of a well-known book, *The Decline of American Capitalism*, in his analysis of the economic collapse thought that "it is useless to make scapegoats of the stock market and the speculators. The recession started before the crash and its cause must be sought in the interacting relations of production, consumption, and purchasing power. . . . " The nub of the problem, Corey declared, was "in the social control of industry." [38]

Felix Frankfurter differed from Corey. He stressed the "profoundly important psychological factor of a growing disbelief in the fairness of our capitalistic scheme," and urged editor Bruce Bliven to publish factual articles exposing the selfishness and dishonesty of high officials. Although he admitted that the fault was with "the system," Frankfurter argued:

> One of the basic aspects of "the system" is the authority wielded by "big men"—the geocentric position accorded to the successful business men and financiers. Nothing, I believe, sustains the present system more than the pervasive worship of Success and the touching faith we have in financial and business messiahs. Therefore it is that I believe it to be profoundly important to undermine that faith. . . . Undermine confidence in their greatness, and you have gone a long way towards removing some basic obstructions to the exploration of economic and social problems. *You* don't have to worry about "what next?"

"You cannot reconstruct the whole of society at one fell swoop," Frankfurter warned Bliven, "and you and I will be in our graves before there is a planned society in this country. But you can do a great deal towards it by dealing with the concrete issues that carry your general philosophy forward." [39]

The hopeful and expectant mood of watchful waiting in which intellectuals observed the aftermath of the Great Crash could not survive the evidence of growing depression. Whereas previous economic slumps had affected the agricultural or industrial population, now in the 1930's all classes and all sectors of the economy were hurt in some way. The middle class, traditionally the bulwark of American society, succumbed to the mounting unemployment and drastically reduced incomes of its white-collar workers and professional people. As stock prices tumbled to ever lower levels, doctors, lawyers, teachers, clerks and skilled laborers, writers and artists, all felt the reality of the depression and the pangs of poverty. Authors and publishers especially found a declining market for their wares. John Steinbeck, for example, recalled later that, being without a job during the first years of the depression, he kept on writing—"books, essays, short stories. Regularly they went out and just as regularly came back. Even if they had been good, they would have come back because publishers were hardest hit of all. When people are broke, the first things they give up are books." [40]

While the circulation of the larger metropolitan newspapers and more popular magazines held up amazingly well, the book industry experienced a severe blight. By 1933 sales were only half of what they had been in 1929. Reviewing the twelve months just past, his publisher informed James Truslow Adams that "It was a very tough year and so far as we are concerned will go down as the worst so far since the firm of Little and

Brown began publishing books in 1837." Although distribution of Adams' *Epic of America* had not achieved the predicted figure of a thousand copies a week, still it had enjoyed a "larger sale than any new book we published." [41]

Americans, of course, notoriously purchased few books even in good times—about two per person in 1929, for example, with several more borrowed from libraries. With the depression this personal buying fell off and libraries as well suffered reduced budgets. They faced the unhappy situation of having to curtail their own purchases at a time when the demand for their facilities was never higher, and when idle millions were re-discovering the public library as a kind of poor man's club, "a warm quiet place to browse or drowse." Some people merely sought escape in reading fiction, the great gainer in circulation at first, but gradually more serious interests took over. With total circulation of library books increasing by nearly 40 per cent from 1929 to 1933, readers in ever greater numbers consulted educational and technical works in their often pathetic quest for jobs or self-culture. Later circulation fell off slightly, perhaps because the libraries were not acquiring enough new books or because people were again beginning to secure jobs. [42]

Among a number of American cities that no longer cared or were unable to support their public libraries, Chicago was the greatest and the worst. There in 1932, "Through an un-premeditated bit of irony the same year which found Chicago celebrating a century of progress by an exposition costing many millions of dollars found the Chicago Public Library for the third consecutive twelvemonth without a book fund." In the midst of a lavish exhibition of costly art and culture, the public library was starving for books. [43]

Formal education also suffered severely from the effects of the depression. Public schools were affected by the sharp decline in tax revenues, and in Chicago a combination of tax delinquency and bad government forced teachers to go unpaid for the school year 1932–1933. Across the country budget cuts meant shorter school terms, ill-paid teachers, and fewer classrooms. By 1933 the United States Office of Education estimated that fifteen hundred colleges and commercial institutions devoted to vocational or professional education had closed their doors. College enrollments, despite an increase in the graduate schools, fell by approximately 250,000 students from pre-depression totals.[44]

Students, worried by their own frequent lack of funds and the dismal prospects of pursuing the careers for which they had prepared, also showed the shock of the depression. Alternately accused of being aloof and cynical, with no concern for politics except in presidential years, and of being too radical in their protests and demands, college youth shared the intellectual confusions of their time. According to William Allen White, who defended their actions against conservative criticism, increasing student riots were evidence of a healthy intellectual growth. "Youth should be radical," White urged.

> Youth should demand change in the world. Youth should not accept the old order if the world is to move on. But the old orders should not be moved easily—certainly not at the mere whim or behest of youth. There must be clash and if youth hasn't enough force or fervor to produce the clash the world grows stale and stagnant and sour in decay.
>
> If our colleges and universities do not breed men who riot, who rebel, who attack life with all the youthful vim and vigor, then there is something wrong with our colleges. The more riots that come on college campuses, the better world for tomorrow.[45]

As the economy continued its rapid descent into the darker labyrinths of the depression, confidence in the automatic fulfillment of the American dream all but vanished. No one was able to see the ravages of the hard times more closely than the social workers and journalists in America's large cities. They knew the facts of poverty. In the slums of New York, Lillian Wald, for years director of the Henry Street settlement house, commented darkly upon "the long-unemployed bread-lines which are a disgrace to this so-called civilization of ours. I don't know what civilization is," she wrote in the early 1930's, "but whatever its concept, it isn't insufficient food and relinquishment of bathrooms for cheaper houses or bread-lines, however 'unworthy' the men in the line may be. . . . Have you ever heard a hungry child cry? Have you seen the uncontrollable trembling of parents who have gone half starved themselves for weeks so that the children may have food?" Summing things up, the *Nation* commented that the year 1931 was one "of suffering, bitterness, and increasing disillusionment." Americans, confident that prosperity would be "our vassal for all time," had shown an astonishing self-control in the general lack of riots and disorder. Clearly, however, the republic was in jeopardy—even though the *Nation's* editors also affirmed that "we have not lost faith that it can be rescued and set upon the right paths through the instrumentality of the present form of government, adequately altered to meet the needs of the situation." [46]

From his vantage point in London, to which he now made more frequent retreats, James Truslow Adams continued to question some of the false business values and perverted democratic ideals which, he felt, prevented the realization of the American dream. His correspondents in the United States were, however, too concerned by business failures and political futility at home to join Adams in philosophizing on the general state of civilization and culture. From these literary friends Adams therefore received a most gloomy picture of affairs. A few weeks after the crash, the newspaperman and historian Claude Bowers noted already that "The conditions here are bad. The press generally is lying outrageously, heroically trying to prevent depression. The cancellation of Xmas orders has been unprecedented. In every nook and corner are the victims of the market—ruined." Denouncing Hoover and his Republican predecessors, Bowers feared that the Democrats would win the next election by default. "The Republicans are utterly demoralized and if there were a militant, constructive, united Democratic Party it could sweep the country in three years." [47]

Allan Nevins, who had recently left his editorial position on the *New York World* to become professor of history at Columbia University, was an old Adams friend and frequent correspondent. "Times are hard here," Nevins reported in 1930 following the November elections. "Merely in walking the streets one sees many distressing sights. At every corner unemployed men are selling boxes of apples at 5 cents each; they make $1.75 a box, and thus keep alive. Beggars are numerous, and I understand that the suffering among the white-collar class is really appalling. The election showed how the people feel about the Hoover administration, and most Republicans think they were lucky to get off so easily." In the new year Nevins, upon returning from the regular annual meeting of his fellow historians, passed on to Adams the pessimistic mood of the nation's scholars:

> This country remains pretty low down in the trough of depression. There are just two bright aspects of the whole affair: it has brought the Hoover Administration and the Republican party into an unpopularity which on other accounts it richly deserves, and it has reduced retail prices of all kinds. . . . I might add that it has taken from America an arrogant cockiness that was growing very offensive. . . . However, it is depressing to hear constantly of bitter personal hardships, and to see the long bread lines that gather nightly in Columbus Circle and Times Square.[48]

Adams himself, in the midst of the successful publication of his *Epic of America*, with its sweeping historical interpretation of the configurations of the American dream, continued to comment on the passing scene for the popular magazines which eagerly sought his articles. In *Harper's* he urged readers to exercise perspective in regard to the stock market, pointing out that in mid-1931, if stocks were compared to the prices of 1925 instead of to the artificially high levels of 1928 and 1929, their descent was not so great; some, he noted, had even risen. At the same time in *Forum*, Adams criticized the bankers unsparingly, pointing to their unwise investments and misuse of funds entrusted to their supposedly expert care. In the *Atlantic Monthly*, in response to an editorial suggestion for an article on "The Decay of Liberalism" or "A Century of Democracy," he wrote about the decline of liberalism and democracy in America as well as Europe. While Britain looked toward Moscow and the United States to Rome, the lesson of the century seemed to be that "in every crisis democracy has to give way to autocracy or a dictatorship." Personally, however, Adams was beginning to see some signs of progress. "Something has at last *got* to be decided about Germany before many weeks, and I believe will be," he informed Henry Hazlitt from London. "America appears to be in a complete funk again but over here sentiment is rather better." [49]

In 1931 Lincoln Steffens, like Adams, published an important book—his famous *Autobiography*, which vied with Adams' *Epic* as one of the most popular works of serious nonfiction in the early 1930's. A veteran journalist who had first captured attention in the Theodore Roosevelt era, Steffens had gone on to report at firsthand the revolutions and wars in Mexico and Europe. Always managing somehow to be at the scene of the latest dramatic moment in world history, Steffens was able to achieve some of the same rapport in interviewing European dictators that he had enjoyed in his earlier personal contacts with American political bosses. Though it was therefore no doubt true that the experienced Steffens had long since lost any youthful illusions he may have had about politics, the *Autobiography* —at once hailed as a classic—managed to convey that sense of disenchanted idealism which was so tremendously appealing to the new depression generation of the 1930's.[50]

Back home in the United States, after a decade of wandering in Europe where he had watched the developing political crisis with a growing admiration for the Soviet way of life, Steffens, after the crash of '29, largely lost his earlier notion that America and Russia were headed in the same fundamental direction. If the depression killed the remnants of his lingering faith in the reform possibilities of the new business capitalism, it did not destroy his belief in the efficacy of technocracy and mass production as harbingers of a socialist society. "We can be free, or democratic, or safe, but not by wishing; only by economic arrangement of the circumstances of life. . . . We have to get rid of our old moral culture and learn the new culture. . . . No more thinking, nothing but theorizing and experimenting. . . . American business is nearer right than American ideals." [51]

During the thirties, until his death in 1936, Steffens continued to comment vigorously on the severity of the depression and the breakdown of capitalism. Although he refused to accept membership in the Communist party, out of his conviction that ex-liberals were not suited for leadership and action, his conception of the American dream and his hopes for the future all pointed toward Moscow. Noting in June of 1932 that the depression was growing worse and worse, with stocks "down almost to their real value" and his neighbors complaining of a cut to one-third of their incomes, Steffens wrote: "It looks as if we might not have to have a bolshevik revolution at all. We are getting there by the swift process of evolution which is not so slow and gradual as the optimists predicted. It is, as a matter of fact, very, very funny." "I am elated over the world news," he told Theodore Dreiser later that year. "You bulls don't understand us bears. I'm selling capitalism short; and morality, too; and . . . liberalism and culture, so I can sit in the sun, watch my neighbors read Technocracy and feel no drive to run the world down and the minds of men up." [52]

Throughout America the prevailing mood in the last two

years of the Hoover administration was one of profound pessimism. With people dazed and bewildered by the turn of events since 1929 and national morale growing weaker, the country's leading spokesmen and men of affairs rose to render their solemn verdict on an economic catastrophe unprecedented in its severity. "Among the fatalities of the depression were the capitalists and the intellectuals," Gilbert Seldes noted in his contemporary *Years of the Locust*, and after the first months of the economic crash "hardly an authoritative word was spoken in defense of the capitalist system. . . ." Yet it was also true that, as Edmund Wilson observed of the writers and artists of his generation "who had grown up in the Big Business era and had always resented its barbarism, its crowding-out of everything they cared about, these years were not depressing but stimulating. One couldn't help being exhilarated at the sudden unexpected collapse of that stupid gigantic fraud. It gave us a new sense of freedom; and it gave us a new sense of power. . . ." [53]

In this spirit, with the intellectuals in the van, the American people engaged in a desperate search for salvation, hoping to discover in the darkest days of the depression the means by which they could recover the lost hopes of the American dream.

TWO

The Search for Solutions

THE DEPRESSION and the accompanying crisis in the American dream forced the American people to try to find some way to check the continuing disintegration of the nation's economy. Liberal critics of the business civilization of the twenties were caught, as Arthur Schlesinger, Jr., has observed, "almost as short by the depression as was American business itself. . . . Depression confronted both groups with a radically new challenge. Assuming the inevitability of economic growth, they failed to anticipate economic collapse. Few among them were ready with either diagnosis or cure." [1]

As the seriousness of the national catastrophe became steadily more apparent, the search for solutions widened, and the American people were impelled to consider ideas that were revolutionary in their probable impact. The undoubted crisis in capitalism seemed to demand, at the very least, new and fundamental reforms. The traditional relations of government and business were called into question, and solutions that previously would have been rejected as dangerously socialistic were given a sympathetic hearing. Confronted by the growth of totalitarian governments abroad, American leaders in business and politics, in the churches and the universities, sought alternatives that might preserve the essentials of democracy and free institutions in the midst of their transformation and redemption.

While some Americans sought relief in communism and flight to Moscow, others toyed with the idea of fascism and an authoritarian type of society at home. Characteristic of almost all levels of social and political thought was the conviction that drastic changes had to be made in the American economic and business system. For the first time since the Populism of the 1890's, radical fiscal and political theories enjoyed widespread support. Significantly, no important economic interest group or social class appeared willing to let natural forces take their way. In contrast to the state of affairs in the nineteenth century, when the business cycle was allowed to run its course, there was now a general demand for some form of economic planning and government action.

The very severity of the depression at once spurred the search for solutions and precluded the resort to easy, time-honored panaceas. Previous depressions in the nation's history, largely confined to agriculture or industry, had not reached the broad strata of the middle and upper classes. But in the interdependent economic structure of modern capitalism all segments of society were affected. Moreover, the traditional consolations offered in time of stress by science and religion no longer seemed satisfactory or realistic. In an age of economic depression, ruled by relativism and indeterminism in thought, the idea of progress was neither an obvious fact nor an acceptable theory.

Members of the clergy, scientists, and educators were themselves uncertain and filled with doubts concerning the future. Rendered still more pessimistic and self-conscious by their disillusioning experience in the Great War, and armed with the knowledge of the failure of past civilizations, intellectuals found recent history a far from happy or hopeful guide to the future. But a growing number of American leaders, familiar with the mobilization of economic and human resources in World War I, and impressed by the apparent success of the Russian experiment, turned to the government to solve the depression. In any case, it was clear that only an extraordinary effort could restore prosperity. Progress, therefore, if it could no longer be regarded as inevitable, would seem to have to depend henceforth on man's own collective efforts to avert a general disaster.

If the federal government was to shoulder the major responsibility for pulling the United States out of the depression, the American people could account themselves fortunate that, in this period of economic stress, Herbert Clark Hoover was their newly elected President. With a broad background of administrative experience in business, social service, and government, and possessed of a disciplined technical knowledge of engineering and economics, Hoover easily surpassed most of his associates and contemporaries in the range of his intellectual capacities and practical achievements. After the Peace Conference he had impressed John Maynard Keynes, the brilliant young English economist, as "the only man who emerged from the ordeal of Paris with an enhanced reputation." [2] Indeed, one could say without much exaggeration that it was Hoover who, more than anyone else in the public life of his time, personified the American dream. Left an orphan at the age of ten, he rose above his obscure Quaker family origins in Iowa to work his way through Stanford University and secure an engineering degree. In his chosen career, unusual opportunities plus real ability brought quick success. As a valued employee, first of British mining interests, and then as a consulting engineer and shrewd businessman in his own right, Hoover traveled extensively over four continents and amassed a sizable fortune by the time he was forty.

The shock of the First World War destroyed the comfortable, upper-class, cosmopolitan way of life that Hoover had come to enjoy and appreciate. But the business talents and engineering skills he had applied with so much success in private enterprise were now in even greater demand for public service. As the efficient chairman of the relief commission in war-torn Belgium, as War Food Administrator in the United States, and then as director of American postwar relief activities in Central Europe, he acquired impressive international esteem. Upon his permanent return to the United States in the fall of 1919, he was accordingly a national political figure considered by both major parties as a possible nominee for President in 1920.

Even though the honor of the presidency was deferred, Hoover as Secretary of Commerce in the Harding and Coolidge administrations was able to exert considerable influence in shaping Republican policies. In his own department he built up a large and efficient bureaucracy of experts dedicated to the advancement of business interests at home and abroad. In this process he specifically encouraged business to organize itself into trade associations and to develop its own codes of fair competition. "We are passing," Hoover said, "from a period of extremely individualistic action into a period of associational activities." [3] Though the United States in the twenties sealed itself off from many foreign products through its return to the Republican program of higher protective tariffs, markets for American exports were nevertheless carefully cultivated. Political isolation implied no accompanying economic indifference to Europe or Asia, while in Latin America the United States continued to be active in both spheres.

Hailed by enthusiastic Republicans as the prophet of a new era of capitalism, whose engineering and business skills and experience would keep the nation on a permanently high plateau of unequaled prosperity, Hoover entered the White House with high expectations—only to have to face the supreme challenge of his lifetime when the stock market collapsed less than eight months after he had assumed office.

It was unfortunate, of course, for the new President that the depression, striking so quickly, came well before his own confident and optimistic political oratory could be forgotten. Speaking at Palo Alto on August 11, 1928, Hoover, in accepting the presidential nomination of his party, had made specific reference to mankind's long struggle to abolish want. "We in America today," he noted, "are nearer to the final triumph over poverty than ever before in the history of any land. The poorhouse is vanishing from among us." Though this goal admittedly had not been reached everywhere in the United States, Hoover concluded that "we shall soon with the help of God be within sight of the day when poverty will be banished from this nation. There is no guarantee against poverty equal to a job for every man. That is the primary purpose of the economic policies we advocate." Touching again upon this subject in his Inaugural Address, Hoover declared: "I have no fears for the future of our country. It is bright with hope. . . . The larger purpose of our economic thought should be to establish more firmly stability and security of business and employment and thereby remove poverty still further from our borders. . . . We have need further," he added, "to perfect the means by which Government can be adapted to human service." [4]

With no clear premonitions or forewarnings of disaster, President Hoover shared the optimism of the overwhelming majority of the citizenry. Any misgivings he may have had about the national economy, he confined to cautious admonitions regarding certain of the more speculative and inflationary practices of Wall Street. So long as business held up, no one in official circles wished to question the prevailing financial wisdom. Yet, if the Republicans had claimed credit for prosperity, it seemed plainly their function also to rehabilitate the country's sagging economic structure. And, as President Hoover had indicated in his Inaugural Address, government had a responsibility for human service. Accordingly, whatever its original hopes or inclinations, it was clear that the Hoover administration would be judged in terms of its success or failure in finding a solution to the depression. It was only natural, moreover, that the American people, conditioned in the twenties by the notion of presidential prosperity, should look expectantly to President Hoover for guidance and leadership.

In his own personal outlook, Hoover was conservative but not reactionary. Considered one of the more progressive Republicans after the First World War, he thought of himself as a believer in what he liked to call true liberalism. A self-made man, intensely individualistic in his background and experience, Hoover's natural opposition to socialism had been reinforced by his observation of postwar Europe. In 1922 he summarized his views in a small volume entitled *American Individualism.* Denying that he was a doctrinaire believer in classical laissez faire, Hoover defined American individualism as a progressive middle way between the radical extremes of socialism and anarchism. It was not the function of government to exercise overall control of the lives or property of its citizens. But government might help individuals and business to prosper in their legitimate concerns. As Secretary of Commerce, therefore, he had urged business to advance its interests through the formation of trade associations, and he had encouraged the idea of government support of a limited program of public works.[5]

The Hoover policies for dealing with the depression were in large part an outgrowth of his individualistic philosophy of business and government as well as a continuation of the type of economic program he had already envisaged before the stock market collapse. Ever hopeful that 1929 would follow the pattern of the short-lived recession of 1921, Hoover was opposed at the outset to government policies that might interfere with the chance of a natural economic recovery. At the same time, he did not agree with Secretary of the Treasury Andrew Mellon who contended that the depression, if it were to correct the abnormal conditions of the twenties, would first have to be allowed to run its course.

The basic causes of the disaster that had overtaken American business, Hoover believed, were rooted in Europe and in the inflationary aftermath of the World War, rather than in any organic defects of the American capitalist system. Nevertheless, it soon became apparent that the fall in stock prices was bound to have severe repercussions for the general state of the economy. Moreover, despite the understandably hopeful public statements of certain business and political leaders, many segments of the economy quickly began to show grave internal weaknesses. Agriculture in the United States, for example, had been in an almost continuous state of depression since the close of the war. But the work of Hoover's Farm Board, established in 1929 by Congress in a vain effort to support agricultural prices without acreage controls, resulted only in mounting surpluses. The increased tariff rates of the Hawley-Smoot bill proved equally useless to the farmer and invited reprisals against American industrial exports. Meanwhile, other Hoover policies, particularly his opposition to federal operation of Muscle Shoals on the Tennessee River, drew bitter criticism from progressives in Congress.

Instead of a program of positive federal controls, Hoover preferred voluntary association and cooperative action by business and government. As much as possible he worked on these premises in seeking to shore up the tottering economic structure of the country. Calling business leaders to a series of conferences at the White House within a few weeks of the stock market crash, Hoover exacted promises that industry would try to maintain existing levels of wages and employment. Government loans and relief funds were also made available for public works and for distribution to private and local agencies. But Hoover was implacably opposed to direct federal expenditures for unemployment relief, a policy he likened to a government dole and which he believed would subject the administration to improper social and political pressures.

At first the voluntary policy seemed to work as employment and wage levels held up despite a further fall of stock prices. But continuing declines in industrial production led inexorably to increasing unemployment by the fall of 1930. Although Hoover appointed a distinguished special advisory committee— the President's Organization on Unemployment Relief, headed by Walter S. Gifford, president of the American Telephone and Telegraph Company—and called upon local and private agencies to redouble their efforts, the varied problems of the depression were too vast and complex for the resources of the cities and states. Whatever small hopes remained for a quick economic recovery were foreclosed by the deepening financial crisis in Europe and the political impasse at home. Both the Democrats and progressive Republicans in Congress were at odds with the President over his opposition to direct federal spending for unemployment relief and more extensive works projects. Thus constructive planning or legislation proved almost impossible.

However justified the President's theories, they seemed out of touch with the political and social realities of the depression with its intense human problems and its multiplying examples of individual needs and suffering. The restricted relief and unemployment policies of the administration, moreover, stood in sharp contrast to the ambitious lending program established primarily for banks and private business concerns under the Reconstruction Finance Corporation. The RFC, which quickly became the country's chief weapon against the depression in 1932, won enough bipartisan support to be continued under the New Deal. Hoover had agreed to it originally with some reluctance, even though he could accept its program of loans more readily than any system of direct federal grants. In any case, the RFC appeared at first to be another unfortunate example of the inner confusions and contradictions of the administration's search for some solution to the depression.

Much denounced by progressives in both parties for favoring big business and a select number of larger banks in its loans, the RFC was perhaps more justifiably criticized on the grounds that it did little more than provide emergency resuscitation for the economy, while it prevented needed reforms. This was the judgment of the popular financial writer John T. Flynn, whose January 1933 article in *Harper's Magazine* helped to expose the aura of secrecy surrounding RFC loans. Flynn, convinced of the folly of attempting to preserve the existing wage-price structure of the economy, contended that "prices must come down to bring goods closer to the size of the available income . . . , income itself must be freed for purchasing by the extinguishment of excessive debts. Whether we like it or not," he continued, "this is what takes place. Any attempt to hold up prices or to save the weaker debtors necessarily prolongs the depression." The best way to relieve the stricken railroads of the country, for example, was through the "inevitable curative processes" of receivership. "The quicker the correction comes," Flynn wrote, "the quicker the regeneration of the road will come. This the R. F. C. has wholly ignored as a part of its depression surgery. Many roads are saddled with impossible, rigid bond loads. Instead of permitting the correction of this fatal flaw to take its course, the R. F. C. has actually added to the bond load. The roads," Flynn concluded, "will come out of the depression in the matter of debt worse than they went in." [6]

In support of Flynn's general line of argument, James Truslow Adams, the financier turned historian, wrote that "our railroads and other corporations should have scrapped more or less of the unwise and hampering debts they had incurred on false assumptions. That done, they would have entered the new race stripped to win." As Russell Leffingwell, a partner of J. P. Morgan and Company, later observed: "For a fatal year and a half the Reconstruction Finance Corporation continued to lend money to the banks on adequate collateral security and gradually bankrupted them in the effort to save them." [7]

Thus the RFC, dedicated to the effort to maintain the existing corporate structure of American business without major changes or reforms, may actually have retarded recovery. By pouring more funds into weak enterprises with large debts, the RFC burdened the remainder of the economy. It was ironic, indeed, to think that continued depression was perhaps therefore the price the country had to pay to preserve American capitalism. On the other hand, the enormous stake held by the American people in the nation's banks, railroads, and insurance companies dictated the resort to economic palliatives and preventive medicines rather than to drastic social surgery.

Whether financial policies that were applied too late, and which then offered too little, were worse than laissez faire is an intriguing question. In any case, Hoover's acceptance of the economic theory that a prosperity triggered by government subsidies and aid to business would eventually trickle down to the average citizen in the form of increased production and new jobs was less acceptable politically than the alternative concept of direct government unemployment relief and public works projects with high labor requirements. More than anything else, Hoover's stubborn, if principled, opposition to such federal spending helps to explain his overwhelming defeat in 1932. Whatever his administrative abilities, they were doomed to futility by his political ineptitude and failure to understand better the tremendous psychological havoc wrought by the depression.

The Hoover economic policies, although they may be regarded as the first comprehensive plan to meet the depression, were attacked from all sides as too timid, belated, and orthodox. Inadequate certainly in terms of quick results, their essential failure nevertheless helped spur others to advocate more satisfying reforms. And compared with former Presidents who had been in office in periods of depression over the last half-century, Hoover's course was positive and even radical. Curiously, this is equally the judgment of those who have praised him for anticipating the New Deal or condemned him for his departure from the tenets of laissez faire. From the latter point of view, economist Murray N. Rothbard in his book *America's Great Depression* has written that "Any propping up of shaky positions postpones liquidation and aggravates unsound conditions." Rothbard believes that Hoover, by abandoning the laissez faire to which he, in theory at least, was originally loyal, made the depression worse and contributed directly to the disastrous years of 1931 and 1932. Unfortunately, Rothbard contends, Hoover's training as an engineer, his reputation as a progressive Republican, and his belief in expertise, all inclined him toward planned action:

> Mr. Hoover met the challenge of the Great Depression by acting quickly and decisively, indeed almost continuously throughout his term of office, putting into effect "the greatest program of offense and defense" against depression ever attempted in America. Bravely he used every modern economic "tool," every device of progressive and "enlightened" economics, every facet of government planning, to combat the depression. For the first time, *laissez-faire* was boldly thrown overboard and every governmental weapon thrown into the breach.[8]

In contemporary comments both Charles Beard and Walter Lippmann commended Hoover's policies for their forecast of the economic philosophy of the New Deal. "It was Mr. Hoover," Lippmann pointed out in 1935, "who abandoned the principles of *laissez faire* in relation to the business cycle, established the conviction that prosperity and depression can be publicly controlled by political action, and drove out of the public consciousness the old idea that depressions must be overcome by private adjustment." From the experiments of the first six years of the depression, Lippmann, in analyzing what he felt might be the more permanent features of the New Deal, concluded that much of the program had been anticipated by FDR's predecessor. More critical of Hoover than was Lippmann, the Beards in their historical account written in the late 1930's still concluded that it was the former President who first rejected a policy of negation for "a program of positive action designed to mitigate, if not prevent, the evil consequences of the depression." Though his program was limited by his own conservative social philosophy, it nevertheless marked a radical and unprecedented acceptance of federal responsibility for the business cycle.[9]

In a crisis more serious in many ways than war, Hoover tried to lead the country out of the depression. His failure, political as well as economic, was perhaps a necessary prelude for the New Deal's later relative degree of success in both these vital areas. Although contrary to Hoover's own intentions, his efforts anticipated some of the political and economic programs of the future. "He had labored to create a psychological climate of opinion conducive to public confidence; instead he succeeded in fostering a necessary precondition for the legislative outburst of the New Deal years: the public's conviction that the job of recovery would require the forceful use of federal power." From this analysis, one of the most recent students of the Hoover administration suggests the plausible conclusion that "Before extreme measures can be considered, more conventional ones must first be tried. Before coercion will be tolerated, the full potentialities of persuasion must be exhausted. The voluntary militia must first thoroughly demonstrate its incompetence before a professional conscript army can be created. Only when voluntaryism has been tried and found wanting will a free, democratic people be prepared for more extreme measures."[10]

Finally, President Hoover himself, in contrast to his later indictment of virtually every aspect of the New Deal, in accepting his renomination in 1932 called attention to his efforts to meet the demoralization of the American economy. "We might have done nothing," he pointed out, but "That would have been utter ruin. Instead we met the situation with proposals to private business and the Congress of the most gigantic program of economic defense and counterattack ever evolved in the history of the Republic. . . . The function of the Federal Government in these times," he noted, "is to use its reserve powers and its strength for the protection of citizens and local governments by support to our institutions against forces beyond their control." Thus Hoover defended the role of his administration.[11]

However progressive was Hoover's record compared with past American practice, its failure—perhaps inevitable in terms of the political circumstances and economic solutions suggested —was most evident in the increasing disenchantment and disillusionment of most of the American people. "In the Hoover years, poverty in the midst of plenty became a daily condition of life, a palpable reality. Americans had merely to peer from their private windows at the world outside to see the economic confusion which gripped their land." [12]

Public pessimism was borne out in the gloomy statistics of the four years from 1929 to 1933: In this span national income declined from $81 to $49 billion, while per capita income, adjusted for the cost of living, fell from $681 to $495. Gross farm income shrank from nearly $12 to $5.3 billion. Salaries decreased 40 per cent, dividends nearly 57 per cent, and wages in industry 60 per cent. In the same period the value of stocks on the New York Exchange slumped from a high of $87 billion in 1929 to $19 billion in 1933. Bank failures in 1931 and 1932 were twice the number of the preceding two years, and general business failures almost doubled. Everywhere, except in the debt structure of the country, there was extreme deflation and a progressive shriveling up of business activity. Unemployment, according to the estimates of the American Federation of Labor, totaled almost three million persons by April 1930; nearly four million by that October; 6.8 million in October 1931; and close to eleven million a year later. In brief, by 1933 about one of every four in the labor force was out of work, and the gross national product was nearly a third less than in 1929. In human terms, one indication of the disastrous effect of the depression was the revelation that in the single month of February 1933, New York City alone spent $9.5 million for relief, nearly ten times the amount of October 1929.[13]

Faced with an economic disaster of such dimensions, the nation's leaders in thought and action began a common search for solutions that went far beyond the Hoover administration's own break with the past. Although conservatives continued to raise the dangers of a dole as evidenced in Great Britain, the desperation of homeless men seeking work and the presence of bread lines and soup kitchens in American cities were more convincing arguments for the spokesmen of reform. As "the contagion of fear" spread across the country, business executives, prominent churchmen, and noted educators, no less than labor leaders, progressive economists, and popular journalists, became the proponents of planning for a new social order.

Indicative of the country's changing temper and that of the top echelons of American business was an address on March 27, 1931, by Daniel Willard, president of the Baltimore and Ohio Railroad, at the fiftieth anniversary of the founding of the Wharton School of Finance in the University of Pennsylvania. America's intelligence and business skills were challenged, Willard asserted, by the great gap between its productive capacities and wealth and its dire unemployment and economic want. This contrast, in turn, raised important questions about "the very foundations of our political and economic system." Such a system

—"call it what you will—under which it is possible for five or six millions of willing and ablebodied men to be out of work and unable to secure work for months at a time, and with no source of income, cannot be said to be perfect or even satisfactory." As for himself, Willard declared that if he were placed in the circumstances confronting many idled workingmen, "I would steal before I would starve."[14]

At this time of crisis in the national economy, an important incentive to industrial planning was the recollection of the experience of the United States in the First World War. Despite the nation's disillusionment with the Great Crusade, it became popular to compare the struggle against the depression with the earlier fight to win the war. President Hoover, mindful of his own important wartime services, utilized the imagery of war and military terms to describe the policies of his administration. As Gilbert Seldes noted in 1933, Hoover "repeatedly used the figures of speech of war in his description of the depression. It was a skillful association of ideas, for the war was a difficult time which ended happily; it was exciting; and it was the last time the whole nation was united." [15]

To Hoover the war provided an example of both the mutual association of independent business units and their voluntary cooperation with the government. Accordingly, while he cited wartime precedents in asking Congress to establish the RFC, he was unwilling to draw upon the example of the war to justify centralized economic planning accompanied by government controls and heavy federal spending. "When Hoover invoked the analogy of war, he had in mind the spirit of unity and cooperation of a people at war, and not the vast expansion of federal authority that many others recalled and urged. In leading America in a war against depression, the President mobilized the nation as a voluntary militia force and not as a conscript army." [16]

National leaders outside the administration were more eager than the President to call upon the example of economic planning from the late war. "Must we wait for war to bring about effective cooperation between business and government?" asked Dean Wallace B. Donham of the Graduate School of Business at Harvard. William Gibbs McAdoo, Wilson's Secretary of the Treasury and head of the wartime Railroad Administration, proposed a Peace Industries Board. Otto T. Mallery, a leading advocate of public works in World War I, now recommended a federal bond issue, akin to the old Liberty Loans, to finance a public works program for the depression. Richard T. Ely, the University of Wisconsin economist, who had been impressed with Germany's economic planning, took the idea of William James's "The Moral Equivalent of War" to suggest a peacetime industrial army recruited from the ranks of the unemployed. Another academic figure, the distinguished Columbia University economic historian Edwin R. A. Seligman, reasoned that "If it is permissible for government to expend billions in wartime in the organization of production, it is no less legitimate for government in a great emergency of peacetime to do what it is also impossible for private individuals to accomplish." [17]

For a general reading audience, a few popular economists drew upon the analogy of war in their suggestions for economic planning. Stuart Chase advocated "A Ten Year Plan for America" with a blueprint for a Peace Industries Board to function in the present crisis and perhaps for years to come. Like the War Industries Board, the new organization should be staffed, Chase urged, by leaders drawn from private life as well as from government agencies. Undoubtedly such a plan would require revision of the antitrust laws. George Soule also claimed that the war had shown that planning was not at odds with American values. "Many of those who now advocate economic planning have been doing so, in one way or another, ever since the experiences of 1917–18. . . . " Citing some of the achievements of the government's industrial mobilization in World War I, Soule argued that "The lessons of this experience cannot be escaped. . . . If that military and industrial army had been mobilized not to kill, burn and shatter, but to substitute garden cities for slums, to restore soil fertility and reforest our waste regions, to carry out flood control, to increase the necessities of life available for those in the lower income groups, we could have achieved in a short time a large number of really desirable objectives. . . . It is nonsense to say that there is any physical impossibility of doing for peace purposes the sort of thing we actually did for war purposes," he concluded. According to William Trufant Foster, former president of Reed College and a popular writer on economics,

> If anyone still doubts that our economic troubles are mainly mental, let him consider what would happen if the United States declared war today. Everybody knows what would happen. Congress would unquestionably stop this interminable talk and appropriate three billion dollars—five billion—ten billion—any necessary amount. . . . Some day we shall realize that if money is available for a blood-and-bullets war, just as much money is available for a food-and-famine war. We shall see that if it is fitting to use collective action on a large scale to kill men abroad, it is fitting to use collective action on an equally large scale to save men at home. But that will require a change of mental attitude.[18]

In the book *America Faces the Future* (1932), Charles Beard, the noted historian, put together from varied sources a number of contemporary ideas for industrial planning. Beard himself advocated "A Five Year Plan for America," with a National Economic Council and a Board of Strategy and Planning modeled upon "the War Industries Board and other federal agencies created during the titanic effort to mobilize men and materials for the World War." The most important of the different economic blueprints edited by Beard was probably Gerard T. Swope's plan for revamping American industry. As a young man Swope had worked with Jane Addams at Hull House, and later he had served with Hugh Johnson in the War Department's Service of Supply. Now, as president of the General Electric Company, he submitted to President Hoover early in the depression a memorandum reminding him that "If we were faced with war, the President would immediately call a special session of Congress to declare war [and] to raise armies. . . . This unemployment situation in many ways is more serious even than war. Therefore it is suggested," Swope advised, "that an extra session of Congress be called and the President request it to issue a billion dollars of bonds, bearing a low interest rate, and that then a campaign be organized to sell these bonds, much as the Liberty Bond campaigns were organized when we entered the war thirteen years ago." [19]

In the face of mounting unemployment, Swope believed that business enterprise itself must take action or face coercive planning by government. To his fellow executives, therefore, he offered a plan calling for the inclusion of all major business firms within a complex of self-governing trade associations. By getting the various companies to cooperate with each other and to coordinate their business practices and techniques, Swope hoped the associations would be able to adjust supply to demand and to stabilize prices. Employees would get pensions and unemployment benefits, and at the top of the system there would be an overall national economic council. In short, what Swope proposed was the planned cartelization of a large part of American industry with certain guarantees and benefits to labor.[20]

In accord with Swope's suggestions, his General Electric colleague Owen D. Young pointed out that the American people and businessmen faced three alternatives: To do nothing, continuing the "system of intensified individualism which, because of its disordered action, necessarily brings great peaks of prosperity and valleys of depression." Or industry could acquiesce in government action "providing the means for employee protection through the power of taxation." Or industry itself could assume the responsibility for planning and stabilization.[21]

If the depression disillusioned business leaders with the effects of unrestricted competition, it also offered them an unparalleled opportunity to urge revision of the antitrust laws. Such revision would enable industry to go beyond the voluntary trade associations of the twenties in order to enforce economic self-planning. Thus there was much business support for Swope's scheme, illustrated in the comment "excellent" pronounced by Silas Strawn, president of the Chamber of Commerce in 1931. In December of that year, the Chamber of Commerce published a report of its committee "on continuity of business and employment." The outcome of a lengthy study by the Chamber of the effects of unemployment, the report pointed out that the United States had left the era of individualism and entered upon "a period in which the national economy must be recognized as the controlling factor. . . . To an onlooker from some other world," the Chamber's report declared, "our situation must seem as stupid and anomalous as it seems painful to us. We are in want because we have too much. People go hungry while our farmers cannot dispose of their surpluses of food; unemployed are anxious to work, while there is machinery idle with which they could make the things they need. Capital and labor, facilities for production and transportation, raw materials and food, all these essential things we have in seeming superabundance. We lack only applied intelligence to bring them fruitfully into employment." [22]

Henry I. Harriman, elected the incoming president of the Chamber of Commerce in 1932, also believed that a new era of intelligent planning was at hand. With the proper modification of the antitrust laws, business could be organized efficiently through its own trade associations. But American corporations, in turn, would have to assume greater responsibility for the social and economic security of their employees. "The men who, by reason of their broad experience, have been obliged to view business in this larger perspective," Harriman concluded, "have been conspicuously zealous in promoting the effort to carry into practical effect the philosophy of a planned economy, which, after all, is only the wider recognition of mutual responsibilities." [23]

To the editors of *Business Week* the depression meant, bluntly, the end of laissez faire. Asking "Do You Still Believe in Lazy-Fairies?", they asserted:

> This deflation has let the wind out of a good many grand old ideas. The grandest is the philosophy of letting-George-do-it, summed up in the fine French phrase, laissez-faire. . . .
> The one thing clear to men of candor everywhere, and at last to us in our maturity, is that it no longer works. . . . The legend of an "automatic equilibrium" upon which we can rely to correct chaos lingers only in the myth and magic of those financial air-castles where the enchanted princesses of political economy lie. In real life we know that someone pulls the strings and pushes the buttons before anything happens.

Planning, *Business Week* suggested, had "become the catchword to unlock the secret of safety from a Soviet 'menace.' . . . Politicians may peck at the issues," it concluded, "but to plan or not to plan is no longer the question. The real question is, who is to do it." [24]

American labor leaders, concerned mainly over jobs, moved in this same direction. Cautious at first, and slow to recognize the existence of mass unemployment, William Green and Matthew Woll, president and vice president of the American Federation of Labor, both espoused the planning and coordination of American industrial production in 1931. Woll, also the acting head of the conservative National Civic Federation, declared: "We need to meet the cold-blooded communist five-year plan with a warm-blooded ten-year plan of democratic idealism woven into the very pattern of our national fabric." In more specific terms, John L. Lewis of the United Mine Workers rejected the old notions of competition, laissez faire, and rugged individualism in favor of central planning for the coal industry.[25]

Like Lewis, Sidney Hillman of the Amalgamated Clothing Workers was a leader of a union in an industry ruined by ruthless competition. "Really to control unemployment," Hillman wrote, "we must think and act in terms of *economic planning* and of the coördination of the industrial endeavors of the nation." Voluntary cooperation was not enough, and "if we are to have more effective handling of our economic endeavors human intelligence must be backed by authority and power. That authority and power lie within the Congress of the United States. . . . The responsibility for national economic planning," Hillman concluded, "should be vested in a board representing labor, capital and the public." [26]

Ideas of planning and reform put forward by business and labor were also in the forefront of the American churches' thinking about the problems created by the depression. Under the impact of hard times, economic issues supplanted the older concern of the Social Gospel over such questions as prohibition and world peace. The middle-class philosophy that had characterized the churches' stand on these problems, as well as its attitude toward labor and the Negro, now gradually shifted toward the left. Although this was more true of individual clergymen than laymen, the governing bodies of some churches did not hesitate to take a forthright stand for sweeping social reforms.[27]

For instance, the Federal Council of the Churches of Christ in America, titular parent body of the major Protestant denominations, through a special study commission prepared a document to be read in the churches on Labor Day Sunday in 1931. Here it presented a severely critical picture of what the depression was doing to the lives of the American people. Specifically, it declared that grave imperfections in the existing economic system necessitated a new public attitude toward labor, as well as the reconstruction and planning of social and economic life according to true religious principles. Characterizing competition as "nothing more than a partly conventionalized embodiment of primeval selfishness," the council pointed out that the Christian ideal demanded, in contrast, "hearty support of a planned economic system." In conclusion, the council's spokesmen asserted:

> The facts of the situation themselves constitute a challenge to the churches to assume their rightful place of ethical leadership, to demand fundamental changes in present economic conditions, to protest against the selfish desire for wealth as the principal motive of industry, to insist upon the creation of an industrial society which shall have as its purpose economic security and freedom for the masses of mankind "even these least, my brethren," to seek the development of a social order which shall be based upon Jesus' principles of love and brotherhood.[28]

The following year, 1932, through its Social Service Commission, the Federal Council explained that "if our individual system of ownership and control of property is to continue, those who hold economic privileges must adopt a new attitude of intelligent social concern. . . . Up to the present time there is no adequate answer to those who contend that privileged classes do not surrender their privileges until they are taken from them. It remains to be demonstrated whether social conscience and social intelligence can together bring about our economic salvation." [29]

The depression also helped to encourage individual statements of a more radical theology. While many of the clergy continued to agree with Harry Emerson Fosdick's warning of the dangers of idealism and reforms without God, others went beyond Fosdick's criticism of capitalism to adopt a more complete socialist view. Harry F. Ward, professor of Christian Ethics at Union

Theological Seminary in New York City, deplored what he believed was a separation of religion and economics. Growing since the time of the Reformation, the split had now reached the point, he wrote, where "The antagonism between these two solutions for the problem of associated living is indeed irreconcilable. One will in the end give way to the other. Industrial society cannot continue in its present divided, inconsistent, increasingly futile state—partly humane and partly callous, now democratic and now imperialistic. Nor," he added, "can a religion whose function it is to develop the ethic of Jesus remain half bound to, and half free from, the living death of this acquisitive society. It must either transfuse our failing economic order with new life or die with it." Shifting ever further toward the radical left, Ward in 1931 indicted organized religion for its alliance with capitalism and nationalism. Still, Ward was hopeful that American Protestantism, with its traditions of protest and dissent, might yet recover its heritage and move in the direction of radical reform.[30]

Like Ward, Reinhold Niebuhr under the duress of the depression espoused a more radical social and political position. As pastor of a congregation ministering to unemployed auto workers in Detroit, Niebuhr was able to see firsthand the disastrous social and economic effects of the business crisis. On a broader scale he was impressed with the stark contrast between man's moral code as an individual and his cruel and brutal behavior in society. No longer confident in the automatic victory of the historic moral and ethical forces in the world, Niebuhr believed that power, used as intelligently as possible, was necessary to restrain and control the increasingly irrational elements in society.[31]

In the thirties Niebuhr became the major exponent of a juncture between "a more radical political orientation and more conservative religious convictions." He saw the depression as part of the paradox of capitalism, now ever more untenable as "its system of wealth production and unequal distribution" spread throughout the world. The competitive freedom of laissez faire was being supplanted in England and America by a form of state capitalism. Although the class struggle in the United States had not yet reached the fascist stage, continued dangers from overproduction and economic stagnation pointed in that direction. Thus there was need for planning and government controls, while the individual, in turn, became ever more "a unit in the crowd which is harangued by the political demagogue and supplies the political force by which reactionaries and radicals fight the political battles of the modern day. If he desires escape from the workday world he must find it in the standardized cinema and commercialized amusements. As modern civilization disintegrates and involves itself in national and civil wars he is called upon to become a unit in a great mechanical slaughtering enterprise. So modern civilization creates and destroys the individual." [32]

Niebuhr's critique of capitalism in the midst of its economic crisis was part of the same search for solutions that persuaded many of his fellow intellectuals to look hopefully to Soviet Russia. In communism and the Soviet experiment they believed they saw a workable alternative to the ills of capitalism and the fluctuations of the business cycle.

By the end of the First World War, the Russian Revolution had already stirred the idealism of radical intellectuals in the United States. Full of romantic enthusiasm for change and reform, and eager to see firsthand what was taking place under Bolshevik rule, the journalists John Reed and Lincoln Steffens, the amateur diplomat William C. Bullitt, and Isadora Duncan, votary of the modern dance, were among the first interested Americans to visit the Soviet Union. Frustrated at home by the

59

contrast between the old prewar progressivism and the postwar capitalist era of Harding and Coolidge, American liberals experienced a new surge of hope from the socialist struggles of the Soviet regime. Social workers, progressive educators, religious leaders in the Social Gospel, crusaders for sex freedom, and all types of reformers accordingly made their pilgrimage to see the new communist world. Symbolically, or so it seemed, American relief workers in famine-stricken Russia in 1921 were followed by hundreds of American experts and technicians, until the beginning of the depression in the United States found more than a thousand American engineers busily engaged in helping Russia to achieve its industrial Five-Year Plan.[33]

Especially significant was the estimate of the Soviet experiment by some of America's leading educators and academic figures. John Dewey, for example, wrote an influential account of his visit to Russia in 1928, which was first serialized in the *New Republic* and then reprinted in his *Impressions of Soviet Russia* (1929). Dewey saw in the Russian society and schools the fulfillment of some of his philosophic hopes and pragmatic educational ideals. The revolutionary "release of courage, energy and confidence in life" was transmitted to education and the work of the Soviet schools. Despite the many elements of propaganda there, Dewey was moved by the attitude of the students. "Those whom I met," he noted, "had a vitality and a kind of confidence in life—not to be confused with mere self-confidence —that afforded one of the most stimulating experiences of my life."[34] Dewey's admiration for some features of Soviet education was shared by other progressive educators in the United States, notably George S. Counts of Teachers College who published in 1931 *The Soviet Challenge to America* and a translation of *New Russia's Primer*.

Like the progressive educators, American social scientists were favorably impressed by their personal observations of Russian society. In 1927 two young economists, Rexford Tugwell of

Columbia University and Paul Douglas of the University of Chicago, were able to go to the Soviet Union as a part of the so-called American Trade Union Delegation. From this visit the social scientists in the delegation received a tremendous emotional stimulus. Douglas, who had described for his Russian hosts the difficulties of organized labor in the United States, felt his faith in socialism strengthened. There was a sense of national unity, of purpose, and of ideals in Russia now which Douglas, like Tugwell, accepted as an excuse for the Soviet dictatorship.[35]

Stuart Chase, who also contributed to the report of the delegation written mainly by Douglas, was concerned by the low output and poor working conditions of Soviet industry. Yet he, too, was impressed by the revolutionary zeal of the workers and by the even more ferocious drive of the plant managers, spurred on by the demands not of importunate capitalist stockholders but of Communist party functionaries. The Communist party representative, he wrote, requires "no further incentive than the burning zeal to create a new heaven and a new earth which flames in the breast of every good Communist. It is something—this flame—that one has to see to appreciate. There is nothing like it anywhere in the world today. . . . Will it last? I do not know. All I can report," Chase concluded, "is that after ten lean years it still scorches the face of the curious onlooker. So must the flaming sword of Allah have come over the plains of Mecca." Chase, whose book *A New Deal* helped to popularize the term in 1932, ended his volume with the famous comment: "Why should Russians have all the fun of remaking a world?" [36] This query touched the heart of the influence of the Soviet experiment, whether it was considered an example for the United States or a challenge to the American way of life.

Until 1930, two years after it was begun, Russia's Five-Year Plan had attracted little attention in the United States. But, with the depression as a catalyst, Americans contrasted economic stagnation at home to the surge of industrial progress under the Soviets. In 1932, with the economic descent approaching its nadir, a number of pro-Russian books appeared, including Joseph Freeman's *The Soviet Worker*, Waldo Frank's *Dawn in Russia*, William Z. Foster's *Toward Soviet America*, and Thomas Woody's *New Minds, New Men: The Emergence of the Soviet Citizen*. The Soviet example was also implicit in suggestions for economic planning by American socialists. Kirby Page's *A New Economic Order*, Norman Thomas' *America's Way Out*, Harry W. Laidler's *Socialist Planning*, and Sherwood Eddy's *Russia Today, What Can We Learn from It?* were some of the suggestive titles that contrasted the scientific planning of a collectivist order to the chaos of capitalism in the throes of the depression.[37]

American intellectuals were, however, by no means always uncritical admirers of Russian collectivism and economic planning. Nor did all accept the pro-Soviet view that violations of political liberty that would have been intolerable in America were justifiable as weapons in Russia's struggle to achieve a socialist society. William Henry Chamberlin, a veteran American newspaper correspondent in Moscow, pointed out that unlike the easygoing Soviet New Economic Policy of the 1920's, the new phase of the revolution under the Five-Year Plan entailed sacrifices for the Russian people not unlike those suffered by Americans in the depression. The Five-Year Plan, under which Russian life "has become harder, blacker, more intense, more practical . . . ," Chamberlin reported, "is inspiring or terrible, or both, according to the location of one's sympathies. It is an age of steel. . . ." In similar fashion, Maurice Hindus, the author of several popular works on Russia, defined the issue in his comment that, "If by the word liberalism we mean tolerance of opposition, then there is not a vestige of it in Russia. But if we mean by it advanced ideas and practices in social accommodation, then the Russian dictatorship has outliberalized the most liberal statesmen in the world." According to the Soviet apologist Lincoln Steffens, fascism was forcing more Americans "to see that 'free speech' is not an abstract 'right.' We want liberty for us, but not for Hitler and Mussolini. And the liberals can't make that 'right.' They can't see that time is a dimension; as it really is; and as the new culture of Soviet Russia can see. Treason to the Tsar wasn't a sin, treason to Communism is." [38]

Calls for economic planning and widespread references to the precedents of World War I and the example of Soviet Russia reflected an increasing disillusionment with individualism and a turn toward some form of collectivism as a pattern for American life. Deriding what he called "The Myth of Rugged American Individualism," Charles Beard cited historical instances of government intervention. Although there was a good side to individualism, including the need of its initiative and energy for the success of any effective enterprise, its philosophy and practice had become confined in the United States to getting more money. "The cold truth," Beard wrote, "is that the individualist creed . . . is principally responsible for the distress in which Western civilization finds itself. . . . The task before us, then," he concluded, "is not to furbish up an old slogan, but to get rid of it, to discover how much planning is necessary, by whom it can best be done, and what limitations must be imposed on the historic doctrine of Manchesterism." [39]

Guy Stanton Ford, the University of Minnesota historian, also tied American individualism to the historic past of the frontier and its perversion in the super-business individualism of post–Civil War days. Now, however, this was changed by science, which "is not interested in individuals." Convinced of the necessity of scientific planning in contrast to the haphazard methods of the past, Ford asked: "If our democratic craft is waterlogged with the individualism, localism, and laissez faire suitable to that bygone day, will it reach port in safety?" "The gist of the whole matter," concluded sociologist Henry Pratt Fairchild in *Harper's Magazine*, "is that, whether we like it or not, modern life has become so highly integrated, so inextricably socialized, so definitely organic, that the very concept of the individual is becoming obsolete." [40]

Even intellectuals and educational leaders less starry-eyed than some of those who had visited the Soviet Union in the 1920's were impressed by the significance of Russian economic planning. Like American business leaders, they thought such planning might be necessary if the United States were to avoid complete collectivism and a socialist society. "The danger in our situation," Dean Donham of the Harvard Business School noted, "lies not in radical propaganda, but in lack of effective business leadership." The example of the Soviet Union, he suggested, showed the advantages of "a general plan for American business. . . . For capitalism," he warned, "is on trial, and on the issue of this trial may depend the whole future of western civilization. The justification of capitalism is efficiency, not the efficiency of separate companies as producing and distributing units, but broad social efficiency." [41]

Like Dean Donham, Nicholas Murray Butler, president of Columbia University, was uneasy with the conservatism of business and the procrastination of government officials. "Gentlemen," he announced to his audience at the American Club of Paris in the summer of 1931, "if we wait too long, somebody will come forward with a solution that we may not like." The characteristic feature of the experiment in Russia, Butler declared, "is not that it is communist, but that it is being carried on with a plan in the face of planless opposition. The man with a plan," he added, "has a vast advantage over the group sauntering down the road of life complaining of the economic weather and wondering when the rain is going to stop." Butler believed the

United States should call an international conference to deal with the depression's paradox of poverty in the midst of plenty.[42]

A notable refutation of the arguments for planning which American liberals deduced from the First World War and the Soviet experiment was offered by Walter Lippmann in his widely featured newspaper column. Chiding the American people for their "hankering for supermen" and their demand for abnormal political methods, Lippmann contended that war and totalitarianism implied a singleminded purpose which was impossible in a free society. "In war the objectives are concrete and simple. You have to mobilize men and munitions at a point where you can force the enemy to sue for peace. The whole nation is agreed on the objective, and minorities are silenced." The Russians, Lippmann noted, were at least realists in not tolerating differences of opinion over their fundamental objectives. On the other hand, Americans were misled "by a false analogy between engineering and politics into thinking that human society can be planned the way an ocean liner, for example, is planned." In engineering the objectives were clear, but in a free human society, division of opinion was a natural and necessary part of politics. Planning, in other words, according to Lippman, was not a substitute for statesmanship.[43]

Having accepted the coercion inherent in planning, the Russians, Lippmann wrote, "are proceeding under a dictatorship with the most gigantic experiment in centralized control in all human history." The question facing the American people, therefore, was "whether the advantages of planning can be had without paying so terrible a price for them." Out of this dilemma, he believed that the Swope GE plan, for example, was "an illustration of the irreducible minimum of surrender required to inaugurate a stable and socially responsible industrial order on the foundation of capitalism and political democracy." Critical of President Hoover's efforts to maintain or restore the old price and wage levels of the twenties, Lippmann saw in the depression a necessary purgative effect which would act as a stimulus to new energy and enterprise.[44]

While most Americans—however desperate their economic plight—still sought solutions independent of foreign ideas and ideologies, the counsels of despair and the prophets of totalitarian utopias were becoming more strident and convincing. John Strachey's *The Coming Struggle for Power*, already popular in England, had an equal impact in the United States upon its publication here in 1933. In the contemporary conflict between fascism and communism, Strachey argued that the "capitalist system is dying and cannot be revived," and that communism, in contrast, was "the only method" by which human civilization "can be maintained at all. . . . Even to-day in the Soviet Union, during the very brunt of the initial struggles of a working-class dictatorship, before a classless society has fully emerged, there is perceptible," he noted, "an exhilaration of living which finds no parallel in the world. To travel from the capitalist world into Soviet territory," he declared, "is to pass from death to birth." [45]

Other widely read critiques of traditional capitalism viewed fascism rather than communism as the most likely outcome of the depression crisis. To John Chamberlain the United States's past, of which he wrote so pessimistically in *Farewell to Reform*, was an example of "the technique of liberal failure." It could only prepare the way for fascism and an eventual revolution. "The situation, looked upon with intelligence and considered as a long-range proposition," he decided, "can lead to but one of two personal conclusions: it can make one either a cynic or a revolutionist." Mauritz A. Hallgren, a Baltimore journalist and an associate of Mencken on the *Sun* newspapers, wrote: "A revolutionary crisis is inevitable. *The* revolution is not." Yet, if the revolution according to Marx was unlikely, Hallgren still believed that the price of preserving democracy would come too high for the United States. In the various extreme suggestions of planning by American intellectuals and businessmen, he discerned an unmistakable fascist tone.[46]

This was also the thesis of Lawrence Dennis' *Is Capitalism Doomed?* The charm of capitalism had been its variety and balance, according to Dennis, but now the business community in the United States had largely destroyed that. Yet its leaders continued to talk confidently of a rebirth—from the frontier, from science, or from another war. Only the last of these, he predicted, could provide the necessary strong leadership to revive American faith and spiritual values: "Keeping six to eight million men unemployed in America for several years is the best known way to prepare for war. The day a war starts somewhere in the world, millions of unemployed, farmers and industrialists, will heave a grateful sigh of relief. As American business picks up, American idealism will get acquainted with the moral issue of the new Armageddon, and history will repeat itself." [47]

If, indeed, America turned to fascism, some type of corporate business or managerial state was likely to prepare the way. As in Mussolini's Italy, economic-interest groups or blocs would comprise the foundation for politics, supplanting the traditional forms of representative or parliamentary government.[48] Without accepting political fascism as the necessary outcome of such economic changes, two intellectuals soon to take important places in the councils of the New Deal provided a classic analysis of the contemporary revolution in the corporate structure of American business. Their *Modern Corporation and Private Property*, first published in 1932, was reprinted some twenty times over the next thirty years.

To its authors, the lawyer Adolf A. Berle, Jr., and the economist Gardiner C. Means, corporations were the most significant institutions in modern society—what Veblen had called "master instruments of civilization." Convinced of the inadequacy of traditional economic theory, Berle and Means saw the modern corporation competing on equal terms with the political state. "The corporation has, in fact," they wrote, "become both a method of property tenure and a means of organizing economic life." While ownership was dispersed among thousands of stockholders, economic power was concentrated in a few dozen of the largest corporations, controlled not by their owners but by their managers or executive officers. "The future," Berle and Means predicted, "may see the economic organism, now typified by the corporation, not only on an equal plane with the state, but possibly even superseding it as the dominant form of social organization. The law of corporations, accordingly, might well be considered as a potential constitutional law for the new economic state, while business practice is increasingly assuming the aspect of economic statesmanship." [49]

Like Berle and Means, though with less clarity, Rexford Guy Tugwell also stressed a coming age of group management and socialization in industry, with business in turn dominated by technicians and experts and disciplined by government, trade associations, and the market. "It is apparent," he observed, "that what may be good business may also be bad economics." Convinced therefore that comprehensive national economic planning must supplant laissez faire, Tugwell contended that it was "a logical impossibility to have a planned economy and to have business operating its industry, just as it is also impossible to have one within our present constitutional and statutory structure." In the depths of the depression he was not afraid to face the radical implications of his views. "There is no denying," he wrote in March 1932, "that the contemporary situation in the United States has explosive possibilities. The future is becoming visible in Russia; the present is bitterly in contrast. . . ." [50]

The old Veblenian contrast between business and industry,

accepted by Berle and Means and Tugwell, was given great popular currency in one of the more extraordinary panaceas advanced as a solution to the depression. This was Technocracy, a set of ideas for supplanting the price system and eliminating unemployment advanced in the twenties by Howard Scott and a small group of industrial engineers and management consultants. In the Technocrats' new world, certificates to measure industrial energy and labor services would replace money, while skilled technicians and efficiency experts assumed the task of adjusting production and consumption to insure the highest possible standard of living for the entire population. With the depression, Scott received enough backing to put some engineers and architects to work at Columbia University on what was called an "Energy Survey of North America." Without revealing any clear or concrete political steps for achieving its program, Technocracy attracted an amazing amount of serious attention in the late fall of 1932. The books of the deceased Thorstein Veblen, who was still listed as an original member of the group, suddenly shot into popular demand, as well as articles about the movement by Scott and others. Scott emphasized the integration of the physical and social sciences, but most significant was Veblen's seminal work *The Engineers and the Price System* (1921), with its classic distinction between production for use and for private profit. Although experts ridiculed Scott's theories, the technocratic idea, fitting the depression mood, seemed to offer an answer—something new but not at odds with American traditions, as were fascism and communism.[51]

With the advent of the New Deal, Technocracy was quickly forgotten. But in the long, unhappy interval between Roosevelt's election and inauguration, it served as a useful outlet or catharsis for public discontent. Technocracy also raised the basic question of whether, in the grip of the depression, the great discoveries in science and engineering could continue to be applied to the welfare of mankind. Thus it popularized the problem—later explored in detail by Lewis Mumford and Stuart Chase, among others—of how the potential riches of an economy of abundance could be used to overcome the poverty and scarcity of the existing social and political order.[52]

Two years before the presidential contest of 1932, the midterm congressional elections already indicated that a political change, even more than new economic ideas, would be necessary to meet the depression. The prospects for radical politics in the United States, in eclipse since La Follette's defeat in 1924, now suddenly revived with the onset of the depression. In 1928 third-party presidential candidates had received less than 400,000 votes, the smallest percentage of the total popular vote since 1872. But from this dismal showing, and from an increasing disillusionment with both old parties, the League for Independent Political Action was formed in September 1929 to work for the creation of a new party.

Backed chiefly by liberal intellectuals, with some labor and socialist support, the league enjoyed a distinguished leadership with John Dewey as chairman, Oswald Garrison Villard as treasurer, and Paul H. Douglas as one of the vice-chairmen. Especially critical of the unequal distribution of the national income, the league proposed "a new political alignment whereby economic progressives will leave the old parties to the conservatives, and will together with those already outside the old parties unite to build a new party based on the principle of increased social planning and control." Although the league at first disavowed any intention to become in itself a new political party, the stock market crash and the 1930 congressional elections raised its hopes of converting American progressive leaders to the idea of a third party. John Dewey accordingly wrote to Senator George W. Norris on December 25, 1930, asking if he would not renounce the two major parties "and help give birth to a new party based upon the principle of planning and control for the purpose of building happier lives, a more just society and that peaceful world which was the dream of Him whose birthday we celebrate this Christmas Day." [53]

Norris' prompt reply to this Christmas missive was an admonition of political realism. Though he agreed with Dewey's indictment of the old parties, he pointed out that the time was too short and the expense too great for the organization of a new third party by 1932. As Dewey himself was compelled to admit in the series of articles on a new third party that he wrote for the *New Republic*, "Discontent with the two old parties does not of itself compel the formation of a new one." Nor, as Paul Douglas pointed out in his book *The Coming of a New Party*, was the Socialist party the answer to America's discontent.[54]

What was clear, however, was that the American people in their search for solutions to the depression wanted a political change, too. Economic reforms to be successful require effective political leadership. Only a dramatic political personality can arouse the popular backing needed to bring to fruition new and radical ideas. The intellectuals' quest in 1930 for a new party was thus less realistic than the people's preference for a dynamic political leader. It was in this light that Franklin Delano Roosevelt, without attracting widespread support from American intellectuals in 1932, nevertheless became the most important instrument for the success of their ideas.

THREE

🏴

Roosevelt in a Word

FRANKLIN DELANO ROOSEVELT as President of the United States was neither demigod nor devil. Too much of a politician to be a true charismatic leader or father figure, he was also too firmly a part of the American democratic tradition to become a dictator in the European pattern. Yet, as both his devoted disciples and diehard detractors agreed, it was Roosevelt who epitomized and characterized the New Deal. "If ever the right man came to occupy the right office at the right time," writes Heinz Eulau, "Franklin D. Roosevelt was that man. Indeed, so close was the contemporary identification of the New Deal and FDR, and so close does it continue to be in the perspective of history, that it is difficult to think of the one without the other." [1]

In 1932 it was Roosevelt's good fortune to be the most attractive and available candidate for the presidency at a time when victory for the Democratic party was virtually assured. It was also fortunate that the American electoral system did not postpone longer the opportunity for a sweeping shift in political power. Certainly it was clear by 1932 that the crisis in the American dream had reached a climax and that the Hoover Administration was unable to give meaningful direction to the country's search for some solution to the depression. Only the prospect of a political shift softened the angry temper of the nation. Happily, therefore, the presidential election gave the people the chance to solve their problems democratically under a changed political leadership. Even if the New Deal did not inaugurate a revolution in American life, it was apparent that the Hoover administration marked the end of an era and that psychologically the country was ready for a fresh start.

The symbol of the New Deal, Roosevelt in his personality and background was also an ideal representative of the popular hopes and aspirations of the thirties. Born into the Hudson River Valley aristocracy at Hyde Park, New York, he had enjoyed a singularly happy and privileged youth, culminating in his schooling at Groton and graduation from Harvard in 1904. His father, twenty-six years older than his mother, and a man of modest attainments, died in 1900 when Franklin was eighteen. Thus, like so many important historic figures, including most American Presidents, Roosevelt did not suffer the competition of a dominating or highly successful father. At the same time, however, he enjoyed the full attention and love of his mother, Sara Delano Roosevelt, a woman of great force and driving personality.[2]

In contrast to Hoover, Roosevelt's early career was comparatively sheltered. Neither poor nor orphaned, he never felt compelled to prepare for the kind of competitive business activities in which Herbert Hoover won success. Even in World War I, Roosevelt's duties as Assistant Secretary of the Navy kept him mainly in Washington, while Hoover through his relief work witnessed the harsher, more brutal side of the Great Crusade. Again during the twenties, Hoover, although he conformed comfortably enough to the business philosophy of the new era, was burdened nevertheless with the responsibilities of high office in an age of prosperity and depression.

To a much greater extent than Hoover, Roosevelt was able to ride with his times, offering little challenge to his environment. In his first entrance into politics, he was elected to the New York State Senate in 1910, the year of the Republican nadir under President Taft. Invited three years later to join Woodrow Wilson's official family, Roosevelt moved easily in the currents of the New Freedom and the World War. As the vice-presidential candidate in 1920, he was not personally affected by, or blamed for, the Democratic defeat. Then during the next eight years of the Republican high tide, Roosevelt was safely removed from the political scene as a result of the devastating and debilitating attack of polio he suffered in August 1921. In itself, Roosevelt's confinement did not work any major or magic transformation in his main ideas or interests. "The evidence," a biographer writes, "is that Roosevelt's illness did not alter but strengthened already existent or latent tendencies in his personality." And in the long run, it has been further suggested that Roosevelt's tragic blow even became a political asset, enhancing his appeal to those "who suffered, who had calamities, and who aspired to overcome them. Polio made an aristocratic Roosevelt into an underdog. For him it replaced the log cabin." [3]

That Roosevelt, aided by his wife and political friends like Louis Howe, was able, despite his crippling illness, to preserve his essential character and self-confidence was a tribute to his strong personality, as well as an indication of his enormous capacity for leadership and power. More than Hoover, Roosevelt possessed the patrician attributes of the aristocracy with the accompanying sense of *noblesse oblige*. His feeling of responsibility for public service was quite different from Hoover's pursuit of relief administration and government work as an exercise in technical business efficiency. Finally, as a politician Roosevelt had a greater confidence than Hoover in the democratic process. Without the latter's dogmatic adherence to certain fixed ideological principles, Roosevelt could believe that a Democratic party victory would make possible the type of broad reforms that would enable the country to climb from the depths of the depression. Thus the oft-noted juxtaposition of Hoover's successes with Roosevelt's business failures, in the rather dubious enterprises to which he lent his name in the twenties, is really of minimal significance when measured against Roosevelt's superior political skill and his understanding of the popular temper of the thirties.

Few politicians are intellectuals, and, indeed, it is probably not desirable that our leading statesmen be philosopher-kings. Scholarly devotion to ideas for their own sake can inhibit action and the constant need of the political leader to execute policies. Perhaps President Hoover had too many of the self-limiting traits of the intellectual, while Roosevelt, in contrast, was able to use ideas realistically to support and carry through his program. This is not to say, of course, that Roosevelt was hostile to ideas. At Harvard, in his courses in economics and history, he had been exposed to several notable teachers, and he wrote a good deal as editor of the *Crimson*. From his own family background and such friends and colleagues in the Wilson administration as Felix Frankfurter, Roosevelt also became accustomed to the mutual associations of the intellectual and political spheres. Both Eleanor and Sara Delano Roosevelt, with their dislike of the coarser side of politics, encouraged contacts and friendships with persons from the world of arts and letters, and Roosevelt as President continued to enjoy the stimulation of representative intellectuals who were invited to the White House.[4]

According to Frances Perkins, an old friend as well as the

first woman to become a member of the Cabinet, Roosevelt's working methods were those "of the common man as opposed to the intellectual and uncommon man." Dissenting from the popular fallacy that a statesman studies all the reports and evidence in scholarly fashion before making a decision, Miss Perkins noted:

> I have never seen a man of action proceed in this way. . . . Roosevelt's mentality was not intellectual in the sense in which that word is ordinarily used. He was a man of high intelligence, but he used *all* his faculties when he was thinking about a subject. He did not enjoy the intellectual process for its own sake as many educated, perhaps overeducated, men do. He did not enjoy debate and argument based on principles of logic so as to achieve superior position by marshaling facts and overcoming an opponent.

"During all the time I was associated with him," Raymond Moley adds, "I never knew him to read a serious book." But Moley admitted: "This is a pattern quite common among politicians." [5]

As Governor of New York in the four years preceding his presidency, Roosevelt began the practice of consulting professors and of appointing experts drawn from the colleges to serve in state administrative posts. In Albany, although he did not make the same crusading impact as had his predecessor, Roosevelt was still able to consolidate a number of the Alfred E. Smith reforms. He thus built a viable base for the New Deal program, and some of the seeds planted by Smith and Roosevelt in New York later flowered in Washington.[6] President Hoover, of course, also used academic advisers. At the outset of his administration he appointed the important President's Research Committee on Social Trends whose report, published in 1933, became a classic document in American social theory. But the Hoover administration, beset by increasing political hostility, was unable to translate the studies of its experts into relevant social reform legislation.

Early in 1932, in the midst of his active effort to secure the Democratic presidential nomination, Roosevelt again went to the colleges in search of help. Samuel I. Rosenman, his legal counsel in Albany, first consulted Raymond Moley, professor of politics at Columbia University. Moley, who had already enjoyed some contact with Roosevelt, then enlisted the support of his Columbia colleagues Rexford Guy Tugwell and Adolf A. Berle, Jr. These three, with Rosenman and such later additions as Hugh Johnson, formed the core of what came to be called the Brains Trust. They functioned primarily as idea men and speech writers, and helped to work out the important intellectual rationale for FDR's nomination and election campaigns.[7]

Probably too much has been made of the so-called pragmatism and ideological innocence of the New Deal. Thus, although Roosevelt naturally did not think of politics in intellectual terms, his general political philosophy and outlook nevertheless drew from the progressive and reform traditions in United States history. These, of course, were strengthened immensely by the depression. More influential, however, than the historic liberalism of the Democratic party of Jefferson and Jackson and the early Woodrow Wilson were many of the ideas of Theodore Roosevelt's New Nationalism. Illustrated in the social welfare legislation in some states and again in the economic mobilization of World War I, the New Nationalism's concept of positive government action was congenial to the theoreticians of the New Deal. Like John Dewey and Charles Beard, they believed society could be reformed through intelligent and organized political action. No member of the Brains Trust, according to Moley, accepted any longer the old Wilson-Brandeis version of liberalism with its faith in a free and competitive market economy. In the spirit of C. R. Van Hise's *Concentration and Control* and Herbert

Croly's *Promise of American Life*—major intellectual formulations of the Progressive era's New Nationalism—Roosevelt's key advisers in 1932 upheld the philosophy of government as a positive agency of social reform.[8]

For FDR, an early opportunity to speak out on national issues, after his own re-election in New York by an unprecedented plurality of 725,000 votes, came at the Conference of Governors in June 1931. There Roosevelt called for "concerted plans for the better use of our resources and the better planning of our social and economic life in general." The state governments, he emphasized, might serve a useful purpose as laboratories for social experimentation to cope with the depression. "In the long run," he asserted, "state and national planning is an essential to the future prosperity, happiness and the very existence of the American people." A month later, however, Roosevelt in an address at the University of Virginia complained of excessive costs and taxes in local government. The challenge to democracy in the late war was being repeated in administrative inefficiency and in the average citizen's dislike for the detailed and hard work necessary to secure good government.[9]

Probably the most significant of Roosevelt's pre-nomination speeches, and the one that most effectively captured the imagination of the public, was the famous "forgotten man" radio address, early in April 1932, which Ray Moley had drafted. Referring again to the experience of the United States in World War I, Roosevelt pointed out that the nation's mobilization then included not just the AEF and the Navy but economic, industrial, and social resources as well. "It was a great plan because it was built from bottom to top and not from top to bottom." Instead of the Hoover administration's efforts to revive big business, Roosevelt called "for plans like those of 1917 that . . . put their

78

faith once more in the forgotten man at the bottom of the economic pyramid." Of the vital changes he considered necessary to meet the depression, Roosevelt's specific suggestions—"restoring farmers' buying power, relief to the small banks and home-owners and a reconstructed tariff policy"—were all rather conventional and conservative.[10]

Encouraged by the Brains Trust, Roosevelt in the final months before his nomination continued to develop the broad theme of social and economic planning. At the Jefferson Day dinner at St. Paul, Minnesota, in April, he disassociated such planning from either selfish class interests or national regimentation. Citing the needs of an emergency "more grave than that of war," he declared:

> I plead not for class control but for a true concert of interests. The plans we make for this emergency, if we plan wisely and rest our structure upon a base sufficiently broad, may show the way to a more permanent safeguarding of our social and economic life to the end that we may in a large number avoid the terrible cycle of prosperity crumbling into depression. In this sense I favor economic planning, not for this period alone but for our needs for a long time to come.[11]

A month later at Oglethorpe University on May 22, Roosevelt offered his most specific commitment to the concept of the general planning of the nation's economy. Stressing the waste and want that came from the overproduction of goods and from unemployment in such professions as teaching, he urged the need for foresight and planning. The average citizen, he was confident, would accept a smaller return on his capital, and the loss of the thrill of trying to become a millionaire, in exchange for the security of his principal. "I believe," Roosevelt said, "that we are at the threshold of a fundamental change in our popular economic thought, that in the future we are going to think less about the producer and more about the consumer. . . . The country needs and, unless I mistake its temper, the country demands," he concluded, "bold, persistent experimentation. It is common sense to take a method and try it: If it fails, admit it frankly and try another. But above all, try something. The millions who are in want will not stand by silently forever while the things to satisfy their needs are within easy reach." [12]

The importance of the Brains Trust in applying Roosevelt's ideas to conditions in the United States in 1932 did not mean that FDR was dependent upon them for his own political philosophy. On the whole, the most helpful advisers were those who seemed to share his general outlook. Like most politicians, Roosevelt developed his philosophy not from books but through people and conversation. In contrast to the intellectual Woodrow Wilson, for example, he hated to be alone and seldom was. But despite the thoughts that he borrowed and the many ghost writers that he used, Justice Rosenman, one of his principal literary aides, has maintained that the ideas in Roosevelt's speeches were essentially his own. Ernest K. Lindley, a journalist who, like Rosenman, was close to Roosevelt, and who had drafted the Oglethorpe address, also pointed out that, in spite of the wide publicity they received and the speeches they wrote, the Brains Trust did not provide Roosevelt with either his political philosophy or his point of view.[13]

In fact, of course, the Brains Trust was only one of the many intellectual influences upon FDR. Its adherence to the philosophy of positive state action and comprehensive national planning ran counter to the more conservative and traditional forces within the Democratic party, heavily committed to economy and a balanced budget. And Arthur Schlesinger, Jr., suggests that after Roosevelt's nomination at Chicago the Brains Trust became somewhat less important. Roosevelt "was now the candidate of the entire party, not just of its liberal wing." Though the conservatives could not convert him, "they could at least keep him from excessive commitment." [14]

But against such conservative figures in his own party as Al

Smith, Senator Carter Glass, and vice-presidential candidate John
Nance Garner, there were ranged several prominent defecting
Republican progressive Senators—including Hiram Johnson,
Robert M. La Follette, and Bronson Cutting—backed up by
the maverick Democrat Huey Long. Despite their conflicting
economic views, each of these highly individualistic political
leaders supported FDR on election day. Meanwhile, Felix Frankfurter, a disciple of the Brandeis belief in trust-busting, in visits
to Hyde Park urged upon Roosevelt an updated version of the
New Freedom as a counterweight to Tugwell and Berle's espousal
of national economic planning. Roosevelt himself tried to appease
the varied ideological interests within his party. His speeches
after his July nomination accordingly seemed to face in different
directions and to uphold contradictory points of view. In Schlesinger's words, "with the campaign scarcely under way, the
candidate found himself in the center of a triangle of advice:
at one corner, integration and social planning; at another, re-
trenchment, budget balancing, and laissez faire; at a third, trust
busting and government regulation." [15]

Amidst these pressures, Roosevelt adhered mainly to a middle-
of-the road philosophy which he undoubtedly felt would be
safer politically and would conform to his own preference for
a progressivism without radical extremes. Under Moley, its
administrative chief, the Brains Trust was able to carry out the
difficult role of maintaining a semblance of intellectual consistency despite a welter of often discordant ideas and conflicting
counsel. Still the contradictions were sometimes striking, particularly between Roosevelt's criticisms of the Hoover administration for its failure to economize, and his own calls for some
form of social and economic planning.

In his speech accepting the Democratic nomination after his

dramatic flight to Chicago, Roosevelt coupled demands for economy with his pledge of "a new deal for the American people." He also adopted the position, which Hoover likewise asserted later in the campaign, that "Never before in modern history have the essential differences between the two major American parties stood out in such striking contrast as they do today. Republican leaders," Roosevelt charged, "not only have failed in material things, they have failed in national visions, because in disaster they have held out no hope, they have pointed out no path for the people below to climb back to places of security and of safety in our American life." [16]

On the whole, in his campaigning in the fall of 1932, Roosevelt acceded to the politicians' desire for caution. He thus took the expedient course of compromise between the traditional forces in the Democratic party and the Brains Trusters' view that the people wanted radicalism to combat the depression. At Columbus, Ohio, Roosevelt excoriated Hoover's economic policies and called for a program centered on federal regulation of banks, securities exchanges, and holding companies. To Tugwell it seemed that the Columbus speech was a throwback to the Progressive era and a reversal of the Brains Trust's carefully worked out ideas of social planning.[17] Only in his farm address at Topeka, Kansas, in mid-September, and later that month in his Commonwealth Club speech at San Francisco, did Roosevelt return to this theme. Otherwise, with his victory all but inevitable, Roosevelt wisely avoided specific commitment to any one set of ideas.

At Topeka, Roosevelt made it clear that because defects were found in certain governmental economic plans was no reason to despair or to abandon further studies of these problems. But there ought to be overall planning in agriculture to avoid scattering efforts through various federal agencies and unnecessary jumping from one expedient to another.

> We need unity of planning, coherence in our Administration and emphasis upon cures rather than upon drugs. . . .

Planning of that kind, designed primarily to gain a better and less wasteful distribution of agricultural productive effort, inevitably will point the way to readjustments in the distribution of the population in general. The pendulum is swinging back from the intense concentration of population in cities. We know the possibilities for the greater ease and comfort of modern rural and small town living. This does not mean a "back-to-the-land" movement in the ordinary sense of a return to agriculture, but it does mean definite efforts to decentralize industry.[18]

A week after his Topeka farm talk, Roosevelt at San Francisco, speaking with a minimum of change from a text composed by Berle, made his most controversial analysis of the need for comprehensive national planning. Tracing the rise of the modern political state, Roosevelt noted that the concept of limited government had developed as a protest against the centralized powers of absolute monarchs. Monarchies, in turn, had arisen from the semi-anarchy of the feudal period. While American tradition had long favored limited government, in the past half-century the growing consolidation of economic power in large industrial units had forced the government to assume the task of modifying or controlling big business. As America built up the West and reached its last frontiers, individual freedom and economic competition no longer operated automatically.

The Roosevelt argument was based directly on the historical assumption that the age of American economic expansion had come to a close. "A glance at the situation today," Roosevelt declared, "only too clearly indicates that equality of opportunity as we have known it no longer exists." Drawing upon the analogy of Frederick Jackson Turner's concept of the close of the frontier, FDR pointed out that such older safety valves against depression as the free lands of the West were gone. The economic and industrial freedom enjoyed under the laissez-faire philosophy of the nineteenth century was now impossible to pursue, and government restrictions henceforth must be accepted "not to hamper individualism but to protect it." The government as an enlightened administrator had to step in to preserve both liberty and prosperity. It was the task of government to help business formulate "an economic constitutional order," and Roosevelt added: "Happily, the times indicate that to create such an order not only is the proper policy of Government, but is the only line of safety for our economic structure as well." The time had come, Roosevelt concluded, "for a reappraisal of values. . . ."

> The day of the great promoter or the financial Titan, to whom we granted anything if only he would build, or develop, is over. Our task now is not discovery or exploitation of natural resources, or necessarily producing more goods. It is the soberer, less dramatic business of administering resources and plants already in hand, of seeking to reestablish foreign markets for our surplus production, of meeting the problem of underconsumption, of adjusting production to consumption, of distributing wealth and products more equitably, of adapting existing economic organization to the service of the people.[19]

It is doubtful that either Roosevelt or the Brains Trust accepted the pessimistic implications of the Commonwealth Club speech. Later, however, it seemed to historians that this address, more than any other, foreshadowed the economic philosophy of the New Deal. At the time, President Hoover took particular umbrage at Roosevelt's espousal of the closed-frontier, overbuilt concept of the American economy, and at Madison Square Garden in New York on October 31, he directly challenged

> the whole idea that we have ended the advance of America, that this country has reached the zenith of its power, the height of its development. That is the counsel of despair for the future of America. That is not the spirit by which we shall emerge from this depression. That is not the spirit that made this country. If it is true, every American must abandon the road of countless progress and unlimited opportunity. I deny that the promise of American life has been fulfilled, for that means we have begun the decline and fall. No nation can cease to move forward without degeneration of spirit.[20]

Again in his *Memoirs*, Hoover singled out Roosevelt's notions of a planned economy as an example of an approaching American collectivism—something "far more sinister," he wrote, "than even the miasmic climate of depression or a political campaign." But Hoover's view, like his comment that Roosevelt's first historic achievement was to raise "economic and social planning to the status of a recognized national policy" during his campaign for the presidency, was based more on hindsight and a knowledge of New Deal policies after the election than on what had been asserted in the fall of 1932.[21]

The initial reaction of American intellectuals to Roosevelt was critical: they liked his possible commitment to radical ideas but thought he was lacking in vision and too willing to go along with any policy that promised political dividends. "Is Roosevelt a Hero?" queried the *New Republic* early in 1931. This was admittedly always an unrealistic expectation of Americans assaying the prospects of their presidential candidates. In the case of Roosevelt, as the *New Republic's* editors pointed out, he could claim to be a progressive and liberal-minded successor to Governor Smith. But he was also involved with Tammany Hall in New York City politics. Although not personally tied to any sinister interests or hard-shelled prejudices of the past, he was nevertheless "not a man of great intellectual force or supreme moral stamina." Similar in tone to the *New Republic's* view were remarks in the *Nation* characterizing Roosevelt as "a charming person . . . who does not advance the cause of reform one whit." He "calls for palliatives . . . not cures . . . hauls down banners under which he has marched in the past and unfurls no new ones to the skies." [22]

One of the most celebrated, and also one of the most unfair, critical commentaries on Roosevelt before his nomination was that of Walter Lippmann in his column of January 8, 1932. There he accused Roosevelt of invoking "two-faced platitudes" in an effort to hold the support of both the right and left wings of his party. Regarding him as "a highly impressionable person, without a firm grasp of public affairs and without very strong convictions," Lippmann went on to characterize Roosevelt as "an amiable man with many philanthropic impulses," who "is not the dangerous enemy of anything. He is too eager to please." FDR, Lippmann concluded, "is no crusader. He is no tribune of the people. He is no enemy of entrenched privilege. He is a pleasant man who, without any important qualifications for the office, would very much like to be President." [23]

Such unflattering estimates of FDR as the prediction by Maxwell Perkins, Scribner's literary editor, that should he be elected "we *shall* have a woman president," with Franklin "ridden with both whip and spur" by Mrs. Roosevelt, were, of course, paralleled by equally dismal portraits of President Hoover. Ellery Sedgwick, editor of the *Atlantic Monthly*, came away from a few minutes' talk with the President, "who looked flabby and discouraged," convinced that "he is a man of no resources of mind or spirit beyond his administrative duties. He never reads except along lines that may prove 'useful.'" From Paris, the historian Worthington C. Ford, dubious of repeated assurances that business was solid and really sound while he lost a third of his income, wrote: "What a lot of cowards they are—from the President down." Robert Morss Lovett, professor of English and an editor of the *New Republic*, wrote that Hoover's re-election would be "a disaster to the nation, a danger to the world." In his opinion the President had "no conception of the state as an organ of general welfare. . . ." [24]

In the spring of 1932, on the eve of the Democratic convention, Oswald Garrison Villard, editor of the *Nation*, addressed an open letter to Roosevelt posing a series of "iffy" questions and demanding "Yes or No" answers. In personal reply to Villard, an old family friend, Roosevelt wagered that the *Nation,* without waiting for his formal answer, would advise its readers to vote for Norman Thomas on the grounds that Roosevelt's views would not be progressive or liberal enough to satisfy its editor. Roosevelt felt such an outcome probable even though "you and I go along together on more matters of national policy than you do with any other candidate of the Republican or Democratic parties. . . ." [25]

After Roosevelt's nomination at Chicago, the *Nation* noted his great opportunity but was still dubious of his abilities: "We respect him in his integrity, in the moral heroism that he has shown in the face of what would have been for most men a final physical disaster. But we can see in him no leader, and no evidence anywhere that he can rise to the needs of this extraordinary hour." Like Villard, Bruce Bliven, editor of the *New Republic,* was inclined to prejudge Roosevelt during the campaign. Citing his excellent chances for the presidency even before his nomination became a fact, Bliven wrote that "such a consummation would be no calamity for the American people." Yet Bliven announced that while Roosevelt was intelligent, honest and "notably progressive for one of his background . . . , if you don't want four years of disappointment as the result of your vote, I suggest that you might well vote for the Socialist candidate, whatever individual (named Norman Thomas) he happens to be!" [26]

This lack of enthusiasm for Roosevelt and support of Norman Thomas' candidacy by the *Nation* and the *New Republic* reflected a widespread attitude of intellectuals in the election of '32. Under Thomas, also its candidate for President in 1928, the Socialist party had begun to shift its main base from labor to the intellectuals. In 1932 an independent committee of ten thousand to back the Socialist slate gained such support from intellectuals that it was renamed the Committee of One Hundred Thousand. Paul Douglas, professor at the University of Chicago and a prime mover with John Dewey in third-party politics, was the Committee's chairman, while among the other officers were Morris R. Cohen, Dewey, Francis J. McConnell, Villard, and Reinhold Niebuhr. Equally impressive were the names of some of those who announced their affiliation with the Committee, including Elmer Davis, Henry Hazlitt, Lewis Gannett, Stuart Chase, Joseph Wood Krutch, W. E. Woodward, Stephen Vincent Benet, Robert Morss Lovett, Van Wyck Brooks, Lorado Taft, Ordway Tead, W. E. B. DuBois, Ben Huebsch, Kirby Page, Franklin P. Adams, Alexander Wolcott, Deems Taylor, George Gershwin, Eva Le Gallienne, Edna St. Vincent Millay, and Irwin Edman. Among the liberal clergy publicly behind Thomas were such stalwarts as John Haynes Holmes and Rabbi Stephen S. Wise. And on college campuses Roosevelt seemed sometimes to run third in the wake of the conservative backers of Hoover and the liberals with their Thomas-for-President Clubs.[27]

Even more surprising than the degree of intellectual support for Thomas was the extent of support in such circles for William Z. Foster, the Communist party candidate. Lewis Mumford, in reply to the urgings of his fellow literary critics Edmund Wilson and Malcolm Cowley that he read the Communist party platform, wrote in August 1932 that he saw no point "in being tied up even temporarily with a party whose official ideology—dialectical materialism—seems to me as unsound as it is cocky and self-confident, and whose political tactics are so transparently opportunist. We must have something better than the official Communist Party in this country," he added, "even if you and I have to take off our shirts and create it." Mumford, however, announced a few weeks later that "if I vote at all, it will be for the Communists, in order to express as emphatically as possible the belief that our present crisis calls for a complete and drastic reorientation in both the personal and the political life of the community." [28]

More positive than Mumford, some of his fellow intellectuals organized the League of Professional Groups for Foster and Ford, the Communist candidates for President and Vice President. In a statement, later expanded into a pamphlet entitled *Culture and the Crisis,* they publicly aligned themselves "with the frankly revolutionary Communist Party, the party of the workers." Denouncing the two major parties as "hopelessly corrupt" and the Socialists as a do-nothing party, the manifesto called for the kind of "practical and realizable ideal, as is being proved in the Soviet Union." "It is capitalism," the writers concluded, "which is destructive of all culture and Communism which desires to save civilization and its cultural heritage from the abyss to which the world crisis is driving it." Among the signers of the open letter were the novelists Theodore Dreiser, Sherwood Anderson, John Dos Passos, Erskine Caldwell, and Waldo Frank; and such critics and journalists as Edmund Wilson, Newton Arvin, Malcolm Cowley, Granville Hicks, Lincoln Steffens, and Matthew Josephson; as well as Professors Sidney Hook and Frederick L. Schuman.[29]

In the face of the number of well-known authors presumably voting for Foster or Thomas, it appeared that Roosevelt's backing in the literary world came chiefly from disaffected Republicans or conservative Democrats. Worthington C. Ford told James Truslow Adams that he was the only one in his family of prominent Republicans, mustering thirty-five votes, who favored Roosevelt. Adams, although at first ready to support FDR, by late summer found "it hard to stomach Roosevelt, and with him, Garner and the Democratic showing in the last Congress. . . ." Allan Nevins observed cautiously that "Nearly everyone in my circle of political and journalistic friends regards Roosevelt's election as highly probable." Yet he added: "My own opinion of Roosevelt is low, but so is my opinion of Hoover, and I am so sick of the alliance of the Republican party and the most selfish and reactionary element in Big Business that

I shall vote the Democratic ticket with pleasure if not enthusiasm. Roosevelt has been a lucky fellow; his name alone is worth a million votes. . . ." William Allen White, of course, despite his perennial avowals of progressivist sympathies, decided to vote for Hoover because, like George Norris, he "has made his life count." White also remarked: "I don't believe Franklin Roosevelt is going to give us a new day or a new deal. I fear that he will take us down rather than up." [30]

White was one of the company of journalists, including Lippmann and Villard, whose unfavorable opinion of FDR shifted substantially in the months after his election and inauguration. Villard, for example, in an election eve article "The Pot and the Kettle," had called "Roosevelt and Hoover Militarists Both." Afterward he rejoiced in "The End of Herbert Hoover." For Hoover's defeat, he wrote, "we give profoundest thanks. Even though the change to a Democratic Administration offers no real relief, . . . we cannot but take heart at the verdict. It quickens our faith in the essential right-mindedness of the electorate. . . ." In a post-election analysis for the English *New Statesman and Nation*, Villard pointed out that in contrast to Roosevelt the candidate, Roosevelt the President "has shown remarkable readiness of decision, vigour of leadership, and enough resourcefulness to make many of us who have known him long and well ask ourselves if this is the same man." Like Villard, H. L. Mencken found that the "utter collapse of Hoover gave me great delight." Roosevelt, he added, "is a weak sister, but he'll be better than Hoover." Uncharacteristic of the changing opinion among intellectuals was the acerb comment in the new radical monthly *Common Sense* that, though the "laughing boy from Hyde Park will soon replace the great glum engineer of Palo Alto, . . . for all our desire to express a smashing protest we only succeed in getting a new deal with the same old cards of political favors. The forgotten man has already been forgotten again and will only be remembered at the next election." [31]

Most interesting and perceptive was Walter Lippmann's view that there were good and bad crises in history. "The American people," he wrote, "have at last had a lucky break. The culminating crisis of the depression has occurred at the precise moment when they are in the best possible position to take advantage of it." In a dramatic contradiction of his earlier estimates, Lippmann declared: "The inauguration of Mr. Roosevelt has brought to the Presidency a man who is fresh in mind and bold in spirit, who has instantly captured the confidence of the people, whose power to act in the emergency will not be questioned." A good crisis, he concluded, such as the nation now faced, was one from which there came the will and the power to fashion solutions.[32]

Summing up the new intellectual climate among liberals, William Allen White, always as much an opportunist as he accused FDR of being, noted in the late spring of 1933 that "These are grand days, worth living for all these fears. . . . How do you account for him?" he asked Harold Ickes. "Was I just fooled in him before the election, or has he developed? As Governor of New York, I thought he was a good, two-legged Governor of the type that used to flourish in the first decade of the century under the influence of La Follette and Roosevelt. We had a lot of them . . . , and I thought your President was one of those. Instead of which he has developed magnitude and poise, more than all, power!" "As I see it, the President is our only hope," White told Frederic C. Howe. "Right or wrong, he is trying earnestly, honestly and courageously to do something, and if he makes five good hits in twelve, it is better than the human average." [33]

In his Inaugural Address Roosevelt, asserting his "firm belief that the only thing we have to fear is fear itself," called boldly for action and a popular forward movement "as a trained and loyal army willing to sacrifice for the good of a common discipline. . . . I assume unhesitatingly," he said, "the leadership of this great army of our people dedicated to a disciplined attack upon our common problems." The American people, he concluded, "have asked for discipline and direction under leadership. They have made me the present instrument of their wishes. In the spirit of the gift I take it." [34]

Desperately eager for salvation and reassurance, the greater public accepted with seemingly little question Roosevelt's almost warlike, quasi-totalitarian plea for disciplined action under strong leadership. "Official Washington was in the grip of a war psychology as surely as it had been in 1917," Ray Moley recalled. With amazing speed, in the midst of the frenzied pace of New Deal legislation in the "Hundred Days," the nation regained its confidence. A grim Congress accorded Roosevelt's bills the near-unanimous consent usually reserved for war legislation. Thus the banking crisis was surmounted with the passage of needed regulatory and reform legislation. And even devaluation of the dollar appeared to have no untoward effects except among those Americans living abroad who were now forced by their diminished incomes to return to the United States. Back home, the expatriate intellectuals quickly became caught up in the movement for social and economic reforms and in the new surge of cultural nationalism.[35]

There was general support across the country for the recovery and relief programs of the New Deal—the NRA, AAA, and the emergency public works and unemployment measures. Even business leaders, paralyzed and shaken by the crisis, offered little or no resistance to the unprecedented concentration of power in the office of the President. Never before in the United States, Beard and Smith concluded in their contemporary history of the Hundred Days, "has anything like such a drastic program of legislation and administrative orders been accepted with as little bitter and dogmatic opposition." [36]

Meanwhile, intellectuals of varied backgrounds were flocking to Washington. In a spirit and number reminiscent of the old World War I days, liberal reformers came prepared to work under the New Deal and to fight the battle against the depression. After a visit to the Department of Agriculture, where as he stood in an office "at least ten of my old western friends came in, old radicals, young ones, newspapermen, etc.," Sherwood Anderson concluded: "There is certainly a curiously exhilarating feeling. You cannot be there now without a feeling of the entire sincerity of many of these men." The frustrations of the intellectuals in the prosperity and depression of the previous decade were being resolved by entrance into public service. For many this step occurred at the right time to enable them to abandon Marxism and the liberals' drift toward the Communist party. Others from minority groups, or Jewish or Catholic in religion, were now welcome in Washington for the first time.[37]

Under the New Deal, Negro leaders, making up what was called Roosevelt's "Black Cabinet" or "Black Brains Trust," were added to various governmental departments as special consultants on race problems. Befriended also by Mrs. Roosevelt, and constantly assuming a more potent political influence in the larger Northern cities, the Negro was ready in the thirties to abandon his traditional allegiance to the Republican party. Harold Ickes, Secretary of the Interior and a former president of the Chicago branch of the National Association for the Advancement of Colored People, in hiring Negro intellectuals as advisers set an example which other Cabinet heads and bureau chiefs gradually followed. Often unhappy in their difficult role of seeking to further the kind of integration which their own special position in the government contradicted, the Negro advisers nevertheless had the satisfaction of seeing the number of Negroes in the

93

federal civil service more than doubled in the 1930's. (In terms of absolute numbers this increase was, of course, comparatively insignificant.) At the same time the traditional segregation of Negroes and whites in government offices and facilities also began to be abolished.[38]

Mostly of the middle class and born in the decade after 1895, the common bond of the New Dealers was that they were all at home in the world of ideas. Not necessarily specialists or scholars, they were rather generalists convinced of the importance of intelligence as an instrument of government. Progressive in their outlook, they harked back ideologically to the Square Deal of Theodore Roosevelt or to Wilson's New Freedom. Mostly, however, they accepted the Brains Trust's view that modern technology made bigness in business and government inevitable. The regulation and control of combination and monopoly, accordingly, was more practicable than any attempt to restore competition. Other New Dealers had gained their reform ideas from government service in the First World War or from their study of Beard, Dewey, or Veblen, or from the practical reforms of the Social Gospel, with perhaps settlement house work in New York or Chicago. Finally, the New Deal was a beneficiary of a social and economic revolution: the depression shifted business and finance from Wall Street to Washington and enhanced the political influence of American cities and of previously excluded urban ethnic groups.

However varied their social and intellectual backgrounds and job profiles, what was important was that "Roosevelt gave the New Dealers an opportunity to put ideas to work." Even if the President was not a good administrator in a narrow technical sense, he proved able to attract talented individuals into government service. "Little wonder it was, therefore," concludes historian Arthur Link, "that a generation of intellectuals should have regarded the New Deal Era as a time bright with the hope of good things." [39]

Veteran Democratic politicians and old-line bureaucrats, surveying the changed scene, naturally resented the influx of bright young men with their plans for remaking American society. The optimism of the new arrivals contrasted jarringly to the outlook of older official Washington. Harold Ickes, for example, came away from a dinner with a group from Congress struck by the pessimism of Senators Wheeler and Thomas. The latter confided that the Civilian Conservation Corps "might be found to have served as concentration camps for men marching against the Government, unless the situation improved rapidly. He also made the statement," Ickes remembered, "that in case of any serious outbreaks, those marching against the Government would not be headed by rioters but by Ph.D.'s and the educated classes." [40]

For jobs the intellectuals particularly favored the newer federal agencies or the research divisions being created in the traditional departments. In the old established bureaus it might take years to get ahead. A number of young government lawyers, many trained at the Harvard Law School and recommended by Felix Frankfurter, were much publicized because of their reputed influence and supposed radicalism. Unfortunately, more or less by chance, some were part of a nucleus of Communists in the office of the general counsel of the AAA under Jerome Frank. But the Agriculture Department of Henry Wallace and Rex Tugwell was also notable for its trained experts and old-line government intellectuals. Men like the economists Howard Tolley in the Bureau of Agricultural Economics and Assistant Secretary M. L. Wilson were able to institute long-range New Deal reform efforts despite the resistance of the more conservative farm organizations.[41]

As it happened, the bright and enthusiastic young New Deal intellectuals became the new men of power, not too different from some of the older bureaucrats they had supplanted. Many, indeed, eventually left Washington, disillusioned with the inevitable infighting and bureaucratic routines. But, although the exuberant mood of the New Deal could not be sustained throughout the thirties, the first years were an exciting time. And the New Deal, "one of the most buoyant movements in American history," even if it accomplished nothing else, "changed the mood of the country from the inert despair of the depression to a revival of self-belief more characteristically American." [42]

Thus at the time American intellectuals pretty much ignored the kinds of doubts later expressed by Walter Lippmann over the advisability of college professors becoming entangled "in the determination of policy and in the administration of government. . . . It is only knowledge freely acquired that is disinterested," Lippmann declared in an address at the University of Rochester in 1936. "When, therefore, men whose profession it is to teach and investigate become the makers of policy, become members of an administration in power, become politicians and leaders of causes, they are committed. Nothing they can say can be relied upon as disinterested. Nothing they can teach can be trusted as scientific. It is impossible to mix the pursuit of knowledge and the exercise of political power and those who have tried it turn out to be very bad politicians or they cease to be scholars." [43]

Despite the reliance of New Deal administrators on the colleges and universities for training personnel, President Roosevelt was reluctant at first to provide federal assistance to college students "because it would start the Government on a policy of paying for education, which has always been a state and local matter." Nevertheless, beginning in December 1933 the colleges and universities were granted funds from the Federal Emergency Relief Administration, and in 1935 the WPA was able to channel more funds and jobs to college students through the National Youth Administration. Outside its relief and public works measures, however, the New Deal showed little inclination either to help or interfere with the administration of higher education, while the President himself stressed the importance of maintaining the traditions of academic freedom in the nation's colleges.[44]

Though the depression enforced strict personal restraints on college campuses, it also heightened the intellectual unrest and growing social consciousness of many students. The undergraduates of the thirties were financially insecure and concerned over jobs and their own economic future, but they were also greatly interested in the new political leadership and philosophy of the New Deal. Enrollment in the social sciences soared in the thirties, and these courses in turn buttressed student criticism of the status quo. Left-wing youth groups, merged by December 1935 into the American Student Union, stressed particularly their sympathies with the labor and peace movements. Yet it was probably also true that most students—as James Wechsler, one of the young rebels of the thirties, later observed—harbored their own private dreams and, appreciating the personal sacrifices entailed in gaining an education, were content to prepare themselves for conventional success in life. They were also confident that, despite the depression, the world was going to hold together.[45]

At the center of the stage, the President and his advisers from the Cabinet and the Brains Trust assumed responsibility for giving direction and focus to the stream of legislation and ideas that characterized the early New Deal. Likening himself in a press conference to the quarterback of the team who calls the plays but who cannot predict the outcome or direction of the game, Roosevelt was the prime mover and catalyst, as well as the institutional embodiment and beneficiary, of the changing psychology of the American people. Determined to retain the initiative and hold his political advantage, he made effective use of public opinion. "Above all," concludes a recent scholar, "Roosevelt could persuade. This was his prime political asset. . . .

He created a sense of intimacy, of special sympathy and concern, or else a sense of comradeship, of being on a good team, or unified in support of a worthy and mutual cause. Variously a coach with a pep talk, a preacher with simple but pointed moralisms, or a military commander giving encouragement to the weary, he attained a sense of community with even hostile audiences." In his messages to Congress and formal speeches, and more especially in his press conferences and "fireside chats" over "I think it is a fact," wrote Frederick Lewis Allen, editor of *Harper's Magazine* and author of *Only Yesterday*, after his first meeting with the President, "that he is too charming—I mean that he so completely adjusts himself to people and circumstances as to give his policies a rubbery aspect; but one does not feel it when with him. There is no feeling of being seduced, so to speak; he is simply a thoroughly attractive and engaging man." [46]

The key measure in the New Deal's program was the National Recovery Act, which Roosevelt himself hailed as "the most important and far-reaching legislation ever enacted by the American Congress." Publicized by an enormous amount of pageantry and propaganda, with large parades by its supporters and badges and labels to indicate the businessmen's compliance with the labor and price provisions of the act, the NRA used social pres-
the radio, Roosevelt was able to marshal support for his policies.
sure and political coercion to try to reverse the disastrous deflationary spiral. General Hugh Johnson, picked by Roosevelt as its head, was an old World War I officer who had helped organize the draft and then functioned as a liaison between the Army and the War Industries Board. More than any of the New Deal agencies, the NRA utilized as models the industrial controls and regulatory methods of the First World War, including the labor provisions patterned on the War Labor Policies Board. In a radio talk from the White House, one of his first fireside chats, the President explained this aspect of the NRA. "In war," he pointed out, "in the gloom of night attack, soldiers

wear a bright badge on their shoulders to be sure that comrades do not fire on comrades. On that principle, those who cooperate in this program must know each other at a glance. That is why we have provided a badge of honor for this purpose. . . . While we are making this great common effort," he noted in concluding, "there should be no discord and dispute. This is no time to cavil or to question the standard set by this universal agreement. It is time for patience and understanding and cooperation." [47]

Not only in the NRA but in other important agencies as well, the New Deal drew heavily upon the experience of the First World War. The Civilian Conservation Corps, directed in part by Army officers and "about 85 per cent prepared for military life," was regarded as the depression's "moral equivalent for war." Secretary of Agriculture Wallace later pointed out that he had been ever mindful that the mechanism of the Agricultural Adjustment Act, established to cut back the farm surplus in peacetime, could also be used to encourage greater production in a war emergency. Similarly, the Tennessee Valley Authority, vastly expanding upon the Muscle Shoals dam built by the government in World War I, showed the possibilities of carrying wartime projects into a new era of social and economic planning. In asking the Congress to create the TVA, Roosevelt affirmed his picture of the broad rehabilitation under public control of the entire region with the comment: "In short, this power development of war days leads logically to national planning for a complete river watershed involving many States and the future lives and welfare of millions. It touches and gives life to all forms of human concerns." [48]

William Leuchtenburg, in calling attention to how much the New Deal owed to the legacy of World War I, points out that the "war provided a precedent for the concentration of executive authority, for the responsibility of government for the state of the economy, and for the role of Washington as the arbiter among social groups. It originated the practice of shunting aside the regular line agencies and creating new organizations with dramatic alphabetical titles." Yet the New Deal and the analog of war, as Leuchtenburg recognizes, was never a completely compelling argument. The examples were not really the same because the problems the country faced in 1917 and 1933, despite certain similarities, were actually quite different. War required and, in turn, stimulated via higher prices a tremendous surge of production. In a depression, on the other hand, prices kept falling so that overproduction or underconsumption became the immediate problem with a consequent need to try to reduce output and stimulate demand.[49]

Although Tugwell and some of the younger New Dealers hoped to use the example of wartime planning to help establish a new collectivized social and economic order, the World War I experience actually pointed more clearly in the direction of voluntary compliance by business and its cooperation with government through its own trade associations, now given renewed vigor through the NRA codes. The greatest usefulness of the example of war to the New Deal, therefore, was probably the support it generated for Roosevelt's call for national unity and for his concept of the government as a harmonizer of the varied economic interests of the country. In this way the rhetoric of war helped to still some of the voices of dissent until the initial economic emergency of 1933 and 1934 could be overcome and until the developing New Deal program could generate solid public approval.

As part of his emphasis on national unity in the fight against the depression, Roosevelt tried to preserve his image as a bipartisan national leader. The New Deal, the President told a Wisconsin crowd in August 1934, "seeks to cement our society, rich and poor, manual worker and brain worker, into a voluntary brotherhood of freemen, standing together, striving together, for the common good of all." Earlier that year Roosevelt, adhering to his strategy, refused to take part in the Jefferson Day celebrations. "Our strongest plea to the country in this particular year of grace," he said, "is that the recovery and reconstruction program is being accomplished by men and women of all parties —that I have repeatedly appealed to Republicans as much as to Democrats to do their part." [50]

In practice, the New Deal adopted a version of "the broker state," in which all politically important groups were to be included. Sometimes, however, too much attention was paid to the exaggerated claims of various economic blocs and pressure groups. Then the New Deal resembled the businessmen's government of the twenties which Roosevelt had criticized effectively in the 1932 campaign. In any case, it was clear that the New Deal Democrats had moved far from old-fashioned liberal ideals of limited government. Roosevelt was convinced that American freedom stood in greater danger from the vast aggregations of private wealth than from governmental abuse of individual rights. The New Deal philosophy accordingly denied the older American assumption that the people themselves could preserve their liberties from any type of interference except what might come from a centralized government. The emphasis of the New Deal was on a type of liberty that minimized individual freedom in favor of a greater social security and economic equality of the whole.[51]

In a survey of the first year of the NRA, Roosevelt denied that the reforms of the New Deal were heading the nation toward communism or fascism. Confessing that he was both amused and a little saddened at such charges, he declared: "The real truth of the matter is that for a number of years in our country the machinery of democracy had failed to function." Shortly thereafter, in some informal remarks, FDR complained about the country's lack of enthusiasm for planning. Perhaps, he suggested, this was because planning was not spectacular and offered no panacea "which would cure all our troubles in thirty days. We do not like to think ahead," the President concluded.

"And yet," he said, "this is the only solution!" Much of the problem was to keep progressives and liberals united in their willingness to accept change and combat reaction. "Democracy," he noted, "is not a static thing. It is an everlasting march. When our children grow up, they will still have problems to overcome." Dubious that the opponents of the New Deal would "want to return to that individualism of which they prate," Roosevelt warned of the danger that the new instruments of public power might be used for selfish purposes. "In the hands of a people's Government this power is wholesome and proper. But in the hands of political puppets of an economic autocracy such power would provide shackles for the liberties of the people." [52]

To conservatives the President's aggressive leadership and demands for national unity and social planning to achieve a vital, living democracy raised fears of a coming era of personal rule and democratic despotism. Radicals, on the other hand, though frankly doubting that Roosevelt could save American capitalism, tended to admire his personal qualities. Illustrative of conservative opinion was Worthington C. Ford's comment from Europe, after he had been associated with Hitler for nine days at Bayreuth, that "Roosevelt is getting his higher prices for the time and at the cost of a dictatorship that no one can measure." Though William Allen White supported the early New Deal measures, he too was troubled by the trend toward centralization of power and authority in Washington. "I am concerned about the danger to the Bill of Rights," he wrote to Allan Nevins. The President's courage, unless it was marked by greater intelligence and purpose, could become arrogance, he feared. Invited to dine at the White House, James Truslow Adams conveyed to the President, with polite expressions of appreciation and wishes for his success, the dismal statement that "personally I am far more worried about America than I have been at any preceding period of the depression." [53]

From a left-wing point of view, Mauritz Hallgren, in his critical, but not totally unsympathetic, book *The Gay Reformer*, stressed Roosevelt's essentially conservative purpose. "It should be obvious," he wrote, "that Franklin Roosevelt has been and is no revolutionary, nor yet a reactionary radical of the Bryan or La Follette or Villard school." Conceding FDR's sincere desire to preserve capitalism and correct some of its weaknesses, Hallgren argued that the President "has believed it wise to keep the submerged classes satisfied with a modicum of bread and an unusually spectacular and noisy circus." Watching Roosevelt in the newspapers and on the movie screen, Lincoln Steffens got "the impression that there is no dictatorship in him." On the other hand, believing that the President had failed to gain the cooperation of business, he predicted that the next step would be some form of compulsion. Summing up the hopes and fears of the dissenters, H. L. Mencken observed sarcastically: "I begin to believe seriously that the Second Coming may be at hand. Roosevelt's parodies of the Sermon on the Mount become more and more realistic. The heavens may open at any moment. Keep your suitcase packed." [54]

Most ironic of all, perhaps, in light of the varied criticisms of Roosevelt from radicals and conservatives, was the way the New Deal reforms wrecked the Socialist party. In the worst crisis in the history of American capitalism, the party was unable to reap its expected electoral reward, and instead its membership began to drift away. In the words of its modern historian, "The story of the decline of the Socialist Party since 1933 is, for the most part, the story of the political success of the New Deal." Looking back years later, Norman Thomas noted that "What cut the ground out pretty completely from under us was this. It was Roosevelt in a word. You don't need anything more." [55]

Yet the radical appeal of the New Deal's collectivism hardly indicated a victory for creeping socialism or the demise of capitalism. Clearly Roosevelt, in pursuing a middle way, was able at once to preserve capitalism and at the same time disarm both its revolutionary and reactionary critics. Thus the new political economy which emerged in the thirties was apparently destined to be an interesting mixture, an amalgam of private enterprise and government controls, an American version of state capitalism and social democracy.

FOUR

Toward a New Public Philosophy

THE DEVELOPING political economy of the New Deal was part of a new public philosophy in the United States which emerged most clearly and directly from the crisis of the depression. With President Roosevelt as its effective national leader, the New Deal undertook to formulate a set of ideas and ideals to supplant the older ideologies governing American life and thought. Although notably practical and eclectic in its search for solutions, the Roosevelt administration's varied program of social and economic reforms was also related to a worldwide intellectual upheaval. "The crisis of the nineteen-thirties, which opened for Americans as a financial panic and as a sudden stop to the gluttony of the boom period, marked," as Alfred Kazin has pointed out, "the opening phase of a revolution in world society more comprehensive but no more significant than the transformation it effected in American life."[1]

In this sense, then, there was a new public philosophy, derived it is true from the American democratic tradition, but also part of a great transformation in concepts of government and economic policy that had begun to take form in Europe even before the First World War. In other words, in a figure of speech more usually applied to the American colonial period, the New World in the twentieth century continued to be cast in an Old World mold. And the New Deal itself had an important part of its heritage in European intellectual history.

From the Old World the nationalism of the nineteenth century gradually spread in the next half-century around the globe. But nationalism in terms of the self-determination and unification of peoples was also paralleled by an increasing mercantilism and statism in almost all countries. The concentration and control, within the confines of a narrow political nationalism, of citizens or subjects accordingly became one of the distinguishing characteristics of the modern world. This phenomenon—most conspicuous in the totalitarian states that followed the dictates of communism or fascism—was, however, by no means lacking in the combination of social democracy and state capitalism that prevailed in other Western nations. It was, indeed, the national state and the worship of nationalism that formed the hard core of the new public philosophy of the twentieth century, supplanting in its triumph both the secular philosophy of the natural rights of man and the traditional faith in supernatural religion.

Although the nationalism of the New Deal in its early years was essentially isolationist, concentrating first on economic recovery at home, the challenge from abroad was never wholly absent. Within a few weeks of each other, Roosevelt and Adolf Hitler took high office, and in the comparison between European and American economic recovery the Nazis provided the stimulus of an adversary. Thus the reciprocal trade treaties, espoused by Secretary of State Cordell Hull, served both a nationalist and an internationalist purpose, seeking to preserve American foreign markets and attempting to minimize German trade in such regions as Latin America. "Every nation on earth today," Stuart Chase noted, "is drifting, nay flying, towards economic nationalism. . . . The New Deal is but a single engagement on a world-wide battle front." Convinced by the collapse of the London Economic Conference that the old international order of laissez faire was now impossible, the *Nation* concluded:

> The New Deal in the United States, the new forms of economic organization in Germany and Italy, and the planned economy of the Soviet Union are merely the latest and most extreme manifestations of a tendency which has been apparent for the greater part of a century—for nations and groups, capital as well as labor, demand a larger measure of security than can be provided by a system of free competition." [2]

Meanwhile, in the rush of innovations which the American public largely accepted as necessary to the recovery and reform program at home, there was a continuing element of national economic planning which gave to the later New Deal, as Richard Hofstadter has pointed out, "a social-democratic tinge never before present in American reform movements." With all Roosevelt's fondness for experimentation and for all his adherence to practical politics, the inner counsels of the New Deal included much eloquent exposition of novel political and economic theories. In the political economy of the New Deal, it was evident that ideas were important and that government action in all its varied forms was to be well supported by a wide range of theory. But what the New Deal lacked in the consistency or rationality of its planning it made up in "a masterly shifting equipoise of interests. . . . If the state was believed neutral in the days of T. R. because its leaders claimed to sanction favors for no one, the state under F.D.R. could be called neutral only in the sense that it offered favors to everyone." [3]

The era of the New Deal thus marked a general attack upon the doctrines of a laissez-faire individualism or Darwinian struggle for survival. No longer were poverty and unemployment to be condoned as the fruits of improvidence; no longer was competition considered superior to cooperation and association as a regulator of the national economy. With the powerful aid of the federal government, farmers and labor gained a new privileged position in the American economy, and progressive reform measures were henceforth not deemed the exclusive interest of the upper and middle classes. For the older isolated individualism there was now substituted, in the Beards' phrase, "an interlaced system of exchange and mutuality correctly described as collectivism." [4]

The new departure in American thought was explicated by a galaxy of intellectuals, functioning both within and on the fringes of the New Deal. Serving alike as the muckrakers and theorists of the 1930's, the intellectuals also became the architects of reform, drawing up the outlines and blueprints of the society of the future. New frontiers, the march of democracy, the open door at home, and insurgent America were some of the slogans of the new public philosophy set forth in the writings of New Deal theorists.

Of the many intellectuals drawn into government service under the New Deal, no one enjoyed a higher estate than Secretary of Agriculture Henry Agard Wallace. Only a decade before, his father Henry C. Wallace had occupied the same office, and both men also continued in the family tradition of editing and managing *Wallace's Farmer*, an Iowa journal begun back in the 1890's by Henry A.'s grandfather. In running their popular agricultural magazine, the Wallaces obviously had a strategic listening post for an understanding of the farmer's many grievances and complaints. As these multiplied again after the First World War, the elder Wallace grew more and more disillusioned over the unwillingness of his fellow Republican leaders to accept suggested reforms. Young Henry, in turn, soured by his father's difficulties in the Harding and Coolidge administrations, and embittered particularly by Herbert Hoover's opposition to any legislation for price-fixing, abandoned the family's allegiance to the Republican party and in 1928 supported Al Smith for President. Four years later, after Rex Tugwell introduced him into the Roosevelt circle, he found himself favored with a surprise appointment to the Cabinet.[5]

Although in the third generation of a family already distinguished in agriculture, Henry A. Wallace's own contributions were outstanding. He was interested in plant genetics even before he attended Iowa State College, and he became widely known for his pioneer work in developing hybrid corn. Also expert in farm economics and a frequent writer on agricultural subjects, Wallace was well equipped for his place in the administration. At the same time, with his interest in science and statistics, Wallace had deep religious feelings which carried him beyond orthodox Christianity and into the realm of the mystical and occult. Extremely practical where agriculture was the major concern, Wallace was, however, something of an evangelist and crusader for the other causes that attracted his wide-ranging idealism. His sincerity evidently appealed to Roosevelt, while it also helped him become a significant representative of the reform spirit of the early New Deal. In the midst of the struggles for power continually being waged in Washington by politicians and bureaucrats, Wallace with his informality and modesty was a refreshing, if quixotic, figure.

The Agricultural Adjustment Act of 1933, a companion piece to the NRA, proposed price benefits to the farmer in return for acreage and production controls on the major staple crops of wheat, cotton, hogs, and tobacco. The culmination of much expert thinking by agricultural economists and organizations over the past decade, the act was an effort to adjust farm prices and production and to establish a relative balance between agriculture and the rest of the national economy. Although the

President told Congress that it was "a new and untrod path," [6] and although the Supreme Court declared unconstitutional the processing tax by which it was originally financed, the basic ideas behind the AAA have changed little and remain in general the foundation of the federal government's present-day agriculture policies.

To Henry Wallace the plight of the farmer was part of a general crisis in modern civilization. Accepting much of the analysis and point of view outlined in Roosevelt's Commonwealth Club speech during the 1932 campaign, he related the farm problem to the perspectives of history and the New Deal's own economic program. Implicit in the thinking of the early New Dealers was the view that America was economically and socially a sick society, and that a comprehensive planned regimen of therapeutic reform was necessary. While eschewing the radical programs favored by the left- and right-wing governments of Europe, the Roosevelt administration was nevertheless convinced that voluntary private planning could not restore the country's economic balance. America, in the eyes of Roosevelt and his advisers, had achieved a mature economy in which the major problem was no longer one of increasing production but of the proper distribution of consumer goods. Concentration of wealth had resulted in overproduction, or at least in an inability of the masses of the people to consume their own factory and farm output. By economic and political reforms the New Deal hoped to redistribute the country's wealth and restore purchasing power among the lower classes. The United States, then, without sacrificing capitalism, would be able to achieve a balanced economy and free itself from dependence on world export markets.

Wallace's most important literary contribution to the political economy of the New Deal was *New Frontiers*, a book he published in 1934. Following in the path of the explorers and pioneers who had built America, Wallace considered the possibilities of new frontiers with the religious zeal of an enthusiastic utopian. Likening the world of his dreams to "a new state of heart and mind," he called on his readers to "invent, build and put to work new social machinery. This machinery," he affirmed, "will carry out the Sermon on the Mount as well as the present social machinery carries out and intensifies the law of the jungle." There was no doubt in Wallace's own mind of the disastrous nature of the Republican policies of what he called the "twelve long years" from Harding to Hoover. This new era of a false prosperity for agriculture, in which "one farm in every four was sold for debt or taxes," had disappeared with the fall of the financial gods that America had worshiped before the 1929 crash. "Perhaps," Wallace reflected, "we needed that experience so that our sense for the truer gods and values beyond present frontiers may now receive our whole-hearted allegiance." [7]

But the way in which America had traditionally abused its soil and its agricultural population recalled for Wallace the disturbing parallel of the decline of the Italian farms in ancient Rome. American democracy, he feared, faced a situation not unlike that of the Graeco-Roman world in the time of Augustus. The close of the nineteenth-century westward movement required the substitution of new frontiers if American and Western civilization were to survive. The American people would have to acquire through science and government the kind of harmony they had formerly achieved through natural environmental factors. "An enduring democracy can be had only by promoting a balance among all our major producing groups, and in such a way as does not build up a small, inordinately wealthy class. . . . The complexities and the confusion of modern civilization are such that legislators quickly forget objectives of social and economic balance, and give way to the special pressures of the moment." [8]

Wallace acknowledged that there was "something wooden and

inhuman about the government interfering in a definite precise way with the details of our private and business lives." The World War had given a tremendous impetus to comprehensive planning, but except in the matter of natural resources like farm land, he saw no reason why the United States should adopt such a system unless faced by a continuing emergency. Denying that the NRA and AAA were intended as permanent controls, he asserted: "We are committed to getting the farmer, the laborer, and the industrialist such share of the national income as will put each in a balanced relationship with the other. Without such a balance the foundation of the state sags." Wallace thought the regulatory functions of the marketplace had broken down in both national and international trade. Government, he argued, must provide the substitute, and its regulation would have to extend into new areas. "If our civilization is to continue on the present complex basis," he wrote, "modern democracy must make rules of the game that go beyond tariffs, monetary policy, freight rate structures, taxation and similar policies which have long concerned the central government. The new rules must also get into fields more directly concerning harmonious relationships between prices, margins, profits and distribution of income." This, he felt, represented the essential challenge to Americans, whom he called "new frontiersmen." Wallace also pointed out that "in order to build the ideal democracy we need more people who know and are willing to pay the price that must be paid to bring about harmonious relationships between this nation and other nations. . . ."[9]

It was precisely in this area of foreign relations that America, however reluctantly, would have to choose between the policies of nationalism and internationalism. Exploring this dilemma in detail in a widely read pamphlet issued jointly in 1934 by the Foreign Policy Association and the World Peace Foundation, Wallace was able to suggest a middle ground which he called "New Dealing with the World." Cut off economically from other nations behind a high tariff barrier, the United States, Wallace acknowledged, might be able to enjoy an isolated prosperity by the rigid regimentation and planning of almost every aspect of life and thought. But the spiritual price of such economic nationalism would come too high. "I would hate to live in a country where individual thought is punished and stifled, and where speech is no longer free." Yet, at the same time, there was a danger in the opposite policy of "entangling alliances" and cutthroat international trade. "I see the seeds of war," he noted, "alike in *laissez-faire* accumulating pressing surpluses at home, and in seeking by hook or crook to thrust such surpluses abroad." Thus, in the middle ground between economic isolation and aggressive intervention in overseas markets, Wallace found an "irresistible logic" behind a policy of "trying to build up consumption per capita at home, as a substitute for the continual search for new consumers abroad. . . . Our New Deal," he concluded, "seeks to promote consumption more soundly. It directs purchasing power to those in need, by wage advances and alleviations of debt. It lessens the need to force exports. It looks toward balancing production with consumption at home." [10]

In much of its program the New Deal, it was true, both required and encouraged the subordination of the individual to the group interest. But, in the age-old fashion of American utopians, Wallace was confident that eventually this temporary loss of individuality would lead to a more stable and permanent individualism. Looking back in time as well as ahead to the future, he hoped that the happy experience of the older, small, New England–type town or agrarian community could be recreated in the new planned frontier of the future. "The keynote of the new frontier is cooperation just as that of the old frontier was individualistic competition. . . . Power and wealth were worshiped in the old days. Beauty and justice and joy of spirit must be worshiped in the new." With economic need eliminated in the new communities, much of the traditional pettiness of small towns would disappear. Wallace conceded that it might take more centralized power along the lines of the New Deal experiments to achieve the eventual goal of a greater decentralization of American society. But, accepting this paradox, he concluded: "I cannot help feeling that eventually the physical manifestation of the new frontier will consist in considerable measure of thousands of self-subsistence homestead communities properly related to decentralized industry." [11]

Where Wallace was inclined to a kind of mystical idealism, his coadjutor in the Department of Agriculture, Rexford Guy Tugwell, was a more pragmatic type of ideologue. Thus, while Wallace's economic thinking embraced a certain nostalgia for a Jeffersonian agrarian philosophy, Tugwell's was that of a staunch new nationalist and collectivist, a dedicated apostle of centralized economic planning. The member of the Brains Trust most responsible for Roosevelt's agricultural program, Tugwell, despite his urbane professorial manners, was not out of place as Assistant, then Under Secretary of Wallace's department. In the popular and congressional mind, however, he was soon identified as the most radical of the Roosevelt advisers, and his name was quickly linked with a variety of controversial ideas and agencies. More than any of the New Dealers, including even the militant Hugh Johnson who ran the NRA, Tugwell wanted to use the experience of the First World War as a model for comprehensive planning and government controls. In 1927 he had described the coordination of the United States economy under the Baruch War Industries Board as "America's War-Time Socialism." And Tugwell also expressed regret that the Armistice had "prevented a great experiment in control of production, control of price, and control of consumption." During the war the "normal progress of a decade was compressed into every year," but he suggested hopefully: "Perhaps we shall turn back to these pages some time for a reformulation of industrial policy. . . ." [12]

As a graduate student at the University of Pennsylvania during the First World War, Tugwell had come under the influence of Professor Simon N. Patten, a pioneer advocate of the planned use of natural resources and an early critic of classical economics. Later, during the twenties, Tugwell was impressed with certain aspects of the Soviet experiment in economic planning and with the need to establish new criteria by which to judge the efficiency of American industry. As business and industry achieved greater economic maturity, they became involved, he believed, with the governmental arts and required a new type of social and economic discipline. The first New Deal measures had brought a degree of economic recovery to the country, thus saving the domestic situation, but as a collectivist Tugwell wanted the Roosevelt administration to push further in the direction of basic reforms and centralized planning. The depression, he argued, had resulted merely "in the dusting off of atomistic reforms which had been lying around unused (or safely mismanaged by hostile administrations) for fifty years," while under the New Deal the political and economic institutions of the country were only "catching up to La Follette three decades after the more striking incidents of his battle with 'privilege.' " [13]

Despite his radical misgivings over its limitations, Tugwell loyally defended the first New Deal recovery program in industry, agriculture, and public works as "adequate," though "in many ways unorthodox. . . . It is tentative," he noted, "but still carefully hammered out of the iron of reality. We believe it to be the instrument of our present salvation; but we believe in no part of it so fanatically that we are unwilling to change." Although he felt it quite impossible to predict the future course of the New Deal's economic program, this was not nearly so important as the fact that "we have undertaken a venture which is theoretically new in the sense that it calls for control rather than drift. . . . We are turning away," Tugwell concluded, "from the entrusting of crucial decisions, and the operation of institutions whose social consequences are their most characteristic feature, to individuals who are motivated by private interests." Yet he admitted this might take a long time before it could be accomplished effectively. Meanwhile, the New Deal offered

> a very definite attempt to evolve a new governmental-economic relationship in response to the needs and opportunities created by the past methods of operating our economy. To inhibit further growth of these new methods is, therefore, impossible and to attempt to deny their application is the ultimate folly of fossilized ways of thought. Using the traditional methods of a free people, we are going forward toward a realm of coöperative plenty the like of which the world has never seen. It will be no antiseptic utopia and no socialistic paradise, but a changing system in which free American human beings can live their changing lives.[14]

In the spring of 1935, Roosevelt appointed Tugwell to head a new agency called the Resettlement Administration. Created to combine a number of New Deal organizations and programs concerned with the problems of farm tenancy and rehabilitation, subsistence homesteads, land reforms, and rural electrification, the Resettlement Administration seemed to offer Tugwell an opportunity to apply some of his advanced ideas on economic planning. Yet, as Arthur Schlesinger, Jr., points out, "the Resettlement Administration was a perplexing as well as gratifying assignment." A collectivist who believed that successful economic planning must move with the mainstream of technological progress, Tugwell was hardly enthusiastic over attempts to rehabilitate the family farm via the subsistence homestead approach.[15]

In the long run the solution to the farm problem that appeared soundest to Tugwell and a number of economists was to get more people off the land. Instead, the depression temporarily encouraged a sentimental back-to-the-farm movement. Throughout American history hard times had increased popular demands for cheap lands and homesteads in the West. Now, after the crash of 1929, people again turned to the land. The reaction against the industrial society of machine and factory was illustrated in the pioneer critic Ralph Borsodi's indictment of "This Ugly Civilization," and in his call for a "Flight from the City." At the same time a group of Southern writers and scholars penned a fervent and nostalgic plea for a return of their section to its conservative agrarian traditions. Although their book *I'll Take My Stand* was essentially an appeal for a revival of the values of the Old South, the authors announced they "would be happy to be counted as members of a national agrarian movement." In New York State, where the rate of abandonment of farm lands had averaged 100,000 acres a year since 1880, Roosevelt while Governor had been attracted to the idea of using these tax-delinquent properties for reforestation or subsistence homesteads. And in the federal government, Elwood Mead, commissioner of the Bureau of Reclamation from 1924 to 1936, had long advocated irrigation and reclamation of the soil as a means of rebuilding a healthy rural society, and as a way of putting families back on the land.[16]

The Resettlement Administration itself took over nearly a hundred rural New Deal communities in varying stages of completion and planning. All needed a secure economic base, and many were being criticized because of their high unit costs. At issue were the contrasting views of those who saw the program as a simple relief measure, and of those others who had a vision of the communities as a new way of life and escape from the traditional isolation of scattered family farms. According to the historian of the program, its initiation had been influenced by a quasi-Jeffersonian agrarianism, but its development reflected an open break with traditional individualism and pointed clearly toward collectivism. Although one of the smaller New Deal ventures in planning, it was a significant experiment and a focal point of ideological clash and criticism. To a dedicated planner like Tugwell, who was at the center of the fight over the Resettlement Administration, it was the collectivist community aspects of the program that made it worthwhile. And in the eyes of many of the conservationists in the New Deal, the subsistence homestead program dealt with only one of a number of coordinate problems, including soil erosion, submarginal lands, and ignorant poverty-stricken farmers. By 1937, when the Resettlement Administration was transferred to the Farm Security Administration, the program was slowly disintegrating, and Tugwell himself, as the chief target of vociferous anti–New Deal criticism, had resigned. In its two-year effort to help impoverished farm families not materially aided by the AAA's economic subsidies, little had been accomplished. Only thirty-eight community projects had been completed, with eighty-four more under construction, and only 4,441 families were in residence.[17]

In the nation's poorest section, the rural South, the New Deal's crop and acreage controls served to intensify the plight of Negro sharecroppers and tenant farmers. Yet, in the midst of their poverty and despair—depicted graphically in Erskine Caldwell's *Tobacco Road* and the documentary volume *You Have Seen Their Faces*, and so similar to the human misery in the flight of the Okies from the dust bowl of the Great Plains—there were also the beginnings of hope. The South, as its traditionalists feared while others waited expectantly, was on the eve of an economic renaissance, marked in part by the growing possibilities for industry and agriculture offered by the New Deal.

As a means for the relief and rehabilitation of depressed rural areas, the subsistence homestead projects formed a small part of comprehensive New Deal plans to develop America's natural and human resources. Intelligent planning required the collection and organization of a body of economic and scientific data. Accordingly, under the Public Works Authority headed by Harold Ickes, a temporary National Planning Board was established early in 1933 composed of Frederic A. Delano, the President's uncle and an authority on city planning, and the eminent professors Charles E. Merriam of the University of Chicago and Wesley C. Mitchell of Columbia University. Mitchell and Merriam had already served as chairman and vice-chairman of President Hoover's Research Committee on Recent Social Trends, and Merriam, an expert in both public administration and political science, soon became the driving force behind the Planning Board and its successor agencies, the National Resources Board and the National Resources Committee. Yet, despite its distinguished personnel, neither Board nor Committee ever became more than an academic sort of research agency, unable to gain the funds or political backing it needed to coordinate various administration efforts for conservation and resources planning. It was apparent therefore that the practical work in conservation, in terms of both natural resources and human needs, was that being carried out by such extensive regional developments as the Tennessee Valley Authority.[18]

The concept of the TVA fitted in well with the old Progressive ideals of conservation and government ownership of public utilities and natural resources. During the 1920's the Regional Planning Association, a small group of economists and engineers led by Stuart Chase and Lewis Mumford, had advocated plans for the scientific management and improved social use of unified geographic areas. At the same time, Senator George Norris of Nebraska began his long struggle to have the government operate for hydroelectric power the Wilson Dam at Muscle Shoals on the Tennessee River. Now, under the aegis of the New Deal, these ideas of regional planning of the pre-1930's were expanded far beyond their sponsors' expectations. In Roosevelt's own words, the Muscle Shoals development, "if envisioned in its entirety, transcends mere power development; it enters the wide fields of flood control, soil erosion, afforestation, elimination from agricultural use of marginal lands, and distribution and diversification of industry." [19]

Much praised and attacked, TVA became one of the most controversial, and even socialistic, of all the New Deal measures. Clearly, TVA put the government in business, in direct competition with private enterprise through its sale of surplus electrical power. In the minds of its first chairman, Arthur E. Morgan of Antioch College, and of such ardent collectivists as Tugwell, TVA had been created to serve as a laboratory in broad regional planning and social reform. But, meeting strong opposition from local political interests, including agricultural and industrial groups whose main concern was cheap power and fertilizers, TVA gradually yielded its early radical ideas. Morgan, later the biographer of the utopian socialist Edward Bellamy, was forced to resign, while David E. Lilienthal, his successor, assumed the difficult task of defending the Tennessee Valley Authority by restricting and limiting its original far-reaching goals.

Lilienthal's personalized retrospective account, *TVA: Democracy on the March*, like Wallace's *New Frontiers*, described the idealistic and yet practical side of the New Deal. At odds with the proponents of centralization and control via overall national economic planning, Lilienthal was convinced that the physical achievements of modern science and technology would bring no general benefits unless conceived and carried out with a moral purpose, including the participation and welfare of the people themselves. "Without such a purpose," he wrote, "advances in technology may be disastrous to the human spirit; the industrialization of a raw material area may bring to the average man only a new kind of slavery and the destruction of democratic institutions." Economic progress under TVA was possible because of its concern for democracy at the grass roots and its "effective combination of the advantages of the *decentralized administration of centralized authority*." Fearful that tasks not carried out democratically would be taken over by small elites of politicians, corporations, or managers, Lilienthal declared: "Every important administrative decision need not be made in Washington. . . . The idea of unified resource development," he concluded, "is based upon the premise that by democratic planning the individual's interest, the interest of private undertakings, can increasingly be made one with the interest of all of us, i.e., the community interest. By and large, things are working out that way in the Tennessee Valley." [20]

Some observers of the whole planned experiment in the Tennessee Valley, who were less lyrical in their attitude than Lilienthal, questioned how well his grass-roots approach to the TVA worked out in practice. The democratic tie-in with local sentiment could easily be used to cover concessions to special-interest groups. Thus the original collectivist and cooperative goals of the TVA had been shelved in response to local charges of socialism. Rex Tugwell, for example, who believed that it was precisely these original TVA ideals that justified the venture in planning, summed up his criticism with the assertion that "TVA is more an example of democracy in retreat than democracy on the march." [21]

The differences between Tugwell and Lilienthal over the essential direction and purpose of TVA were also at the heart of the divisions among American liberals and radicals in their attitudes toward the New Deal. Unlike conservative critics concerned over individual rights, or those dissenters who preferred a totalitarian society modeled on fascism or communism, a number of American intellectuals, vaguely classified among the liberal left, were impatient, and yet not unsympathetic, with much of the New Deal. They were enthusiastic over the idea of a planned society and only questioned whether the New Deal was the best means toward such an end. Later, as New Deal goals themselves became more uncertain, considerations of practical politics and the lack of feasible alternatives persuaded many of the once radical intellectuals to accept the economic expediency and partial solutions offered by the Roosevelt administration. Especially significant at first were those intellectuals outside official circles who, though agreeing with the overall concepts and new public philosophy delineated by a Wallace or a Tugwell, were nevertheless inclined to move further in a more radical direction. Under the harsh and continuing impact of the depression, they were convinced that the new political economy could no longer remain capitalist.

Representative of this changing state of affairs in the thirties was a young Yale graduate who returned to the United States early in 1932 after an extensive world tour to found a new magazine, its title borrowed from Tom Paine's old American Revolutionary pamphlet *Common Sense*. Alfred Bingham, just twenty-seven years old when he began his journalistic venture, was the son of a wealthy and scholarly archeologist, Hiram Bingham, who served as a highly conservative and contentious Republican Senator from Connecticut during the twenties. Reared in a patrician atmosphere, and educated like Franklin D. Roosevelt at Groton, before he went to Yale where his father had once taught, the younger Bingham in the course of his trip through Europe confronted for the first time in his life the less happy side of the real world. Impressed by the new economics of Soviet Russia even though the "life was brutal and crude," he came home convinced of the decline of capitalism and of the ultimate triumph of some form of socialism. "I found at the end of my world tour, almost to my horror," he wrote, "that I was arguing the inevitability of revolution with everyone I met." Yet, at the same time, Bingham realized that the Marxism of the Soviets and the traditional Socialist parties had little relevance to life in the United States. In New York City, as he "wandered in Union Square and bought the revolutionary Marxist publications for sale" there, he recognized that "the knot of jobless men clustered near a soap-box orator looked forlorn and hardly sufficient to terrorize the 'bourgeoisie.' " [22]

Convinced of the need of some non-Marxist alternative to capitalism, Bingham decided to publish a magazine and invited a fellow Yale man, Selden Rodman, to serve as co-editor. Rodman's literary experience and his unorthodox tastes in the arts and culture complemented Bingham's wealth and radical social views. Continuing publication into the early 1940's, *Common Sense*, their joint venture, became the best journalistic expression in the New Deal era of an intellectually radical American position. More progressive and at the same time less conventionally left wing than the established liberal weeklies the *Nation* and the *New Republic*, *Common Sense* was also less doctrinaire than the various socialist and communist organs. In a decade when both the *Nation* and the *New Republic* were undergoing a series of editorial shifts, following the semi-retirement of Oswald Garrison Villard and the death of Herbert Croly, *Common Sense* enjoyed the advantage over its older competitors of greater editorial continuity and less intellectual confusion.

Bingham and Rodman included in the first issue of their magazine, in December 1932, a platform or statement of principles. Avowing its lack of connection with any political party, *Common Sense* affirmed its belief that "a system based on competition for private profit can no longer serve the general welfare." At the same time it recognized the need "for immediate emergency measures" and reiterated its faith "in the American ideals of liberty, democracy, and equality of opportunity." Generally, it was clear that the editors and contributors to *Common Sense* agreed upon the need for radical change in American society.

A public opinion poll, addressed primarily to its readers in the spring of 1933, revealed that over 90 per cent of the respondents favored the elimination of the profit system. *Common Sense's* own early utopian visions were outlined in detail in a series of articles by Bingham entitled "The New Society," which he published in the midst of the New Deal's Hundred Days. Basic to Bingham's New Society was his enthusiasm for some of the ideas of Bellamy's *Looking Backward* and Howard Scott's Technocracy, and his acceptance of Veblen's distinction between production for use and production for profit. Useful work, Bingham believed, should no longer have to depend on finding remunerative private employment. Foreseeing a world in which culture, beauty, and leisure would be combined with labor and valued each for its own sake, Bingham noted, even more optimistically, that with the achievements of modern eugenics, "The dream of a race of supermen seems almost within grasp." [23]

Hopeful of his New Society, Bingham nevertheless wished his ideas to be considered in practical rather than utopian terms. Human nature and modern civilization were too complex to reduce to complete harmony, but the elimination of the profit system was to Bingham a necessary first step in the overall improvement of the quality of American life. The end of capitalism, "which led men to compete and fight instead of cooperating," was the "key to change." Curiously, in view of his strictures on private enterprise, Bingham believed that radicalism and progressivism must make their major appeal in the United States to the middle classes. His own most important book, *Insurgent America*, which he published in 1935, indicted Marxism for its failure in this regard. For, he wrote, "if the bulk of the people, in a modern capitalistic country like the United States, think of themselves as being of the middle-class, having interests between those of 'capital' and 'labor,' then there is such a middle-class or middle group of classes." Contrary to Marxist opinion, it was the new and dominant "technical and managerial middle-classes," not the working classes, that would have to be won over to the idea of a planned society.[24]

Marxism, because of its elevation of the workers and its appeal to the class struggle, was repugnant to most Americans. But Bingham believed that the middle classes, with their faith in equality of opportunity and their enthusiasm for civic action and charitable reform causes, could be enlisted in native radical-progressive movements. The foundation for their interest and support, however, would have to be an economic security which now, in the midst of the depression, capitalism could no longer provide. "It is security—security of income, security for home and family, security for old age, security of position—that the middle-class type craves." Against the alternative of fascism, Bingham urged therefore the practicability of extending and expanding conventional forms of social security into what he called a Cooperative Commonwealth. "And as production-for-use proved its superiority for those engaged in it to production-for-profit, the great bulk of the population engaged in private enterprise would clamor for admission to the new system. The life-blood of the old system would be gradually drained away, and it would be left an empty shell. A transition to an economy of abundance would have been effected. . . . America has the means of knowing herself and of knowing her possibilities. If she will use that knowledge and realize on those possibilities she may be privileged to help to lead the rest of the world to a more abundant life." [25]

In keeping with its dream of a New Society and its rejection of both major parties, *Common Sense* became the organ of the League for Independent Political Action, joining in the drive to create a strong radical-progressive coalition party in the United States before the elections of 1936. The Farmer-Labor Political Federation which grew from these efforts included John Dewey as honorary chairman and Bingham as executive secretary. The active chairman of the federation and its top political figure was Thomas R. Amlie, an energetic Progressive party Congressman from Wisconsin. For a brief period there was the possibility that Floyd B. Olson, the Farmer-Labor Governor of Minnesota, or one of the La Follettes in Wisconsin might become the presidential candidate of a major new third party in 1936. Into that year the staff of *Common Sense* continued to write hopefully of a new mass party of radicals, labor, and socialists. But then, when labor's support of Roosevelt and the prospect of a conservative Republican victory in any three-party race ruined the federation's hope of presenting its own presidential candidate, *Common Sense* announced regretfully: "Roosevelt should be supported for re-election. But it should be a support limited only to the next few weeks, and withdrawn the day after Election day." [26]

It was plain, especially after the verdict of 1936, that Roosevelt's political appeal made unrealistic Bingham's utopian notion of a radical upsurge of the American middle class. Shifting its attention temporarily from politics, therefore, *Common Sense* stressed again the vital role that new discoveries and achievements in the physical and social sciences might play in future national planning. Here its intellectualized emphasis coincided with the ideas of such admired thinkers as John Dewey and Charles Beard, whose writings were also an integral part of the new climate of opinion in which the New Deal flourished.

In contrast to Beard, John Dewey, America's outstanding philosopher, was never able to accept wholeheartedly the New Deal. Despite his pragmatism and faith in the importance of experimentation and action, Dewey throughout the thirties continued to indulge in his longtime hope for the establishment of a successful third party. Criticized severely by fellow liberals for supporting American entrance into the First World War and for backing Al Smith in 1928, Dewey had grown wary of further compromise with principle. And the New Deal, despite its steps in that direction, never seemed a satisfactory realization of his ideal of a democratic socialism.

In 1929, on the eve of the Great Depression, in a study of the relations of knowledge and action, Dewey pointed out the difficulties and contradictions in the philosophical quest for certainty. "The attempt to include all that is doubtful within the fixed grasp of that which is theoretically certain is committed to insincerity and evasion," he wrote. But the conflict between the truly real and the merely apparent might be resolved by action. Insecurity generated the quest for certainty, while modern industrial society was brutalized by its failure to become integrated with social and cultural values. It was not surprising, therefore, that economic life in an industrial society, "exiled from the pale of higher values, takes revenge by declaring that it is the only social reality. . . ." [27]

When the depression cast doubt on the claims to predominance of the nineteenth century's so-called Economic Man, it also brought into question the old American faith in individualism. Comparing "Individualism Old and New," Dewey noted that the historic individualism associated with nineteenth-century liberalism had been a very limited boon in which the mass of the people had hardly participated. Despite the talk of rugged individualism, America in the mass society of the twentieth century was moving toward socialism or collectivism, or to what Dewey preferred to call "corporateness." Without the loyalties that once had given the individual a sense of personal focus and direction, he was lost in the crowd. Insecurity, with unemployment, became therefore the most marked trait of modern life. The solution for this crisis in American culture, Dewey believed, was the recovery of a "composed, effective and creative individuality," or a new individualism via a public or democratic socialism.[28]

With his faith in collective social action and shared experience, it was clear to Dewey, as well as to most New Deal liberals, that the older, traditional liberalism was outmoded. Thus, at the outset of the New Deal, in an introduction to a collection of articles from *Common Sense*, Dewey noted that there had been much discussion of intellectuals turning left. "But there is no longer such a discussion; the intellectuals *are* left. . . . The only question is how far left they have gone." Technocracy, the growth of a third-party movement, and the New Deal and NRA—though the latter bore "ominous analogies to Fascism abroad"—were all part of a new and native American radicalism. The imperative need, occasioned by the impasse of liberalism, was a strong third party. The classical liberalism of the eighteenth and nineteenth centuries had stressed freedom from the institutional restraints of an authoritative church or state. This kind of liberalism, Dewey argued, was obsolete. The earlier liberalism which "regarded the separate and competing action of individuals as the means to social well-being as the end" had to be reversed so that people could see that a "socialized economy is the means of free individual development as the end." Thus the modern liberal was forced to think in terms of organized society and of working through government rather than against it.

> The only form of enduring social organization that is now possible is one in which the new forces of productivity are coöperatively controlled and used in the interest of the effective liberty and the cultural development of the individuals that constitute society. Such a social order cannot be established by an unplanned and external convergence of the actions of separate individuals, each of whom is bent on personal private advantage.[29]

Classical liberalism had rendered valuable service to society in sweeping away many of the historic restraints on individual freedom, but it had failed to keep pace with historical relativity and the new needs of the twentieth century. "This absolutism, this ignoring and denial of temporal relativity," Dewey saw as "one great reason why the earlier liberalism degenerated so easily" into what, he believed, was a specious or pseudo-liberalism, illustrated in the social ideas of the Liberty League and former President Hoover. The commitment of liberalism to experimental methods and procedures carried with it the responsibility for action, and for the "continuous reconstruction of the ideas of individuality and of liberty in intimate connection with changes in social relations." Convinced of the "monstrosity of the doctrine that assumes that under all conditions governmental action and individual liberty are found in separate and independent spheres," Dewey, however, also pointed out that "No economic state of affairs is merely economic. It has a profound effect upon [the] presence or absence of cultural freedom. Any liberalism that does not make full cultural freedom supreme and that does not see the relation between it and genuine industrial freedom as a way of life is a degenerate and delusive liberalism." [30]

While Dewey sketched the outlines of a new society in the abstract terms of a philosopher, Charles Beard, with his long and successful career as a historian and political scientist, explored its more concrete possibilities. Convinced, like Dewey, that the prized American rugged individualism was largely a myth, Beard was a staunch proponent of economic planning and an admirer of the nationalism of the early New Deal. A true modern *philosophe* in his stress on science and rationalism, Beard, in the manner of Dewey and the philosophers of the Enlightenment, believed in the power of human intelligence to effect reforms. His major historical work, *The Rise of American Civilization*, which he and his wife wrote in the era between the two world wars, gave special attention to the influence of science and economics in the determination of culture and politics. Ever hopeful, despite the Great Depression, Beard in the introduction to the American edition of Bury's *Idea of Progress* declared that the future advancement of the world would depend, as always, on human will and effort. It was the dynamic quality of modern technology, more than any other force or value, he observed, that made it the supreme instrument for the idea of progress.[31]

For Beard a major threat to this progress, and the subject of his own increasing scholarly concern in his later years, was the institution of war. The national interest to which the cause of war was conventionally ascribed he found in cold truth to be largely a rationalization, useful chiefly to the small elite groups that held a special stake in protecting foreign trade and overseas commitments. The New Deal of Roosevelt's first term, Beard believed, offered a challenge to this historic system by seeking to advance American national interests apart from war. And in his *The Open Door at Home*, published in 1934, Beard himself offered a trial philosophy in the efficient use of resources to achieve national security at home. The trends of the last fifty years represented a crisis in thought as well as in the economy, in which the quest for security was matched by the struggle of the expanding industrial nations of the world for the control of trade and markets. Seeing in much of the world's recent internationalism merely "a covering ideology for the aggressive nationalism of one or more countries," Beard urged instead relative isolationism and a planned economy for the United States. Absorbing its surpluses in a careful balancing of production and consumption at home, America would be relieved of the pressures to expand its foreign trade and of the accompanying danger of war. "Offering to the world the strange sight of a national garden well tended, the United States would teach the most effective lesson—a lesson without words." [32]

Beard's intellectual commitment to national collectivism found expression not only in his support of the early New Deal but in the policies he outlined for the development of the social studies in American schools. Convinced that, "in the United States as in other countries, the age of individualism and *laissez faire* in economy and government is closing and that a new age of collectivism is emerging," Beard and his fellow consultants in the fields of education and the social sciences recommended increased governmental responsibility for the social and economic welfare as well as for the education of American children, youths, and adults. Continued stress on the philosophy of individualism in the national economy, these scholars believed, would merely "increase the accompanying social tensions." [33] The New Deal, however, apart from its appropriations of relief funds under the National Youth Administration, did not disturb the traditional American system of local and state support and control of education.

Beard himself, arguing that "America Must Stay Big," criticized President Roosevelt for his timidity and conservatism in failing to match a truly national economy with effective national planning. Meanwhile, in the Democratic party, he noted, "the cult of littleness and Federal impotence prevails. It is the cult of 'the new freedom' which hurried us on into greater bigness. Only the depth of the crisis of 1933 made it possible for the President to abandon the admitted farce of trust-busting for a moment, and to seek the effective functioning of the national economy by the exercise of commensurate Federal powers." Certain that the whole question of centralized social and economic planning begged for an answer, Beard by 1935 was also, however, beginning to fear that the New Deal might attempt to resolve its problems by war. As early as February he came to the unhappy conclusion that, judged by the experience of the past in which other American reform movements had been terminated in war, Roosevelt would also, in the last analysis, choose salvation from domestic difficulties by resort to a foreign entanglement. To Raymond Moley, to whom he sent antiwar material for the eyes of the President, he declared: "I consider the foreign implications of our domestic policy and the hazards of a futile and idiotic war in the Far Pacific more important than old age pensions and all the rest of it." [34]

After the mid-1930's, Beard's enthusiasm for planning was more and more subordinated to his growing concern over foreign policy and his increasing fears that the vast New Deal spending would be shifted to preparedness for war. In 1932 he had entitled his first book about the New Deal, *The Future Comes*. Eight years later in a more sober analysis, *The Old Deal and the New*, Beard expressed concern over the mounting federal budget and the contradictions between the New Deal's antitrust and foreign policies. If war was a likely prospect, the Roosevelt administration would have to depend on the very monopolistic business enterprises it was attempting, at least in theory, to dissolve. "The present trend toward public spending, heavily befogged as it will be by a huge military program, holds no end of potential possibilities for stock manipulators. If war comes," Beard predicted, "the social disorganization which may ensue will also be rich in opportunities." Concluding his estimate of the lost virtues of the New Deal, he wrote:

> The principal weakness of the whole program is its heavy dependence upon government spending and lending policies. . . . Only one thing seems to be certain. When all the merits and accomplishments of the New Deal are duly appreciated, it remains a fact that this dispensation has been made possible only by enormous increases in the national debt.[35]

As Beard in his disenchantment over the Roosevelt foreign policy turned gloomily away from his early hopes for the New Deal, another scholarly iconoclast left the academic world to accept appointment as Assistant Attorney General in charge of the Antitrust Division of the Department of Justice. Thurman Arnold, a professor at Yale Law School during the thirties, was, like Beard, the scion of an old American family that had achieved prosperity in the West. In Arnold's case it was the Far West of Wyoming rather than Beard's Indiana, but both men, despite the collectivist cast of certain of their writings, possessed a pioneering type of individualism exemplified in their successful careers and independent views. Each in his own way was also a scholar with a strong interest in politics and the public welfare. Arnold, widely regarded as the most significant philosopher of the pragmatic, "hard" side of the later New Deal, was a realist and skeptic who had aired his particular species of disillusionment *before* he entered upon government service.

In the mid-thirties Arnold published two important books analyzing what, he asserted, were some of the popular myths and beliefs about American political and economic institutions. *The Symbols of Government* examined the conservative, ritualistic thinking about law, economics, and government in terms of conventional intellectualized efforts to make much of the irrational behavior in these fields appear logical and sound. Especially during a depression, "when institutions fail to function adequately," Arnold observed, there was a "rush to theories and principles as guides. . . . Everyone becomes a reformer; everyone becomes a social planner." Under the impact of hard times, questions of constitutional law and theories of economics emerged suddenly as matters of public debate. Meanwhile, practical men —those who operated in ignorance or in violation of established and cherished principles and ideals—continued to carry out the constructive work of society. These men were, as often as not, the machine politicians—"the only persons who understand the techniques of government"—and the so-called tycoons and robber barons of the business world, who "raised the level of the productive capacity beyond the dreams of their fathers." [36]

Throughout the world the popular veneration of outmoded ideals constantly threatened to stifle human energy. "It is for this reason," Arnold wrote, "that in a country as bursting with energy as is America, we can predict the general acceptance of a new and more hopeful philosophy of government to replace the confusion of our present idea of law and economics. . . . It is true," he admitted, "that there is little in the present conduct of the governments of the world which can by any stretch of the imagination be called adult. Everywhere we see unnecessary cruelty used to dramatize even humanitarian creeds. Fanatical devotion to principle on the part of the public still compels intelligent leaders to commit themselves, for political reasons, to all sorts of disorderly nonsense." Yet Arnold had faith that "a new public attitude toward the ideals of law and economics is slowly appearing to create an atmosphere where the fanatical alignments between opposing political principles may disappear and a competent, practical, opportunistic governing class may rise to power." [37]

By "The Folklore of Capitalism," Arnold explained that he meant "those ideas about social organizations which are not regarded as folklore but accepted as fundamental principles of law and economics." Paradoxically, such popular institutional creeds or beliefs of a society had to "*be false in order to function effectively*." But these widespread taboos and "phobias against practical commonsense action" also entailed a real danger: "Taboos do not mean that a nation ceases to progress. They only mean that it advances in devious ways with most of its cylinders missing." Arnold personally did not doubt either the desirability of principles and ideals or the fact that a society probably felt more secure with them.

> Yet the belief that there is something peculiarly sacred about the logical content of these principles, that organizations must be molded to them, instead of the principles being molded to organizational needs, is often the very thing which prevents these principles from functioning. The greatest destroyer of ideals is he who believes in them so strongly that he cannot fit them to practical needs.[38]

It was clear from Arnold's analysis that capitalism and the Constitution were prominent symbolic examples of American folklore. Thus, despite the fact that the election of 1936 seemed to demonstrate popular rejection of many of the accepted verities espoused by anti–New Dealers, "Nevertheless, after the election, people continued to talk in the old phrases as before. The political leadership which was demanded was also required to be cast in old formulas and these old formulas continued to confuse its direction." [39]

In view of the obvious relativism and pragmatism of Arnold's thinking, at least as measured in his books, there was a special irony in his being called to Washington in 1938 to administer the antitrust laws. In a suddenly much scrutinized chapter of *The Folklore*, entitled "The Effect of the Antitrust Laws in Encouraging Large Combinations," Arnold had rather cynically termed the laws "the answer of a society which unconsciously felt the need of great organizations, and at the same time had to deny them a place in the moral and logical ideology of the social structure. They were part of the struggle of a creed of rugged individualism to adapt itself to what was becoming a highly organized society." Thus prosecution of the trusts was, in Arnold's opinion, similar to the age-old crusades against vice or crime that periodically agitated American reformers.[40]

Enforcement of the antitrust laws was a part of the shift in policy generally noted between the First and Second New Deals. After the Supreme Court declared the NRA unconstitutional in 1935, the initial New Deal visions of an American type of corporate society were largely given up. In place of a program of central economic planning as envisaged by the Brains Trust and a number of prominent intellectuals and business leaders, the Roosevelt administration turned toward a policy of regulating monopoly and restoring competition. Instead of Tugwell and the economic planners, there were now the young lawyers of the Brandeis and Frankfurter New Freedom school of thought. Acceptable again was Brandeis' hostility to bigness and the old jurist's faith in regulated competition.[41]

Various events combined to shape the administration's new

course. The highly controversial Supreme Court fight, the economic recession in 1937, and the increasing political restiveness among progressives in Congress, as well as the troubled world scene, all helped to strengthen the President's desire for a change of direction and a new issue. Spurred on by his famous anti-monopoly message of April 29, 1938,[42] Congress launched its investigation of the concentration of economic power in the United States by creating the Temporary National Economic Committee, the TNEC. Meanwhile, although Arnold instituted a number of antitrust prosecutions from within the Department of Justice, the outbreak of the European war and the accompanying American preparedness effort precluded any real possibility for a vigorous policy against monopolies.

What the TNEC submitted in its final report to the President in 1941 was already unreal, though still historically significant. Arguing that democracy must extend to "all the organizations through which man operated," the report set forth the thesis that "Political freedom cannot survive if economic freedom is lost." To restore free enterprise and at the same time safeguard efficiency, it urged as government policy the decentralization of industry, stimulation of competition, an end to the "Pittsburgh-plus" system of determining prices, repeal of fair trade laws, centralized government purchasing, a national corporation law, enforcement of the antitrust laws, limits on the restricted sale of patents, and registration of trade associations. Criticized, in turn, for its dogmatic quest of a panacea and its tendency to lay all blame upon monopolies, the TNEC report nevertheless pointed up the problem of reconciling the modern industrial order, tending toward collectivism, with the traditional, liberal, democratic, individualistic, and competitive society of the American past.[43]

In this dilemma it was Arnold as much as anyone who, in his writings and efforts to modernize the enforcement of the antitrust laws, provided a bridge between the ideas of the confirmed social planners and the dedicated followers of Brandeis. Unwilling to damn all economic concentration, and yet anxious to humanize competition, he moved against the monopolistic practices of big business in a practical rather than dogmatic way, securing consent or civil decrees where possible and preferring pragmatic reforms to doctrinaire consistency. Between the members of Congress who doubted that he had any faith in the antitrust laws and the businessmen who accused him of being against big business *per se*, Arnold protested that he was only against its monopolistic tendencies and was interested chiefly in protecting the consumer. "The idea of antitrust laws," he noted in 1939, "is to create a situation in which competition compels the passing on to the consumers the savings of mass distribution and production." In addition to a market economy, there were various ways of distributing goods—by the Army, by European cartels, or by government subsidy. But Arnold noted: "If we want a competitive system we must take measures to maintain it. We must apply our ideal to concrete situations." Unfortunately, he declared in writing later on the subject "Must 1929 Repeat Itself?",

> F.D.R., recognizing that he could have only one war at a time, was content to declare a truce in the fight against monopoly. He was to have his foreign war; monopoly was to give him patriotic support—on its own terms.
> And so more than 90% of all war contracts went to a handful of giant empires. . . .[44]

To the staunch economic nationalists and protagonists of planning in the early New Deal, the so-called Second New Deal of the later thirties had little appeal. For example, Donald Richberg, Hugh Johnson's successor as head of the NRA, wrote to Roosevelt in April 1938: "The philosophy of the NRA was wholly consistent with the New Deal. The philosophy of the fanatic trust busters, their hostility to all large enterprise, their assumption that co-operation is always a cloak for monopolistic conspiracy, this philosophy is wholly inconsistent with the New Deal." Though loyal personally to FDR, Rex Tugwell also complained increasingly of the changed character of the New Deal's economic thinking. Apparently more conventional in its progressivism, and accepting the concept of regulation in lieu of the positive planning and control favored by a Tugwell or a Richberg, the Second New Deal was nevertheless radical in its aid to labor and small farmers and in its broadened program of federal unemployment relief.[45]

The Second New Deal also broke with the past in its espousal of the policy that Harry Hopkins called "Spending to Save." Through the Social Security program, and through the operations of Hopkins' own Works Progress Administration, the administration made large-scale federal expenditures and fiscal innovation into a new kind of public philosophy. By spending, by taxing, and by borrowing, the New Deal was in effect achieving a peaceful revolution without apparent changes in the political or economic structure. Fiscal reforms, or the large-scale infusion of government funds into the economy, represented a managerial revolution more decisive in terms of overall policy than the effort to control monopoly.

Until the prospect of war intervened, the New Deal's campaign against monopoly and its increased spending policies were in no great conflict. A high level of economic activity, sparked by a plentiful supply of money and intertwined with a growing demand for goods and services, could do more than economic planning or limitations on production to create an aura of competitive business activity. Thus the theories of both Thurman Arnold and John Maynard Keynes were able to coexist and win considerable mutual acceptance among New Dealers in the late 1930's. Antimonopoly activities and increased appropriations were also good politics with which to reward the faithful and belabor conservative critics. At the same time, it was also true that the funds pouring from the Treasury seemed to help both the masses and business enterprise, and served to minimize the differences between the two New Deals. The overriding goals of recovery from the depression and higher living standards could, after all, be achieved as much by fiscal innovation as by economic and social planning. As James MacGregor Burns points out in his biography of the President, "Deficit spending was ideally suited to Roosevelt's ideology and program." Neither a doctrinaire capitalist nor socialist, he found that "Keynesian economics was a true middle way—at a time when New Dealers were groping for a middle way that worked." [46]

Keynes, the great English advocate of public spending, probably had little personal impact on Roosevelt. His first influence, therefore, was never very great—indirect rather than direct, and more potential than immediate. Unlike Harold Laski, the English radical socialist who hit it off so well with FDR and who enjoyed frequent access to the White House at Saturday luncheon meetings, Keynes's limited contacts with the President were far from fruitful. But through his teaching of other economists influential in the government, and through the enormous stimulus of his writings—particularly *The General Theory of Employment, Interest and Money* published in 1936—Keynes's financial ideas became ever more compelling to the New Deal.[47]

Large-scale spending seemed especially necessary to insure continued economic recovery after the recession of 1937. Then, when the increasingly radical fiscal policies of the New Deal aroused alarmed conservative protests, the nation's rearmament program and defense spending stifled possible political difficulties. Obviously, major government spending was justified most easily in terms of preparedness and readiness for war. As Keynes himself pointed out to his American readers in 1940: "Your war preparation, so far from requiring a sacrifice, will be a stimulus, which neither the victory nor the defeat of the New Deal could give you, to greater individual consumption and a higher standard of life." [48]

What Roosevelt and the New Deal could not achieve in peace, therefore, was gained indirectly in the Second World War. Until midway in his second term, when the naval rearmament program and increased defense spending became significant, eight or nine millions still were numbered in the ranks of the unemployed. There was irony, and even tragedy, in the fact that only the onset of World War II furnished the social and economic well-being promised so persistently throughout the thirties. Ultimately the fiscal theories of Keynes and his American followers, rather than the utopian visions of the original New Dealers, came to dominate the new political economy and public philosophy of the United States.

FIVE

❧

Life Can Be Beautiful

THE HOPES and plans of the New Deal were not confined to politics and economics. In the 1930's for the first time in American history, aesthetic goals became a part of official thinking and the public philosophy. In the continuing effort to overcome the depression, the Roosevelt administration believed that life in the United States could somehow be made more attractive as well as more secure. This goal of a popular mass culture—as distinct from a society in which the enjoyment of arts and letters was limited to the few—had long been an article of the American democratic faith. But before the 1930's the federal government exerted little influence upon most aspects of American cultural and intellectual life. Now, however, not only did American writers and artists rediscover their native land, but the political leadership of the New Deal also recognized that the depression was affecting these people as much as businessmen, farmers, and laborers. The severe economic plight of thousands of unhappy, frustrated, and talented individuals underscored the need for new forms of patronage, public as well as private, if the artist, or intellectual, or professional man was to survive and maintain his integrity. Thus the environment of the depression created an opportunity for government support of the arts which was congenial not only to the political philosophy of the New Deal but to the changed psychology of many Americans who had never expected to have to seek public aid or welfare.

The role of the government in intellectual and cultural affairs under the New Deal was reciprocated by the social concerns of the artists and writers themselves. In contrast to the individualized protests of the twenties against the materialistic standards of a business civilization, many of the artists and writers of the thirties were eager to join hands in some form of collective action. Enthusiasm over Soviet Russia and generally left-wing political views became prominent characteristics of the literary world and of large numbers of American artists and intellectuals. Novels and paintings, dominated by the social consciousness of their authors, reflected the angry protests and utopian aspirations of the radical left. Then, as disillusionment gradually developed —with the New Deal at home and with the Soviet experiment abroad—the menace of fascism in Europe and the prospect of another world war arose to challenge anew the sensitivity of American intellectuals. Yet Americans, despite the influence of the New Deal and of left-wing politics, were far from being "artists in uniform" during the thirties. The voices of dissent in their midst remained strong and, until their ranks were closed after Pearl Harbor, intellectual life in the United States continued to be enriched by the diverse contributions of many independent and creative individuals.

Although the depression was responsible for the unprecedented ties of the New Deal with American intellectual life, it also, perhaps paradoxically, set limits to the government's role. In the WPA cultural projects, for example, the dominant consideration was the individual's own need for relief and not the political slant, or even technical competence, of his artistic or literary product. While neither politics nor prejudice were always avoided, the government's sponsorship of the arts remained remarkably free of censorious restraints on the freedom of the individual artist or writer. The obvious personal and social concerns spawned by the economic collapse pushed other considerations aside and militated against the kind of political controls that in more normal circumstances would have been almost inevitable. This freedom, while it aroused criticism especially in conservative circles, contributed nevertheless to the spontaneity and individuality, as well as to the social consciousness, of American intellectual life and art during the 1930's.

Symbolic of the new cultural outlook was the hopeful and expectant mood of American intellectuals as they returned to the United States from living or traveling abroad. Thus in the middle of the depression, George Biddle, artist and member of a distinguished Philadelphia family, came home from Europe to find that his friends were all discussing economics, socialism, communism, Technocracy, and the New Deal. Thorstein Veblen and Howard Scott, he noted, were the popular literary heroes of the day along with Rex Tugwell and Stuart Chase. Biddle, however, first concentrated his attentions on Rockefeller Center in New York City where Diego Rivera, the famous Mexican artist, was hard at work on his controversial murals. Eagerly Biddle imbibed the Mexican school of art which, he felt, was different even when government supported. In Europe during the World War every country had controlled its artists, but "No Mexican artist had been mobilized and marched, goose-stepping in rank, at the point of a bayonet. He had been given the uncensored privilege of expressing a social faith." Biddle wondered at the chances of a similar development in the United States. "Life is drab and ugly," he confessed, but "Life can be beautiful." Having stated what, he felt, was the core of the problem, Biddle on May 9, 1933, sent a congratulatory letter to his old friend and Groton classmate now ensconced in the White House. For the President's benefit, he sketched out his idea of a plan for government support for art and needy artists:

There is a matter which I have long considered and which some day might interest your administration. The Mexican artists have produced the greatest national school of mural painting since the Italian Renaissance. Diego Rivera tells me that it was only possible because Obregon allowed Mexican artists to work at plumbers' wages in order to express on the walls of the government buildings the social ideals of the Mexican revolution.

The younger artists of America are conscious as they have never been of the social revolution that our country and civilization are going through; and they would be eager to express these ideals in a permanent art form if they were given the government's co-operation. They would be contributing to and expressing in living monuments the social ideals that you are struggling to achieve. And I am convinced that our mural art with a little impetus can soon result, for the first time in our history, in a vital national expression.[1]

What was new in the proposals of Biddle and his associates for a revival of American mural painting was simply their belief in government aid to artists. In Europe the decoration of public buildings had long been a characteristic art form in ancient empires as well as in modern monarchies. And in the young American republic, Congress as early as 1817 had commissioned John Trumbull to execute a group of historic paintings to hang in the rotunda of the Capitol building. But despite spasmodic efforts to popularize American art, the average painter or sculptor in the United States enjoyed little general patronage, whether private or public, except as he depicted the likenesses of a few rich benefactors. With the economic collapse of the 1930's, the sources of private philanthropy were still more drastically curtailed, and the support that a wealthy elite had traditionally extended to the arts was now diverted to more practical uses. Overnight, as artists and writers joined the ranks of the unemployed and as theatres closed their doors, "the nation was brought face to face with a troublesome question: were the arts simply luxuries that could be lopped off in times of depression? Could a country treat its creative artists as valueless expendables, thus discouraging new recruits from joining their ranks and perhaps creating a cultural vacuum that would last for generations to come? And, if not, how could artists be supported?" [2]

In the summer and fall of 1933, some of the top New Dealers with an interest in the arts discussed this question and some of its possible answers. Once it was decided that it was legally feasible for the government to put unemployed artists to work at their profession, an executive order of November 29 authorized Assistant Secretary of the Treasury L. W. Robert, Jr., an enthusiastic and sympathetic administrator, to organize an Advisory Committee to the Treasury on Fine Arts. In a press release that same day, announcing the members of the committee—Frederic A. Delano, Charles Moore, Rexford G. Tugwell, Harry L. Hopkins, Harry T. Hunt, and Edward Bruce—Robert noted:

> Provision for the encouragement of the fine arts has always been recognized as one of the functions of the Federal Government, and it is obvious such provision should be enlarged in times of depression. The work of artists and craftsmen greatly aids everyone by preserving and increasing our capacity for enjoyment and is particularly valuable in times of stress. [3]

Meanwhile, Harry Hopkins, convinced that artists deserved relief, agreed to allocate slightly over $1 million of Civil Works Administration funds for what became known as the Treasury Department's Public Works of Art Project. Through its Procurement Division, the Treasury was already responsible for the government's public building program, and the completion of many new federal structures in the 1920's had created a need for decoration and adornment. Accordingly, a bureaucratic agreement fastened government responsibility for the arts upon a department primarily concerned with fiscal matters—a marriage of form and function that recalled the largesse of wealthy patrons and monarchs to the artists of European society. Frederic A. Delano, an architect and the uncle of the President, was named initial head of the Treasury committee, but its major guiding influence was Edward Bruce, who served first as secretary and then, in succession to Delano, as chairman.

For executive direction of the Advisory Committee, Edward Bruce had impressive qualifications. A corporation lawyer and financier before he took up painting, he accompanied Cordell Hull to the London Economic Conference in 1933. There, at the suggestion of the Secretary of State, an exhibit of his art was held during the sessions—a pleasant interlude in an otherwise unhappy series of futile meetings. Back home in the United States, Bruce helped win support for the idea of a government-subsidized art project, and the first meeting of the Advisory Committee was held at his Washington residence on December 8, 1933. With Mrs. Roosevelt and a number of eminent directors of great art museums in attendance, the Public Works of Art Project was thus officially launched. To encourage decentralization and help establish local control, sixteen regional committees composed of distinguished citizens and experts from the art world were quickly assembled, and four days after the December 8 meeting the first of a quota of 2,500 artists were on the government payroll. Two months later most of this quota was already employed and, in all, a total of almost four thousand artists from the forty-eight states became at some time a part of the project.[4]

While mural painting was most prominent in the public mind, the Advisory Committee considered any craft that embellished public property. The regional committees, whose chairmen were usually museum directors, had as their major function the choice of the artists to be employed. As the Public Works of Art Project was not merely a relief program, these artists had to be qualified in their profession as well as in their need of a job.

Fiske Kimball, director of the Pennsylvania Museum of Art and one of the regional chairmen of the project, advised Secretary of the Treasury Morgenthau that, in his opinion, "The work secured is . . . much better than the average decoration of public buildings in the past. . . ." It was nonsense, of course, to suppose that the project would unearth 2,500 geniuses who would adorn the federal structures with masterpieces. Nevertheless, the program was no school for amateurs or avocationists, and men of national reputation were not too proud to accept the government's modest stipends. There was an outcry, however, in the New York City newspapers when such well-known artists as John Sloan were placed on the PWAP rolls at $38.25 a week.[5]

In art circles the federal government's patronage provoked varied reactions. Bruce and Forbes Watson, technical director of the Treasury Project, each offered assurances that artists would enjoy complete personal freedom in their work. But, at the inception of the project, the presidents of eight artists' organizations protested that "It would be tragic if the creating artist should be required to perform his work at the rate of $40 a week. . . . It would be distinctly against public policy if he should do so." In tart rejoinder Watson replied: "Clearly before one can raise oneself to be the president of an art society one must first remove oneself from the problems that confront the true artist." In his defense of the Project, Watson also cited the "thousands of letters from artists proclaiming their delight at receiving regular wages. In their eyes," he concluded, "there is no indignity in this arrangement." For a group of the PWAP artists, Charlton L. Edholm sent a personal note to President Roosevelt expressing their gratitude:

You have given us the opportunity to do the best work we are capable of in the service of the nation. For many of us it is the chance of a lifetime to put our souls into the work by which we gain a living, with no obligation to do less than our best in order to produce something of commercial rather than artistic value.

147

We want to assure you that we intend to meet your challenge and produce something worthy of the new spirit of courage and faith and loyalty to the true ideals of our country.

We hope that the crisis through which the nation is passing may be remembered as the period in which American art grew to full stature and took on a virility and beauty never dreamed of before.

We thank you for relieving our financial worries—not by an act of charity which would humiliate us—but by giving us this golden opportunity to do our best work for our fellow-countrymen.[6]

Technically the Public Works of Art Project was among the shortest-lived of New Deal agencies: it was terminated officially as of June 30, 1934. But less than four months later, on October 16, the precedent it had helped to validate was continued on a more permanent basis with the establishment under the Treasury Department of a Section of Painting and Sculpture—"the first official unit within the United States government devoted to art." Four years later, this agency was transferred into the "permanent" Section in Fine Arts in the Treasury Department. Edward Bruce, guiding hand of the PWAP, continued after 1934 as consulting expert to the Section of Painting and Sculpture, which carried out competitions among artists to determine those who would receive commissions for specific projects in major government buildings. The Section was thus an operating and productive organization, while the Fine Arts Commission of the government, created in 1910, remained as an advisory board to set standards.[7]

Although the Public Works of Art Project and its successor sections in the Treasury Department made a notable start in the decoration of federal places, their operations were limited by the amount of Public Building Funds. By 1935, of some 2,800 edifices which the Treasury Department had under its control, only about three hundred had received any artistic attention. And, under the Treasury's restricted program, too few artists received employment to meet job-relief needs. Moreover, their artistic productions were concentrated in the larger cities, while President Roosevelt, among others, was anxious that art be decentralized and distributed to small communities so that it could be enjoyed by the nation as a whole. Edward Bruce therefore requested the President's permission to use relief funds for art, and on July 21, 1935, the new Works Progress Administration, or WPA, allocated to the Treasury Department over one-half million dollars. Thus there was established the Treasury Relief Art Project which supplemented the more permanent Section of Painting and Sculpture. At first 90 per cent, and later 75 per cent, of its artists were drawn directly from relief rolls. For the most part they did easel paintings which were allotted to government buildings, federal hospitals, embassies abroad, and various other public agencies.[8]

While the Relief Project attempted to hold artists to the same high standards originally set by Bruce for all public work, the large numbers of individuals engaged for the WPA average wage of $89 a month for ninety-six hours of work obviously were not all equally gifted or inspired. On the other hand, there was also objection to the Treasury's alternate, more traditional system of competitions and jury awards to decide what painters should be commissioned to decorate federal buildings. George Biddle complained that the supervisory role of the Treasury's Procurement Division in the PWAP had applied grocer's standards to painting, while judgment by a jury of museum directors tended toward the mean and mediocre. It screened out the obviously unprofessional, unfit artists, but no jury, Biddle avowed, could be trusted to select the best.[9]

The American public and many leading New Dealers, including President Roosevelt, wanted an art that represented the more wholesome, optimistic part of the American scene. Abstract painting was not deemed appropriate, and radical political points of view were certain to provoke local and congressional criticisms. In most of the paintings and murals done for the government, contemporary American subject matter therefore was stressed, rather than classical themes of mythology. Often, however, this work was done in a manner contrary to conventional public taste or to entrenched social prejudices. Inevitably such art occasioned controversy, like the furor touched off in official Navy circles by Paul Cadmus' realistic painting of sailors on leave with their girls along Riverside Drive in New York City. But later, Henry Varnum Poor's somewhat cynical and critical murals in the Department of Justice, showing the penal side of criminology, were accepted for their artistic merits and aroused little objection.[10]

Many artists, however, protested that the Fine Arts Commission was reactionary in its tastes and unsympathetic to the style and content of the Mexican school of muralists which had become one of the major influences on their work. Among native painters a vocal individualist, Thomas Hart Benton, lamented the amount of work and preparation involved in doing murals for the government. Confident that he was as popular as any of his fellows in America, he insisted that he have an opportunity to paint untrammeled by administrative regulations. Thus he pleaded: "Please give me all the breaks possible and have trust that I will do the very best in me." [11]

Despite the complaints of artists like Benton and Biddle, it was obvious that the various Treasury art programs did much to beautify government buildings, especially those in Washington itself. The new Justice and Post Office Department buildings, for example, provided space for a notable collection of murals by George Biddle, Henry Varnum Poor, Boardman Robinson, Reginald Marsh, Rockwell Kent, and others. Later the Interior Department and Social Security buildings were similarly embellished with murals interpreting various facets of American life and history.[12]

At the same time the Treasury art programs decorated a large number of government structures, they also gave employment to needy and competent artists. Yet, in terms of widespread relief for those out of work, or for the encouragement of a popular and democratic folk art, the WPA Arts Projects had greater influence. The Treasury program, limited by official regulations and restrictions governing federal buildings and public construction, was competent and satisfactory rather than innovative or exciting. For this kind of creativity and beauty, Edward Bruce, who believed that no great art had ever been developed without a patron, was confident that there was now a deep popular longing. "In considering our standard of living," he wrote in 1935, under the title "Art and Democracy," "too much weight is being given to the money we have to spend and too little weight to what we are getting out of life. You can't *buy* the kind of life a human being should aspire to." [13]

In a somewhat like vein, John Dewey stated the case for an art drawn from experience which would not be separated from contemporary life, or identified with a type of adornment divorced from reality. Many European museums, he pointed out, were simply memorials of the nationalism and imperialism of past wars. Deploring the notion of a gap between the artist and the intellectual, Dewey argued that the artist must think about his society and that the intellectual, in turn, "has his esthetic moment when his ideas cease to be mere ideas and become the corporate meanings of objects." "In the end," he concluded, "works of art are the only media of complete and unhindered communication between man and man that occur in a world full of gulfs and walls that limit community of experience." [14]

Art as experience, with democratic goals and government sponsorship, received its most important encouragement in American history with the establishment of the so-called Four Arts Projects under the Works Progress Administration. As proposed by President Roosevelt and enacted by Congress in August 1935, the initial WPA appropriation of $2 billion included $27 million for art, divided among the Federal Writers', Theatre, Music, and Art Projects. Hiring for all projects began immediately, and in six months a peak figure of forty thousand persons was already on the rolls—almost 16,000 in Music, over 12,000 in Theatre, 6,500 in Writers', and 5,330 in Art itself. Approximately 75 per cent of these were rated as professionals, while two-thirds were "certified as eligible for employment," a polite way of saying they were on relief or were destitute. An exemption clause provided for older persons who were in need but who could not qualify technically for relief. Actually, however, some 90 per cent came directly from relief rolls, while the remaining 10 per cent included administrators, supervisors, and special outside experts who were paid more than the minimum WPA figure. WPA pay scales varied, in turn, according to geographic location and degree of professional skills, ranging from about $60 to $100 a month. A national committee of one hundred served as informal advisers; there were also local state committees which in many instances were little more than "window dressing." Unlike the other WPA projects, there was no provision for local matching funds, and the fact that the Arts Projects, therefore, had to depend almost wholly on federal support, plus some private contributions, occasioned later adverse criticisms in Congress.[15]

From the efforts of its first year, the Art Project proper under the direction of Holger Cahill, an outstanding critic and authority on folk art, was able to offer an exhibition at the Museum of Modern Art in New York City entitled "New Horizons in American Art." Comments in the metropolitan press were generally sympathetic or enthusiastic, and some critics compared favorably the more exciting quality of the WPA work with the earlier Treasury-sponsored art. Lewis Mumford, who was dubious of "New Horizons" exhibits on principle, wrote that "For once, the title means something. . . . There is not a touch of officialism or nationalistic bumptiousness or academic timidity in the whole show. . . ." Louis Untermeyer, writing as a poet and literary critic also interested in the related arts, confessed to Cahill: "I began as a dubious critic of the W.P.A. Federal Art Project; I have become an unreservedly enthusiastic champion of it. I find myself not only referring to its astonishing program, but lecturing on its even more extraordinary accomplishment." [16]

The primary purpose of the Federal Art Project, like that of its parent WPA, was, of course, to provide work relief. But before the project was curtailed by Congress in 1939, it had already accumulated an impressive range of material and artistic accomplishments. An average of four to five thousand artists was employed annually with the largest number engaged in easel paintings. Over 48,000 oils and watercolors were sent out on permanent loan to schools, libraries, and hospitals, while over 1,300 murals decorated other public buildings. Much was also done in graphic art, sculpture, ceramics, posters, and model buildings. Among the thousands given work in the various art programs, it was estimated, for example, that probably two-thirds of all the really important sculptors in the United States were on the government payroll. Three thousand individual contributions were shown at some five hundred WPA exhibitions, and at dozens of WPA Community Art Centers lectures and demonstrations gave an opportunity to countless Americans to participate in workshops and receive free instruction. Estimates from various sources indicated that government support or federal allocations for art from December 8, 1933, to June 30, 1942, totalled over $74 million. To this could be added more than $9 million contributed by local sponsors of WPA art.[17]

Particularly interesting for its historical and cultural importance was the Art Project's Index of American Design. Employing from four to five hundred artists, this division searched the American past for articles in daily use from colonial times to the close of the nineteenth century. On some ten thousand plates WPA artists copied meticulously for posterity the design of American decorative and folk arts as illustrated in furniture, textiles, ceramics, glass, pewter, silver, and so forth. The Index, when it was collected, organized, and lodged in the National Gallery in Washington, became a vast storehouse of carefully painted and drawn reproductions of Americana. Mary R. Beard, the historian, making a belated discovery of the Art Project and the Index, wrote that she was "genuinely thrilled by its potentialities as a vital cultural movement as well as interested in the designs already unearthed and assembled." And Constance Rourke, an expert in American folkways and a consulting editor on the project, reported delightedly from Michigan, where she was tracking down material, that "the cigarstore Indian belonging to that fire-eating anti-New Dealer, Colonel McCormick, is being recorded for the Index. . . ." When the question of some kind of publication or reproduction of a selection of the plates of the Index was raised in 1941, President Roosevelt gave his enthusiastic approval, not objecting to its sponsorship by the Roosevelt Library at Hyde Park, but suggesting that other avenues of distribution be explored.[18]

Despite its own impressive cultural achievements and its success in convincing Americans that art was something more than the viewing of old museum masterpieces, the Federal Art Project had to be judged in terms of its primary purpose of providing work relief. With even partial economic recovery in the nation, the more skilled artists presumably would be able to find private employment, or could compete for government contracts and awards at self-respecting professional fees. WPA rolls would then become a refuge for mediocrity. Most authorities thus felt it difficult to accept the WPA Federal Arts Project as the best means of continued government patronage.

Yet, at what point the transition to private enterprise, or to a sounder system of government support, might be effected soon became a matter of considerable controversy. The Workers Alliance, a labor union including most of those on WPA rolls, and the American Artists Congress, composed of socially conscious left-wing radical groups, kept up constant pressure for the maximum employment and job security of all eligibles within the WPA. Lewis Mumford, one of the vice-chairmen of the Artists Congress, in an open letter to President Roosevelt in December 1936, ardently defended the Arts Project within the WPA. Writing as "a historical and critical interpreter of the arts in America," Mumford appealed to the President to avert the apparent federal policy of reducing and finally cutting off appropriations. In originally approving these projects, Mumford told the President that he and his administrators had done more than provide relief for individual artists: "You have created a solid public platform for American art and you have furthered a great civilizing influence, capable of solving, as no commercially supported arts can solve, the problem of how to use our collective wealth and our individual leisure with dignity and sanity and permanent delight." [19]

In the spring of 1937, in reply to the Artists Congress' complaint of WPA personnel cuts and layoffs, Holger Cahill was forced to restate carefully the project's essential democratic purpose and, at the same time, to make it clear that "no matter what any of us think about the desirability of a program which would give employment to all artists, irrespective of economic need as established by state and local welfare agencies, need as so established has been basic to the set-up of all projects under the Works Program of which the Federal Art Project is one." In rejoinder to Cahill's contention, the Artists Congress, in identical letters to President Roosevelt and Harry Hopkins, argued: "The Arts Projects must not be sacrificed at any cost to the sniping demands of reaction. They should rather be permitted to continue with increased funds and should be further aided by the feeling of such security as would result from Civil Service status for all those eligible." [20]

As national support for many of the New Deal measures waned by 1938, the recurrent idea of an overall federal agency for the fine arts was suddenly revived by the introduction of two such measures in Congress. The Sirovich joint resolution and the House-Senate Coffee-Pepper bill both proposed to incorporate the Four Arts Projects within a more substantial framework of permanent federal aid. Testimony in behalf of these bills by the directors of the Arts Projects was confined to a defense of their particular areas of interest. Employment facts and figures, plus statistics of the large popular audiences for the varied artistic productions of the projects, were cited to justify continued federal support. Neither Congress nor the country, however, seemed ready to establish a permanent government department devoted to the fine arts. And President Roosevelt, though concerned over the fate of the various WPA Arts Projects, also informed Senator Pepper in the closing weeks of the legislative struggle that he hesitated "to recommend the creation of a Department of Art without further clarification, through experience, of the function which such a Department should serve." [21]

Within the art world influential groups and individuals were hostile, not so much to the idea of federal support as to the particular bills before Congress. Francis Henry Taylor, the art critic who had praised some of the earlier work in the Federal Art Project without, however, accepting the basic ideas of the relief program, termed the bills before Congress "pork barrel" and "class legislation." Favoring intelligent support for the arts that would not continue to subsidize mediocrity, he charged that "no one in authority has been willing to face the issue of where relief ends and art begins." George Biddle, a proponent of federal aid, nevertheless feared that the Coffee-Pepper bill would terminate the happy freedom from political control that had character-ized the first four years of government subsidies for art.[22]

Most damaging was the testimony of Arthur F. Brinckerhoff, president of the Fine Arts Federation, a nationwide group com-posed of seventeen organizations including the National Academy of Design, the New York chapter of the American Institute of Architects, the Society of American Artists, and the American Society of Mural Painters. Confining himself to the general issues involved, and not to the details of the bills, Brinckerhoff asserted that the federation had "the utmost sympathy with the principle that the Government should include artists in its pro-curement and relief activities, as it is now doing; but it believes that wholesome results in the field of relief flow from an organi-zation of art work frankly as relief rather than under the disguise and label of a permanent bureau to raise the standards of and appreciation in the arts, as is done in these bills." But the fed-eration, at the same time, dissented from federal control which it feared "will in the long run substitute journeyman standards of art for truly artistic standards, mediocre common standards in place of the highest individual standards, regimentation of art work in place of individual talent, and personal and political pull in the award of art jobs in place of free and open competition." [23]

The not unexpected defeat of the Sirovich and Coffee-Pepper bills was followed by a general curtailment of the Federal Arts Projects. In 1939 both the Treasury Section in Painting and the WPA Art Project were transferred to the Federal Works Agency, which was gradually closing out all relief programs. Edward Bruce, annoyed by the talk in 1940 that with the world in flames art should be dropped, wrote defensively: "My whole argument for the last six months has been that with art a com-plete blackout in Europe it becomes that much more important for us to make culture an active force in the world. . . ." But art, too, was going to war, and in the last months of 1941, WPA

157

paintings were used for an exhibit at the Library of Congress on "Cultural Projects in National Defense." [24]

The political contentions and controversies that swirled about the WPA and the Treasury Art Programs troubled to an even greater degree another of the WPA Four Arts Projects—the Federal Theatre. Like the fine arts, the performing arts were badly hit by the depression. Among the first activities to feel the effects of the economic debacle of 1929 were some of the more expensive forms of popular amusement and entertainment. For the commercial theatre, as for other business enterprises, the crash dried up the sources of capital investment. On Broadway, playhouses shut their doors as producers sought vainly for rich "angels" to finance their shows. In cities throughout the United States, theatre lights were dimmed or darkened, while actors, playwrights, and stagehands were turned into the streets to join the growing army of the unemployed. Under the auspices of the early New Deal relief agencies, a few plays were staged as benefits for jobless performers, and across the country amateur theatricals enjoyed a new vogue. But these were only stopgap measures, and in the field of mass entertainment the first important relief venture of the New Deal was the Federal Theatre, established with the other WPA Arts Projects in the summer of 1935.[25]

To direct the Theatre Project, which enjoyed the interest and support of both the President and Mrs. Roosevelt, WPA Director Harry Hopkins turned to an old friend and Grinnell College classmate, Hallie Flanagan, head of the highly regarded Experimental Theatre at Vassar College, and fresh from a study of the national theatres in Europe. Mrs. Flanagan approached her job with a verve and enthusiasm that soon carried the project beyond its official objectives as a mere relief agency. Willson Whitman in his study of the Federal Theatre makes the point that it was not founded as a national theatre or as a yardstick for commercial entertainment or to provide culture. "It owes its existence to the assumption that actors must eat." Yet, in time, it did almost all the things for which technically it was not created. In explaining this shift, Mrs. Flanagan pointed out that up to 1935 the New Deal's aid to unemployed theatrical professionals "was entirely a relief enterprise and as such laudably humanitarian. It was not regarded by its founders, by professional theatre people on or off its rolls, by drama critics, or by the public in general as a theatre program." But, in contrast to the more individualistic work of a painter or writer, an actor required a complicated medium or forum. If he was to be given work instead of a dole, obviously some kind of federal theatre had to be created. That it would be venturesome and different, rather than staid and bureaucratic, seemed assured by Hallie Flanagan's own background and interests.[26]

Although its director was the major single force behind the Federal Theatre, she was able to enlist expert help and gain the cooperation of community groups. Thus before the Federal Theatre was started in a town or city, local people were called upon to form a committee to explore the region's interests and possibilities. In the key area of New York City, playwright Elmer Rice served as a regional director and as a general source of encouragement for new ideas. Rice believed there were "but two possible alternatives for the theatre: as a business it will become, more and more, a relatively unimportant subsidiary of a gigantic industry, controlled by Hollywood and by the bankers who control Hollywood; as an art, supported by public funds, it may be made to serve the needs of the community and to play a part of some importance in the cultural life of the nation." [27]

How far it was possible for the Federal Theatre to go when its WPA funds were intended primarily for unemployment relief was, however, a serious question. Mrs. Flanagan was convinced that its achievement "will be measured not only by the number of people put to work, but also by the quality of production and the type of plays produced in the various theatre units." Confident that the primary objective of re-employment was being largely accomplished by 1936, she explained to the regional directors: "From now on our job is to see that the enterprises in which we are engaged are worth the effort." [28]

No one could object that the Federal Theatre was unwilling to experiment. In types of productions and audiences, it covered a wide range. But its programs had to be suited to the abilities of the performers and to the tastes and desires of local communities. In addition to regular theatrical performances, there were vaudeville groups, marionette and puppet shows, dance companies, and even two circuses. Major efforts included Negro, Experimental, Poetic, Tryout, and Children's Theatres. Unusual and novel techniques were attempted, chiefly in New York City. A new technical form of theatre was the Living Newspaper—documentary productions modeled on the moving picture newsreel. Conservative critics complained with considerable justice that the Living Newspaper's politically controversial subject matter voted strongly for the New Deal. Introduced, for example, were the questions of agricultural relief (*Triple-A Plowed Under*); slum conditions (*One Third of a Nation*); public utilities and TVA (*Power*); and labor disputes (*Injunction Granted*).[29]

A production which also aroused contention was the play based on Sinclair Lewis' strongly anti-fascist novel *It Can't Happen Here*. While an earlier Federal Theatre production, *Ethiopia*, had been canceled by Washington on the grounds that it would offend Italy, the extensive staging of *It Can't Happen Here* contrasted to the unwillingness of Hollywood to produce controversial movies that might be banned abroad. Opening in December 1936 in twenty-one simultaneous productions across the nation, *It Can't Happen Here* played to large audiences who paid an average admission price of only thirty cents. In New

York City, Sinclair Lewis himself took the role of his hero Doremus Jessup. Reviews of the play, though friendly in tone, were distinctly "mixed" as to the quality of the various performances. For the WPA Theatre a much greater artistic success was *Macbeth*, staged in a Haitian backdrop with a Negro company. And both a box office and critical triumph was the performance of T. S. Eliot's distinguished play *Murder in the Cathedral.*[30]

An unpleasant episode, reminiscent of the stopping of *Ethiopia* which had occasioned Elmer Rice's 1936 resignation as the Federal Theatre's regional director in New York City, was President Roosevelt's executive order forbidding the performance, three days before the scheduled opening, of Marc Blitzstein's *The Cradle Will Rock*. A musical play or operetta set in a fictitious city, Steeltown, U.S.A., *The Cradle* dramatized sympathetically the cause of the steelworkers. When the bitter steel strike in the spring of 1937 suddenly coincided with the Federal Theatre's plans to produce the play, Washington officials feared the public would assume that Blitzstein's radical point of view reflected government sentiment. After a fruitless appeal to the President, *The Cradle* was produced independently of the Federal Theatre. The last-minute change in plans plus union rules forced the actors to sing their roles from the audience, while Blitzstein sat alone at the piano on stage. Following this uniquely improvised opening night, which Archibald MacLeish called "the most exciting evening of theatre this New York generation has seen," the play went on to enjoy critical and popular success and to become in time a legend in the annals of the WPA Theatre.[31]

In all, the Federal Theatre was responsible for almost a thousand different plays and over 50,000 performances; it employed an annual average of 10,000 stage personnel, with 12,700 in the peak year of 1936. Most of the performances were offered free of charge, while the admission scale of the rest ranged from ten cents to $1.10. Only minimum or no royalties could be paid to authors, so there was a heavy emphasis on revivals or experimental plays. Competition with the commercial theatre was thus avoided, although both Bernard Shaw and Eugene O'Neill allowed the use of some of their dramas. Giving his approval of the Federal Theatre's plan for an extensive program of his work, O'Neill wrote: "It is particularly gratifying coming at this time when illness has, for the past six months, forced me to drop all work on my new series of plays. . . . It gives me a reassuring feeling that while I'm forced to be idle, at least my work will be working, and so I won't feel too much of a loafer." [32]

Both O'Neill and Archibald MacLeish stressed the contribution of the WPA Federal Theatre in bringing together a large group of performers and a new popular audience. It was true that many performances were amateurish, but Broadway also had more failures than successes, and at least the price of admission to Federal Theatre productions was minimal. In answer to the question, "How good is the work?", MacLeish wrote that a surprising amount of Federal Theatre was "very good indeed. . . . From any point of view save that of the old-line, box office critics to whom nothing is theatre unless it has Broadway stars and Broadway varnish, the Federal Theatre Project is a roaring success." [33]

Enthusiastic commentary was, however, tempered by the criticisms of those who resented the tie-up of the theatre with relief or who wanted a federally supported national theatre. Thus playwright Sidney Howard, in reply to Hallie Flanagan's invitation to serve on an advisory committee, commented that "by far the greater part of our unemployed actors should be hurried out of acting as quickly as possible—and I believe the same to be true of the unemployed musicians—and relieved of the continued misery of encouragement in a profession for which they are not qualified. I dream of the day," he added, "when the government will be able to do something substantial for the arts of the theatre and music by establishing permanent Federal theatres in different key cities. . . . How hard one could work on such a scheme as that!" Max Lerner, in a friendly review of *It Can't Happen Here*, pointed out, however, that the Federal Theatre, like TVA, was socialistic in tendency—in the sense of its competition with what private enterprise could conceivably do. It was not government propaganda, but he warned:

> One thing is clear. This new role of the federal government is a double-edged sword. Today a progressive government is lending its strength in the fight against ideas hostile to democracy. Tomorrow a reactionary government may turn about and do exactly the opposite.[34]

From the start, Federal Theatre as the most conspicuous of the WPA Arts Projects drew attacks from hostile Congressmen. Brooks Atkinson, drama critic of the *New York Times*, pointed out that "Art seems like boondoggling to a Congressman. . . . But for socially useful achievement it would be hard among the relief projects to beat the Federal Theatre, which has brought art and ideas within the range of millions of people all over the country and proved that the potential theatre audience is inexhaustible." [35] Members of Congress, particularly those from rural constituencies, were, however, not impressed with Atkinson's views, and they were also naturally much less friendly to the theatre than New Yorkers. In the South some resented the way the WPA Theatre and Arts Projects treated Negro and other minority groups fairly and without discrimination.

After 1937, cuts in WPA appropriations were the prelude to increasing pressures to curtail all the Arts Projects. Then in August 1938, less than three months after it had been created, the House Un-American Activities or Dies Committee began hearing witnesses who testified to communist activities and sympathies within the Federal Theatre Project. Plays and individuals were cited for left-wing tendencies, and the Committee Report in January 1939 charged that "a rather large number of the employees on the Federal Theatre Project are either members of the Communist Party or are sympathetic with the Communist Party." Later that year, the House Subcommittee on Appropriations questioned the finances and spending of the Theatre Project, and despite the protests of members of the New York City delegation, Congress cut off all appropriations as of June 30, 1939. Two months later the Theatre Project was officially closed, with most employees receiving the usual one month's notice.[36]

Hallie Flanagan, who was permitted to testify only briefly on certain aspects of the project, declared: "It was ended because Congress, in spite of protests from many of its own members, treated Federal Theatre not as a human issue or a cultural issue, but as a political issue." To Congressman Vito Marcantonio, a leading supporter of the project in the House, she wrote on the day of its defeat: "On behalf of 7900 employees of Federal Theatre I want to thank you for your courageous and inspiring defense of the Project on the floor of the House of Representatives." A short time later, in a retrospective account of her four years' experience with the project, Mrs. Flanagan summarized the case for federal support of the arts.

> The greatest achievement of these public theatres was in their creation of an audience of many millions, a waiting audience. This audience proved that the need for theatre is not an emergency. Either the arts are not useful to the development of the great numbers of American citizens who cannot afford them—in which case the government has no reason to concern itself with them; or else the arts are useful in making people better citizens, better workmen, in short better-equipped individuals—which is, after all, the aim of a democracy—in which case the government may well concern itself increasingly with them. Neither should the theatre in our country be regarded as a luxury. It is a necessity because

in order to make democracy work the people must increasingly participate; they can't participate unless they understand; and the theatre is one of the great mediums of understanding.[37]

Although the Federal Theatre was abruptly terminated by Congress, in the four years of its operation there was abundant testimony to its influence. Some of its bright young people like Orson Welles graduated to the commercial theatre. The work it had done in gaining a new mass audience for all kinds of live productions presumably stimulated an interest in the performing arts, both professional and amateur. The left-wing views with which it was charged were a part of the literary and artistic climate of the mid-thirties and were not confined, of course, to the personnel or work of the Federal Theatre. The outstanding American plays of the period, like many of the American novels, showed an increasingly radical social concern with national and international problems. In any event, the coming of World War II would have cut back most of the Federal Theatre's operations, while much of its excitement and its new techniques were capable of being absorbed into the world of the commercial theatre.[38]

Of the four Federal Arts Projects, the only one that was able to remain largely clear of political controversy and objection was the Music Project. Musicians, like actors, artists, and writers, were hard hit by the depression. Talking movies and radio furnished increasingly formidable competition, adding the woes of technological unemployment to the ravages of the nation's economic collapse. Yet radio, and especially the cheaper sets which the depression encouraged, did much to stimulate the taste and widen the market for serious music. Deems Taylor, the music critic, quoted the letter of a high school girl in the thirties who kept track of the good music she was able to hear over the radio—"a total of 582 overtures, suites, symphonic poems and ballets, played by practically all of the leading orchestras of the country. . . ." As Taylor observed, the average citizen "will not readily visit an art gallery or a symphony concert. But radio banished his fears. It offered him serious music, free of charge, in his home, under conditions whereby, if it happened to bore him, he could simply shut it off." [39]

Homogeneous in its personnel, easily administered, and enjoying popular appeal, the Music Project under the direction of Nikolai Sokoloff, organizer of the Cleveland Symphony Orchestra, was able to carry through a varied nationwide program. Those on the rolls of the Music Project, numbering some fifteen thousand, were nearly all musicians, mostly members of the Federation of Musicians of the American Federation of Labor. Employed in a variety of performing capacities, they gave thousands of concerts, staged operas, supplied the orchestra for Federal Theatre musical shows, and made radio recordings. Special attention was given to folk music and the works of American composers. In addition, the teaching members of the Music Project gave basic instruction to both children and adults in regions that had lacked the opportunity to enjoy any sort of musical training. Thus the project was able to reach down into local communities and enlist popular participation in such activities as national music week.[40]

As varied in the potential range of its activities as the Music Project, the Writers' Project of the WPA was, however, a much less tidy or manageable enterprise. One difficulty, as the novelist Sinclair Lewis pointed out, arose from the fact that "almost every one sufficiently literate to write a postcard home from Niagara Falls believes that he would be a successful creative writer if he just had the time." Moreover, a writer's professional skill was not easily determinable, and even less apparent might be an individual's latent creative ability. Thus at its peak the Writers' Project "supported over six thousand journalists, free-lance writers, novelists, poets, Ph.D.'s and other jobless persons experienced in putting words on paper. Hacks, bohemians and local eccentrics jostled elbows with highly trained specialists and creative artists of such past or future distinction as Conrad Aiken, Maxwell Bodenheim, Vardis Fisher, John Steinbeck and Richard Wright." [41]

In the late summer of 1934, a year before the inception of the WPA Writers' Project, Edward B. Rowan, assistant technical director of the Treasury's Public Works of Art Project, sounded out a number of prominent American authors on the possibility of such an idea for creative writers. The interesting and varied responses indicated some of the difficulties that were, in fact, later faced by the WPA program. Archibald MacLeish in his reply suggested historical research for unemployed writers. But, he added,

> if you are going to keep them alive as artists you'll have to let them use your money to do their own work. And their own work may be terrible. Or it may be wonderful and strange. You can let a painter paint a state building but you can't hire a poet to write its epic because the taxpayers can see murals but not epics. I don't see in my ignorance that there is anything much you can do but turn yourself into a Guggenheim committee and get the boys to submit projects and back those you believe in even though they may add nothing to the life of the general public.[42]

Other prominent authors echoed MacLeish's concerns. H. L. Mencken, for example, doubted that any "genuine" creative writers were in need of government help, and he feared the subsidies would go to "quacks." In like vein, Hamlin Garland wondered whether Rowan's idea was not in direct conflict with Secretary of Agriculture Wallace's plan of discouraging production. "To be consistent, the government should pay us a bonus for NOT writing or painting," he concluded. A number of those queried—including Sinclair Lewis, Edgar Lee Masters, William Carlos Williams, Conrad Aiken, Marianne Moore, and Dorothy Canfield Fisher—commented on the great difficulty of discovering and supporting literary excellence. But they also agreed that many writers who desperately needed help could be put to work usefully on research and the simpler forms of noncreative writing. To his letter in regard to the plan, Aiken added: "I should like nothing better than to get a job in it!" Only Theodore Dreiser in his answer seems to have suggested the possibility that the government might use the writers for propaganda work, a notion to which he was, however, personally much opposed. "I think," he noted, "that whatever is written should be free, unbiased, untainted by any influence whatsoever, whether emanating from the government or other sources." [43]

Intended at first to be largely a relief measure for unemployed journalists, the Writers' Project was headed by Henry G. Alsberg, a former foreign news correspondent, editorial writer, and director of the Provincetown Theatre. Under the aegis of his national office and the separate state directors, the writers of the project turned out reams of copy devoted mainly to factual reporting of topics related to American regional history and folklore. Vardis Fisher, state director for Idaho, and such established writers as Conrad Aiken, John Cheever, and Richard Wright were on the rolls of the project. And in 1936 and 1937, some of the more personal creative writing done by members of the project in off hours was collected in two volumes called *American Stuff*, edited by Alsberg and published commercially by the Viking Press.

The principal task of the project, however, was its American Guide Series, a unique combination of tourist information, local history, and geography, which eventually covered all the separate states and territories plus certain important regional areas and cities. These guides, a number of which became modest best-sellers, were issued attractively by several commercial publishing houses. Local advisory groups of authors, editors, and critics helped secure support and publication of the guides. In New York City, for an example that was not, however, really typical, the Authors' Guild Committee for Federal Writers' Publications, Inc., included such well-known names as H. S. Canby, Van Wyck Brooks, Rockwell Kent, Lewis Gannett, Mark Van Doren, Malcolm Cowley, and Bruce Bliven.

The writing and editing was a collective job with the consequent anonymity of the various contributing authors. In some cases, though, like the classic account of Deerfield by Conrad Aiken in the Massachusetts Guide, the author was easily discovered. Radical political and social points of view at times colored the factual materials, creating difficulties for the project and arousing congressional criticism. But, on the whole, the volumes made useful and interesting and, in a few cases, even distinguished books.[44] The favorable comment of critics was summed up in Van Wyck Brooks's opinion that the volumes "will still be going strong when most of our current books are dead and forgotten." Brooks added as a postscript: "And when people have forgotten the rubbish about Red propaganda." [45]

The Writers' Project was also responsible for gathering by interviews with aged Negroes a notable collection of ex-slave narratives. But the second major enterprise of the project, after the Guide Series, was the Historical Records Survey, which compiled inventories of some of the less accessible manuscripts and printed materials bearing on the American past. This task was similar to the parallel inventory of physical remains undertaken by the Index of American Design. Records and archives stored in out-of-the-way places, when duly catalogued and listed, became more easily available to historians and other scholarly researchers. At the same time, the inventories provided a start for a comprehensive modern survey of important historical sources located throughout the United States. Historians were quick to recognize the value of the Records Survey, but the often uninspiring, mechanical nature of the routine work tended to dampen the morale of the personnel involved in the endless tasks of inventorying and cataloguing.[46]

In the summer of 1939, when Congress let the curtain drop on the Federal Theatre, it provided that the other Arts Projects might be continued only if local sponsors furnished 25 per cent of the necessary costs. The Writers' Project was able to prove its popularity when in all forty-eight states local sponsors raised the required funds. Neither the WPA nor its Arts Projects survived the war, yet the latter have continued to interest subsequent generations, and it seems probable that the various cultural programs will be judged to have had more enduring worth than the myriad building and construction projects of WPA.

Any considered evaluation of the WPA cultural program depends, of course, very much on the criteria involved. Although the official aim was simply to provide work relief for professional white-collar people, the projects quickly transcended this limited goal. Defined strictly as a relief and employment measure, the Four Arts Projects, after all, cared for a very small proportion of the millions on WPA rolls. Aside from the individual satisfactions at stake, the jobs provided by the program accordingly had little impact on the American economy. Obviously, however, it was not the relief afforded but rather the intrinsic and substantive merits of many of the projects that attracted the interest of the intellectual and cultural world. Already in 1939, several academic groups—the National Council of Social Studies, the American Council of Learned Societies, and the Social Science

Research Council—cooperated to appoint a committee to study ways of making the maximum scholarly use of such WPA projects as the Historical Records Survey.[47]

The belief that scholarship and the arts should reach the widest audience possible was, in turn, related to the whole question of the extent of the federal government's responsibility for subsidizing intellectual and cultural programs. Many of those most vitally interested and concerned with the various depression projects were also ardent advocates of a permanent government center of the fine arts, a national theatre, and other state cultural endeavors. Thus the degree of success or failure of the WPA Arts Projects, judged solely in terms of artistic accomplishments, had an important relationship to possible future government cultural programs. This was evident in the way the experience of the Four Arts Projects dominated subsequent discussions of government support for the arts.

Considered as a precedent for the future, the New Deal experience with the arts must first be appraised in terms of its depression background. The criteria of relief minimized political factors but, at the same time, resulted in the subsidizing of many persons of inferior talent or ability. In a normal, more prosperous period, the government presumably could select artists and writers of proven worth. Yet any direct government aid, not based on the needs of the recipient, might easily succumb to partisan politics. Even in the crisis of the depression, the WPA Arts Projects did not escape political pressures, if not from Washington then from local and internal interest groups. Historian Ray Allen Billington, part-time director of the Massachusetts Writers' Project, has recorded some of its difficulties. While critics tended to judge the projects on political rather than aesthetic grounds, project supervisors themselves frequently had to make decisions on the basis of political expediency. Though administration leaders in Washington kept hands off, there was a "tendency for numerous employees of the Arts Projects to use them as propaganda agencies." And again, although Roosevelt and Washington officials allowed the WPA artists and writers a free hand, except in two instances involving the Theatre Project, "even in the socially conscious decade of the 1930's censorship was a constant threat." [48]

That there were problems in the WPA Arts Projects was readily apparent. But more important and significant was the way in which they illustrated, even with their limited success, the increasing nationalism of American intellectual and cultural life. If therefore, as seemed likely, the future was to witness the growing use of public funds for a greater variety of cultural endeavors, it was to be hoped, in the words of Professor Billington, that "those responsible will devise a system of government aid for the arts that will be free of the defects noticeable in the WPA experiment, yet offer the American people a taste of the finer things of civilization that are today denied to them." [49]

The New Deal's nationalism was exemplified not only in the government's own cultural programs but in the general tenor of American arts and letters in the thirties. Many American writers, profoundly critical of the economic system on which they heaped the blame for the First World War and the depression, gave their sympathetic support to the New Deal. At the same time, the rise of fascism abroad and the threat of a Second World War made most American intellectuals less critical of their own country. This nationalism and patriotism was especially noticeable in a growing emphasis on American culture and American literature. Thus in the first winter of the New Deal, George Biddle, one of the chief architects of government support for the fine arts, sought Roosevelt's endorsement of a plea by a group of his distinguished fellows to museum directors and curators that, for the duration of the depression, they buy only the works of living American artists and craftsmen. And in music, too, there was a new interest in performing the works of contemporary American composers.[50]

Motion pictures, in such striking documentary films as *The River* and *The Plow That Broke the Plains,* and then in newsreels which pictured the approach of World War II, also heightened the sense of loyalty to the American environment and history. Though cautious at first in depicting the depression, the movie makers in Hollywood did try to treat the thirties realistically despite their continued stress on the popular "escape" themes of crime, sex, and love. In contrast to the traditional theatre, the movies proved well adapted to the times. As Gilbert Seldes pointed out, all other arts had been aristocratic in their origins, while the movies with their large varied audiences were essentially a democratic form of mass entertainment. "Never before in the history of the world," Seldes wrote, "has there been an actually universal entertainment. Possibly the gladiatorial combats and the massacres of the Christians in ancient Rome were intended to satisfy all the people of a metropolis at the same time, but no attempt was ever made before the movies began, to please young and old, men and women, rich and poor, learned and ignorant, well-bred and vulgar, urban and provincial, cleric and peasant, by the same means." [51]

In the thirties the American landscape again attracted the attentions of native artists. Especially popular and widely reproduced were the works of the so-called regionalists of the Midwest—Thomas Hart Benton, John Steuart Curry, and Grant Wood. Choosing rural themes in the satiric mood of Wood's "American Gothic," this group constituted a sort of populist revolt against the conventional artistic tastes of the East. Also enjoying a great vogue in the decade were American primitive painters, led by "Grandma Moses," who favored New England farm scenes.

Even when the treatment of the landscape was harshly realistic, in contrast to the mood of the primitivists, it still was capable of evoking nostalgia for the American past. Mexican artists had been painting their country as they saw it. And in the United States now, according to Alfred Frankenstein in the *Magazine of Art*, the American scene was "not merely a matter of subject. Thousands of American artists have been painting the American landscape, American architecture, and the American people for generations past, but without remotely approximating this thing called the American scene. What distinguishes the American scene group—Benton, Curry, Wood, Marsh, Hopper, Burchfield, to name only a few—is a highly complex attitude toward the subject, an attitude compounded of romantic emotion and realistic delineation, of a desire to expose the plain, unvarnished facts of American life plus a strong, even sentimental love for the facts that finally emerge. It is primarily, but not exclusively," Frankenstein concluded, "a phenomenon of the Middle West, where the natural landscape is comparatively unspectacular and offers the artist little challenge. . . . The American scene thus depicted is basically the human scene. . . . It is an art of people and what they do and the places they live in, not an art of mountains, clouds and the sea." [52]

Most important in terms of both intellectual attitudes and popular taste was the American novel of the thirties. Of the leading writers of fiction in the 1920's, only John Dos Passos continued to have a significant and widespread influence. In general, the older giants of American letters seemed unable to come to grips with the depression. At first the hard times acted as a stimulus to works of social protest, to the radical and labor novel. Their authors meanwhile turned to the left, to the Communist party, to the American Writers' Congress, or simply to vague left-wing sympathies and a radical philosophy. While little of the avowedly radical or labor fiction survived as literature beyond the thirties—in contrast to works more personal and individualistic in their approach—there were some noteworthy exceptions. For certain authors a stand on the left at some point in their careers was probably a necessary aid in shaping their insight into American life during the depression. Examples of this kind of novel of social protest written in the thirties that continued to win critical and popular acclaim were Dos Passos' *U.S.A.*, the foremost literary indictment of the old order of the twenties, and James T. Farrell's *Studs Lonigan* trilogy or John Steinbeck's *Grapes of Wrath*—equally devastating pictures of urban and rural poverty and despair in the depression decade.[53]

By the mid-1930's, under the impact of the New Deal and the left wing's new ideology of a Popular Front among liberals, novelists found themselves able to write more enthusiastically about the American scene. With the standard romances of escape there was an increasing vogue of historical fiction. And even the literature of social protest revealed a growing nationalistic emphasis and a confidence that life would be better under the future foreshadowed by the New Deal. The writers themselves were caught up in the excitement of the times. "Gosh, isn't life a whirlwind; and why are there 15 million unemployed when some of us haven't even time to breathe," Martha Gellhorn wrote hurriedly to Hallie Flanagan soon after Roosevelt's re-election in 1936.[54]

Whether truly radical or not, there was youthful exuberance in much of the writing of the thirties: for example, in *Waiting for Lefty* and *Golden Boy* by Clifford Odets, the exciting left-wing playwright uncovered by the Group Theatre; or in the novels, jampacked with life as it was in the depression, by Thomas Wolfe, who enjoyed a success similar to Odets' without the latter's left-wing radicalism. The works of both of these young authors had an appealing messianic note which enabled them to combine fervor and prophecy with social protest, and which also kept their writings close to the American scene.[55]

In sum, the thirties proved to be an enormously complex

decade—intellectually and culturally, as well as politically. To an unprecedented extent, whatever the government did, either directly or indirectly, affected American arts and letters. Even the most individualistic artists and writers could not ignore the times, and much of their work mirrored the sense of crisis with which the thirties began and ended. It was also a decade in which Americans increasingly took pride in their history and culture, including its local and regional customs and traditions. And finally, the New Deal itself gave a strong nationalist tinge to American thought. This rising American national spirit gradually overcame all foreign ideologies, even as the approach of war disrupted the old dreams of further reforms or new utopias at home.

SIX

❦

A Chorus of Dissent

THE NEW DEAL, for all its persuasive political power and broad cultural interests, was almost never without active intellectual opposition. Except in the honeymoon period of Roosevelt's first Hundred Days, his administration constantly faced a varied and vocal chorus of dissent. Even in the midst of the rising tide of electoral support in 1934 and 1936, a broad range of criticism stretched across the political and ideological spectrum. But, significantly, in a decade that began with the Great Crash of 1929 and culminated in the Second World War, the opponents of the New Deal were unable to muster decisive political backing. Their arguments, on the whole, were not convincing to the great majority of American voters. Given the evident appeal of much of the New Deal's philosophy and program, its critics were compelled to assume a defensive posture. Thus the voices of dissent, it was apparent, were fated to remain also largely declamations of despair.

Much of the criticism of the New Deal came from the spokesmen of the upper classes. Franklin D. Roosevelt "was four times endorsed by thumping majorities," writes Henry Steele Commager, "but no student can fail to be impressed with the consideration that on each occasion the majority of the wise, the rich, and the well-born voted the other way." [1] More surprising was the large number of old Progressives, veterans of the struggles of the Theodore Roosevelt and Wilson eras, who turned against the New Deal, sometimes joining the conservative opposition and generally convinced that Franklin Roosevelt had not remained true to the Progressive principles of the early 1900's. Indeed, many of these now conservative or old-fashioned liberal critics of the New Deal, in venting their indignation over FDR's policies, also recalled in a kind of utopian nostalgia the older ideals and traditions of American life. The New Dealers, in contrast, often seemed almost businesslike in their opportunism and search for practical reforms. [2]

The most serious ideological attacks upon the New Deal, however, came first from the radical left. Despite the relatively poor showing of the Socialist and Communist parties in the 1932 elections, left-wing forces were not silenced. The unhappy state of international politics and the uncertain direction of the Roosevelt reforms made it easier for radical critics to point to supposed fascist tendencies in measures like the NRA. At the same time, there was widespread radical objection to what was believed to be the essentially moderate course of the New Deal and its accompanying failure to use the economic crisis as a lever for revolutionary changes.

Speaking for one faction of the literary left wing, V. F. Calverton's *Modern Monthly* expressed some of the radicals' concerns. "An old America is being buried today and a new America is being born," Calverton wrote on the eve of Roosevelt's inauguration. As a result of what he termed "the Europeanization of America," old differences between the two continents had disappeared. "The day of the individual in America is gone; the day of the classes has definitely come in." Sentimentalism over a Jeffersonian individualism and a competitive economic order, Calverton explained, only held back the material progress of the United States and helped to create confusion among modern American liberals. Yet his analysis betokened little sympathy for the initial attempts at social and economic planning of the early New Deal. In "An Open Letter to American Intellectuals," Calverton and a group of left-wing associates avowed:

> Capitalism will resort to reaction, under the name and form of Fascism, or some other, in the U.S. as elsewhere. This country has its own history, tradition and conditions of which due account must be taken, but we cannot by some Rooseveltian trick evade the unfolding of basic economic and political developments under capitalism. . . . Let us not deceive ourselves that we shall not have to face here also the choice between reaction, on the one hand, and a truly scientific economy under a genuine workers' democracy on the other.[3]

A naturally popular leftist assumption of the thirties was that the depression heralded the death of capitalism. Lewis Corey, an orthodox Marxist who was forced to leave the American Communist party in the 1920's as a result of a personal and factional dispute, set forth this thesis in great historical detail in his books *The Decline of American Capitalism* and *The Crisis of the Middle Class.* Paralleling Calverton's left-wing interpretation of American literature with his own radical concept of American history, Corey surveyed the growth of what he regarded as state capitalism masked in the guise of old-fashioned progressive reform. "It took 500 years of struggle to create the new world of capitalism," he wrote. "But the struggle for socialism, in the midst of the dying world of capitalism, is more purposive, easier, more capable of speedy realization." Communism, Corey argued, is the modern Marxist Enlightenment; "it calls to struggle for a new world that is already appearing on the horizon." [4]

179

The question "Will Capitalism Survive?" Jerome Davis answered in 1935 with a categorical NO. Professor Davis, later forced from his teaching post at the Yale University Divinity School because of his pro-Soviet sympathies, offered a lengthy socio-economic analysis of *Capitalism and Its Culture*, in which he defined both as anachronisms. Individual liberty, he argued, had been subverted until "In reality it has come to mean liberty for big combinations of wealthy interests to gouge the common people. . . . No one can be sure," he admitted, "what the next stage of economic development will bring forth. . . ." But experience suggested "an extension of power to the working class . . . , a goal supremely to be desired." Still another alternative, and at least a possibility, was the revamping of capitalism under Roosevelt into a "form of capitalistic fascism." [5]

With Corey and Davis, other well-known writers in the early 1930's viewed the New Deal as part of a right-wing reaction. Roosevelt's version of a planned economy, though more refined than the policies of Hitler or Mussolini, was nevertheless "paving the way for Fascism in the United States," according to I. F. Stone. "The New Deal Is No Revolution, Well Then: What Next?" asked Louis M. Hacker. Among all the possible alternatives, he concluded that "it is difficult to see how war can be left out of any calculation, whether one talks of a resurgent imperialism, fascism, or proletarian revolution as the next development after the New Deal." And David Cushman Coyle, in his economic analysis, observed that "The ultimate question is whether the New Deal will go over into fascism." [6]

Like these American leftist critics, Harold J. Laski, the influential and scholarly British socialist and Labour party official, saw democratic capitalism in a stage of historical crisis. Capitalism, he believed, had to keep expanding in order to avoid the stress and strain of the class struggle. But due to the economic contractions forced by the depression, this problem had become "insoluble in terms of the present social order." The concessions exacted by democracy accordingly appeared to be too high for the assumptions of capitalism. "I do not accept, therefore," Laski wrote in 1935, "such a diagnosis as President Roosevelt makes when he declares that our present difficulties are due to the unethical practices of some business men, and acts upon the presumption that the removal of those practices will restore the health of the body economic." Echoing Laski, the editors of the *New Republic* concluded their discussion of the Supreme Court decision invalidating the NRA with the statement: "Either the nation must put up with the confusions and miseries of an essentially unregulated capitalism, or it must prepare to supersede capitalism with socialism. There is no longer a feasible middle course." [7]

In one of the livelier literary dissections from the American left, Benjamin Stolberg, long active in radical labor circles, and his co-author Warren Jay Vinton criticized the so-called pragmatism of the New Deal for its lack of any coherent economic theory. "Science," they contended in 1935, "performs no experiments which are not guided ideologically, by the strictest possible theoretical background." But the characteristic American social thinker, from Dewey to FDR, "has been a sociological adventurer and opportunist. The New Deal is merely the capture of government by 'scientific' social work. It is merely a remodelling of the White House into a new Hull House. And the Brains Trust are nothing but settlement workers who want the big bad bankers and the good little workers to play together in peace." The NRA and AAA Stolberg and Vinton called bare panaceas, while the New Deal's public works program, they complained, would not cure the fundamental problem of the maldistribution of wealth. Only TVA, the most socialistic of the New Deal measures, found merit in their opinion as "an invaluable lesson to the American people in the possibilities of social control." However, they concluded:

> There is nothing the New Deal has so far done that could not have been done better by an earthquake. A first-rate earthquake, from coast to coast, could have reestablished scarcity much more

effectively, and put all the survivors to work for the greater glory of Big Business—with far more speed and far less noise than the New Deal.[8]

More temperate and forebearing than most of the New Deal's left-wing critics were the moderate Socialists. Believing, as they did, in economic change by evolutionary means, it was easy for many of them to view the New Deal as a halfway house to an eventual American socialism. "The American Socialist party is striving to effect the transition to the socialized order as peacefully as possible," wrote Harry W. Laidler, an old-time party leader and director of the National Bureau of Economic Research. Torn by bitter factional disputes in the early thirties, the party was further weakened by the defections of its more conservative members and traditional trade union supporters. A significant number of the Socialists, wearied by long years of struggle in the ranks of a small minority, welcomed the opportunity to work for the New Deal program. Others outside the party, although sympathetic personally to Norman Thomas whom they had supported in 1932, could no longer see the relevance of the classic socialist position. "I do not believe that Socialism in any form known at present is going to be the actual medium through which a better economic era is ushered in," Henry Pratt Fairchild wrote to Thomas a week before Roosevelt's inauguration. "Its emphasis upon Capital and Production seems to me to be entirely archaic today. What we need is an emphasis upon Business and its Ownership, and on Consumption. The economic theory of Karl Marx is in many respects almost as antiquated as that of Classical Economics, many of the basic postulates of which it accepts." [9]

Socialists in the early thirties concentrated much of their attack on two key New Deal measures—the National Industrial Recovery Act and the Agricultural Adjustment Act. The NRA, according to the party's National Executive Committee, was "an official admission that capitalism can make no recovery without governmental supervision. It marks a new stage in the struggle of workers against exploitation for profits, but falls short of giving them their freedom." Although Socialist spokesmen did not usually denounce the NRA as fascism, they claimed it was an approximation of the Italian corporate state that could easily lead to an American fascism.[10]

In regard to the AAA Socialists were particularly critical, although the party itself had in the past offered little by way of a concrete program of reform to American farmers. The AAA, as Norman Thomas protested again and again, was most open to censure because it failed to provide properly for a division of crop benefit payments between landowners and tenants. Thus it contributed directly to the plight of the Negro sharecroppers in the South and to the flight of John Steinbeck's Okies. Thomas himself was one of the few important political and intellectual figures in the thirties to concern himself with Negro civil rights. His criticisms of the administration reinforced the point that, except as they benefited from the relief and welfare measures of the New Deal, Negroes in the thirties remained a submerged and neglected minority. Despite strong Southern influence in the Democratic party, the Negro did make gains under the New Deal in respect to the share he received of public services. But, in contrast to the militancy that followed World War II, the combination of the depression and New Deal economic aid discouraged an aggressive civil rights movement—at least until the coming of the war.[11]

Continually suspicious of its methods and goals, Norman Thomas insisted that the New Deal was not socialist, except in the vaguest sense. "This new economic order," he wrote in 1934, "is not Fascism, at least not yet, and emphatically it is not Socialism or Communism although some of its measures look more like a distant approximation of Socialist immediate demands than anything contained in any Democratic platform." While not denying the achievements or the idealism of the Roosevelt program, Thomas pointed out that it was a revolution only as a part of the general movement from laissez faire to state capitalism. Neither a revolution nor a dictatorship, the New Deal in most of its legislation, despite its brave talk of the forgotten man, "simply accentuated the inevitable capitalist drift to concentration in its freezing out of the little man." Finally, Thomas believed that Roosevelt's absorption in domestic affairs, at the expense of true international cooperation, indicated a devotion to economic autarchy and nationalism, with an eventual new kind of imperialism on the horizon. "History may yet record," he predicted darkly, "that the nationalism implicit in the New Deal was as disastrous to America as was the capitalism to which it was allied, and that for the increase of this national emotion the workers paid a price out of all proportion to such benefits as they reaped from the reformist idealism which tried to change capitalism but not to build the coöperative commonwealth." [12]

"In sum," according to the party's modern historian, "the Socialists were critical of the New Deal for not being socialist, for building a state capitalism which they held contained dangerous tendencies toward fascism, and for being considerably less than thorough in relieving the suffering of the Great Depression." Norman Thomas, the party's perennial presidential candidate, in reply to a correspondent's comment foreseeing "state capitalism as one of the steps toward some form of socialism," agreed that this might be the case. But, he added: "It may, however, lead to a long interlude of Fascism and a kind of new form of Dark Ages." [13]

Forebodings of governmental support for an American version of a corporate state or fascism, so endemic among spokesmen of the radical left, made less sense after 1935 when the New

Deal abandoned its experimentation along the lines of the NRA's type of corporate planning. New labor legislation, work relief for the unemployed, and social security all indicated strong New Deal sympathies with the underprivileged, as well as a return to some of the older progressive reform causes. At the same time, the Communist party line in the United States shifted abruptly from attack to cooperation with the New Deal in resistance to the conservative right. The new Communist strategy of a worldwide Popular Front with democratic and liberal governments postponed the goal of a worker's revolution against capitalism. Instead Communists solicited a united stand against war and fascism in Europe. In the United States they sponsored organizations appealing particularly to fellow-traveling college students and intellectuals. Offering only token political opposition to the New Deal by 1936, the Communists broadened their influence through such fronts as the American League Against War and Fascism, the American Youth Congress, and the American Writers' Congress.

Despite the New Deal's shifting goals and its newfound popularity in left-wing circles, it was apparent by the mid-thirties that the fundamental economic problems of the country, though much alleviated, were still unsolved. After a fairly rapid reduction in unemployment rolls in the first year of the New Deal, the number of jobless declined only slightly from 1934 to 1935. Labor and agriculture remained restive, uncertain of what the Supreme Court would say about the legislation replacing the NRA and AAA. Politically the administration had been living in the reflected glory of the first Hundred Days. Now in the new Congress, with further legislation awaiting passage, it was necessary for Roosevelt to build support for the changing policies of the so-called Second New Deal. The President's problem essentially was one of maintaining political momentum and of overcoming the criticisms developing in the wake of the New Deal's only partial success in coping with the depression. In the words of Arthur Schlesinger, Jr., "Recovery had proceeded far enough to end despair, but not far enough to restore satisfaction." [14]

Tilling the soil of this political discontent were a number of angry men—insurgents, demagogues, political newcomers, and seasoned politicians—who sought to push their varied programs of radical change by the establishment of a new third party. Traditionally, third-party politics in the United States, at least until the New Deal, had revolved around either the progressive coalitions that rose periodically in the agricultural Midwest, or the radical labor and Socialist party organizations of the country. After the La Follette campaign of 1924, these groups, with increasing support from liberal intellectuals, had attempted to build a new party. Along these lines, the Farmer-Labor Political Federation or the American Commonwealth Political Federation, successor organizations to John Dewey's League for Independent Political Action, hoped to contest the presidential elections in 1936. Without any real organized mass support, or even the backing of the Minnesota Farmer-Labor party or the La Follette Wisconsin Progressives, the ACPF, however, found that no political figure of national stature was willing to challenge Roosevelt. Meanwhile, any radical tendencies on the part of organized labor were forestalled by the formation in April 1936 of Labor's Nonpartisan League. Its chief goal was to further Roosevelt's re-election by preventing the rise of a hostile third party. In New York City the newly organized American Labor party also provided a means by which independent and Democratic voters, reluctant to cast their ballots under the Tammany Hall label, might still support the President.[15]

A more serious threat to the New Deal than the old-line Progressive dreams of a farmer-labor coalition were those new radical movements of the thirties that appealed directly to the special interests of the lower middle class. Variously regarded as demagogic left-of-center movements, or as radical right-wing

186

forerunners of fascism, these groups contained the ingredients for a formidable third party. Although Upton Sinclair, the famous novelist and former Socialist running as a Democrat, was defeated in his EPIC (End Poverty in California) campaign for the state's governorship in 1934, the clamor of angry voices continued to fill the political air. Sinclair, Norman Thomas complained, had "turned Democrat at the very hour when the decadence of capitalism and the hopeless inadequacy of capitalist parties was most manifest." [16]

Riding the tide of what seemed to be a widening popular unrest, figures like Father Charles E. Coughlin, the Reverend Gerald L. K. Smith, and Dr. Francis E. Townsend numbered their followers in the millions. The most important politician, however, among the right-wing radicals, until his assassination in September 1935, was Senator Huey P. Long. The self-styled Kingfish of Louisiana politics and leader of the Share-Our-Wealth movement, Long as a third-party candidate might have been able to draw away enough of the votes of the discontented to defeat Roosevelt and throw the election to a conservative Republican. The Coughlin, Smith, and Townsend forces did combine in 1936 to form the Union party, but its nominee, a comparatively obscure congressman from North Dakota, William Lemke, polled fewer than a million votes. In a sense though, the Lemke backers, with their calls for old-age pensions and share-the-wealth schemes, had already gained a measure of success with the passage of Social Security legislation in 1935. Thus Roosevelt had moved to disarm the challenge of the new radical forces that had clustered around Huey Long.

Though there was little open support for fascism in the United States, thoughtful Americans were alarmed at the spread of such fascist-like societies as the German-American Bund or William Dudley Pelley's Silver Shirts of America. Even more disturbing were the demagogic tactics of such leaders of the extreme right as Father Coughlin, "the radio priest," and the

Reverend Gerald L. K. Smith, successor to Long as leader of the Share-Our-Wealth movement. Sinclair Lewis' widely discussed novel, *It Can't Happen Here*, though its alarm seemed exaggerated, pointed nevertheless to the totalitarian tendencies growing in the midst of American democracy. Moreover, it was not forgotten that, as Huey Long was said to have remarked, if fascism ever took hold in America it would arrive in the guise of antifascism. Father Coughlin, in an interesting exchange with Norman Thomas, pointed out that he had gone "almost as far as Socialists themselves in advocating the nationalizing of those public utilities which according to the teaching of the Catholic Church should not be left in the control of private owners." A radical in his belief that money and banking should be nationalized, Coughlin denied that he was a fascist because, with its dictatorship and ungeographical representation, "Fascism endeavors to protect private ownership and control of money and credit." [17]

During Roosevelt's first term, serious intellectual efforts to analyze the likelihood of an American fascism differed widely in their conclusions. By comparison with Europe, America was not ripe for fascism in the opinion of V. F. Calverton. Nor did the New Deal seem to point in that direction. Everything depended, however, on economic conditions, so that "Fascism may develop in America, but not until the economic situation provokes it." Taking issue with Calverton's point that a radical revolutionary situation like that of Germany and Italy was necessary for fascism, Mauritz A. Hallgren, an editor of the *Nation*, argued that it "can unquestionably come without the emotional hoopla of a Hitler or the stage maneuvering of a Mussolini. Indeed," he wrote, "I am certain that in this country it will come gradually, dressed up in democratic trappings so as not to offend the democratic sensibilities of the great American people. But when it comes it will differ in no essential respect from the fascist regimes of Italy and Germany. This is Roosevelt's role—to keep the people convinced that the state capitalism now being set up is entirely democratic and constitutional. . . ." [18]

In an extended survey of the "Forerunners of American Fascism," based on a series of articles in the *Nation*, veteran European correspondent Raymond Gram Swing described America's right-wing radicals. Fascism, he believed, should be used in an economic sense and not merely as a taunting reference to the violence and repression in Italy and Germany. "I define it," he asserted, "as a reorganization of society to maintain an unequal distribution of economic power by undemocratic means. . . . By this definition of fascism," he added, "the only distinction between our present day capitalist democracy and fascism is that one tolerates the democratic technique of operating the country, and the other does not." Unlike Hallgren, Swing predicted that fascism, if it came to the United States, would be accompanied by force. Not merely a reactionary form of capitalism, fascism was rather, especially in its beginnings, also radical and revolutionary—a revolt against poverty and despair which appealed to primitive instincts and prejudice rather than to reason. American right-wing demagogues, Swing feared, would make an alliance with big business. The remedy, he concluded rather obviously and lamely, was economic recovery and a working democracy.[19]

Frequently labeled by his liberal and left-wing critics as America's leading intellectual fascist, Lawrence Dennis, author of *The Coming American Fascism* (1936), was convinced that traditional liberal capitalism was doomed and could not be made to work short of war. A reserve officer and a staunch nationalist and patriot according to his own standards, Dennis had become progressively disillusioned with the existing economic order during his service in the diplomatic corps and in Wall Street during the twenties. In a war situation the United States, he believed, would be forced into fascism, although it was unlikely to be called by that name. Meanwhile, neither the type of national planning nor the violence associated with European fascism was necessarily un-American. In his own book Dennis undertook to define and rationalize "a desirable fascism . . . before it becomes an accomplished fact in the United States." Coercion, backed by the threat of force, was needed to make economic planning work. Fascism, unlike communism, enjoyed the advantage that it preserved private property and enough of the market system and owner management to enhance efficiency and minimize burdensome government regulations and controls. "The ultimate objective," Dennis concluded, "is welfare through a strong national State, and neither the dictatorship of the proletarian nor the supremacy of private rights under any given set of rules." [20]

In comparison with the active propagandizing of both the radical left and right, the conservative opponents of the New Deal seemed a lost minority. After the Republicans' decisive defeat in 1932, there was understandably a dearth of candidates to succeed Hoover as effective head of the party. In addition, a considerable segment of the business community was willing, at least in the first months of the New Deal, to go along with the Roosevelt economic program, and especially with the NRA. As this initial spirit of cooperation gave way to increasing mutual distrust between businessmen and New Dealers, a group of conservative Democrats, encouraged by members of the Du Pont family, organized the American Liberty League in the summer of 1934. With some of the leading figures in the American business world contributing funds, prominent Democrats such as John J. Raskob, former chairman of the party, and its unsuccessful presidential nominees in 1924 and 1928, John W. Davis and Alfred E. Smith, were enlisted as public spokesmen for the League.

Officially the American Liberty League dedicated itself to a

defense of traditional nineteenth-century liberalism and individualism. These values, it maintained, had dominated the course of
United States history. Although the League stressed its nonpartisan concern for all groups and classes of American life,
in practice its laissez-faire philosophy and intellectualized arguments appealed only to an elite. Moreover, it gradually became
clear that its major purpose was to defeat Roosevelt in 1936.
Refusing, however, to utilize the demagogic techniques of the
Coughlinites and Townsendites, and failing to come to any sort
of terms with the economic and social realities enforced by the
depression, the League never emerged as a serious political threat
to the New Deal. Thus when Al Smith, at a well-publicized
Liberty League dinner in Washington early in 1936, assailed
Roosevelt and the New Dealers as the tools of Moscow, the
speech was easily refuted as a reactionary example of Smith's
personal bitterness and disappointment. Smith himself, despite
his growing conservatism, was an odd figure to be associated
with the leaders of big business.[21]

Unlike the former Governor of New York, few of the
Liberty League's corporate spokesmen had ever enjoyed particular distinction as liberals or friends of civil liberties. Most
liberal intellectuals accordingly remained dubious of the sincerity
of the League's own brand of liberalism. Through Arthur Garfield Hays, counsel of the American Civil Liberties Union, the
Liberty League was asked whether it was prepared to protect
the civil liberties of radicals and of liberal minorities. And John
Dewey, in a letter to League President Jouett Shouse, inquired:
"Can you cite any instance in which property has been taken
without 'due process of law'?" The League, however, had
some support from college students and professors, particularly
several conservative economists.[22]

Speaking from the depths of his own disillusionment, and with
a certain justification to be sure, Herbert Hoover indignantly
rejected a proffered membership in the Liberty League. He could

not forget that Raskob and some of his colleagues had used aggressive public relations techniques, and even smear tactics, to damage the reputation of his own late administration. "They are, therefore, hardly the type of men to lead the cause of Liberty . . . ," Hoover observed tartly. Refraining from further analysis of their motives, he nevertheless declared: "I have no more confidence in the Wall Street model of human liberty, which this group so well represents, than I have in the Pennsylvania Avenue model upon which the country now rides." Patrick J. Hurley, Hoover's Secretary of War, also refused to join the League. Ridiculing its contentions that the conservative class was unrepresented politically, he announced: "I am opposed to minorities trying to rule the nation." Losing interest and support on all sides, and ignored by Republican Alfred M. Landon in 1936, the League returned the favor by not endorsing his presidential candidacy. Then, after Roosevelt's overwhelming victory, the Liberty League suspended active operations and finally disbanded completely in 1940.[23]

Former President Hoover in the meantime summed up his own considered and systematic dissent from New Deal policies with the completion in 1934 of his book *The Challenge to Liberty*. Hoover's old friend, Supreme Court Justice Harlan F. Stone, warned that publication would run "a real risk that it will be misinterpreted and that it will be severely assailed as 'stand pat' in its philosophy and outlook. The country is convinced," Stone wrote, "that the time has come for sweeping reforms, and that these are being, and will be, resisted for selfish reasons by those who have an excessive stake in things as they are or have been in the past. People expect that objection will be made to such reforms on the ground that they infringe the principle of freedom of the individual. Even the man in the street is aware that every important reform in the past seventy-five years has been resisted and assailed as an infringement of individual liberty." Although he too "found little satisfaction in the New Deal," Stone, more than Hoover, accepted the curbs on individual liberty resulting from industrial society. The power of modern corporations, he felt, needed some check. Admittedly there was more scope for individual liberty in the time of Jefferson, but the important question to Stone in 1934 was whether Jefferson was correct in his view that freedom and urbanized industrial society were incompatible opposites.[24]

Hoover, however, remained irreconcilable. The fundamental issue facing the American people was the worldwide attack on individual liberty. In its haste to control the forces let loose by modern warfare and technology, mankind was sacrificing freedom in both the intellectual and economic sense of the term. Placing his critique of the New Deal against the background of an ever-widening decline in liberal values, Hoover specifically attacked the whole program of government planning and regimentation of the economy. "Congress cannot run business," he observed in regard to the NRA, "but business can run Congress —to the bankruptcy of liberty." Seeing the weakening of the legislative arm as the first sure sign of the decay of republican government, he added: "It is in the legislative halls that Liberty commits suicide. . . ."[25]

The general point of view expressed in Hoover's *The Challenge to Liberty* was a surprise to the many intellectuals who regarded the former President as a blind conservative. "Think of a book on such a subject, by such a man!" Albert Jay Nock exclaimed. Formerly the editor of the old *Freeman* magazine, Nock had also written sympathetic biographies of Thomas Jefferson and Henry George. He was unconventional in his own highly individualistic sort of liberalism, and a determined enemy of any government intervention in personal or economic affairs. At the same time he deplored particularly, with their political power, the increasing control over culture by the masses—a fact that he presumed was a result of the wider diffusion of material well-being in modern society. Europe so far had avoided the worst of this, but in the United States publishers in their concern over profits sought the widest possible mass market with the lowest common denominator of popular taste in the arts and literature. Temporarily Nock was willing to suspend judgment on the New Deal, but by the fall of 1933 he had already come to believe that "Roosevelt's policy is Statism, pure and simple. . . ." As such, he felt, it was part of a world revolution that denied to the individual all his natural rights and which was leading inexorably to the totalitarianism of a Hitler or a Stalin.[26]

In 1935 Nock published *Our Enemy, the State*, a book indebted to the thinking of both Herbert Spencer and Ortega y Gasset. Making clear the distinction between an absolutist state and limited government, Nock pointed out that the latter responded to man's social needs and protected him in his natural rights, while the former rested on exploitation and conquest. Although American politicians refrained from using the language of a Hegel or Hitler, the United States in its own way was also drifting toward statism. Nock resented furthermore what he called the naive belief of collectivists that, when the state had achieved all power, as in communism, it would automatically wither away. It was, on the contrary, his observation that the seductive ease with which political power now was often gained merely increased the difficulty of its being yielded voluntarily. Thus he predicted gloomily:

> What we and our more nearly immediate descendants shall see is a steady progress in collectivism running off into a military despotism of a severe type. Closer centralization; a steadily growing bureaucracy; State power and faith in State power increasing, social power and faith in social power diminishing. . . .[27]

Nock's later magazine articles in the thirties grew more shrill in their denunciation of the New Deal, but his autobiography, *The Memoirs of a Superfluous Man*, published shortly before his death in 1945, expressed the mellowed disenchantment of a determined aristocrat. It was this work also, which in its individualistic way, served as a successor to the more famous *Education* of Henry Adams.

Less doctrinaire in their individualism than Nock, and not politically identified with either the extreme left or right, a good many intellectuals by the mid-thirties were uncertain of their attitude toward the New Deal's version of planning. Walter Lippmann, in the Godkin Lectures at Harvard, while noting that "After the collapse of 1932–1933 a New Deal of some sort was imperative," pleaded for a mixed economy to avert the danger of either laissez faire or collectivism. William Allen White, sympathetic to FDR but worried by the possibilities of too much power in Washington, asked his audience at the University of Kansas 1934 commencement: "Can Freedom live in the machine age?" Amos Pinchot, confessing that he was "unable to lie awake long at night contemplating the beauties of the Fundamental Law and the Supreme Court," admitted nevertheless that he was "mortally afraid of what Managed Economy will do to us if the Constitution and the Court don't intervene and stop it. . . ." From the right wing, James Truslow Adams asserted: "In spite of the charming pictures of a Utopia drawn by Socialists and New Dealers, and charted on blue-prints by innumerable college professors, there is no use blinding ourselves to the stark fact that a planned national economy and society means the coercion of the citizenry. . . . The more all-embracing the plan," he added, "the greater would be the amount of coercion required." [28]

Critical of the New Deal from the standpoint of the liberal left rather than the right, John Haynes Holmes also expressed a growing distrust of the President as a personality. "He is essentially a play-boy and not a serious leader. His work is that of improvisation, not of statesmanship." Holmes, a longtime member of the board of the American Civil Liberties Union, shared the Union's original disposition to distrust strong government—

including the New Deal's growing reservoir of "power to do ill." He was particularly disturbed by the contemporary liberal equation of the rights of labor with civil liberties. From the hearings in the late 1930's before the La Follette Committee to investigate violations of civil liberties in American industrial relations, it was clear that big business had used violence and espionage to interfere with labor's right to organize. Holmes, however, was not sure that the ACLU should follow the La Follette Committee's single-minded, pro-labor approach. The committee and the New Deal, he believed, ignored the tradition of civil liberties as a negative check against government in favor of the kind of positive government activism illustrated in the role of the National Labor Relations Board. Holmes warned therefore of those "who are not fundamentally interested in civil liberties at all, but only in the question as to how the advocacy of civil liberties may now be used for the benefit of labor in the current struggle . . . ," and he admitted reluctantly that the ACLU might be guilty of "using the civil liberties principle as a means of fighting labor's battles and the cause of radicalism generally." [29]

From the melange of anti–New Deal criticism, a number of philosophers and political scientists sought to reconcile the older American individualism with what they believed was, more or less inevitably, a coming age of collectivism.[30] "By general consent of the intellectuals," Joseph Wood Krutch noted with some asperity toward his fellows, "a revolution is imminent. The average man . . . now agrees with the editors of left-wing journals that Capitalism is Doomed, and hence, no doubt, it is. But the closer it comes the less anyone seems to know what it will be like. . . ." Unwilling, even in the face of the mounting evidence of the new and all-powerful general will, to take the probable revolution on faith, and dubious of all the reigning generalities about Class Struggle, Planned Economy, Social Control, Means of Production, and so forth, Krutch declared: "I for one, should prefer to form some definite idea of just what it is that I am in for." [31]

On the defensive in the 1936 elections, with no firm intellectual foothold from which to launch an effective political attack, the miscellaneous clusters of resistance to the New Deal were suddenly given an unexpected opportunity by the President's blunt second-term announcement of his program to revamp the Supreme Court. No other political institution enjoyed the veneration popularly accorded the Supreme Court and the Constitution; they were representative of what Thurman Arnold called the symbols or folklore of American government. Because of this traditional feeling, New Deal politicos had looked askance at Henry Wallace's pre-election plans for publishing a book skeptical of the Court's social philosophy. "All criticism of the Supreme Court," press secretary Stephen Early pointed out to the President, "treads on dangerous ground because we know that it seems to be the one institution for which . . . there is popular reverence." Early added that Jim Farley, with whom he had just checked, was "definitely opposed to anyone in the Administration, at this time, going into the writing business. . . ." [32]

But Roosevelt was increasingly restive and annoyed by the tenor of the Supreme Court's decisions declaring unconstitutional key New Deal legislation, and he was determined to fight back. With at least implied presidential approval therefore, Wallace's book, *Whose Constitution*, came out in 1936, and late that year the President reviewed with interest a long memorandum from Donald Richberg outlining a plan for the appointment of new judges to any court of the United States after its incumbents had reached the age of seventy. Wallace's book, in turn, emphasized the contrast between the theories of laissez faire and the general welfare as principles of government. Dissenting from the Supreme Court's acceptance of laissez-faire beliefs, Wallace called for the regulatory controls and social cooperation that, he believed, were necessary to realize the promise of America's natural resources and economic opportunities. "Today we need," he noted, "a great many persons who will become as deeply motivated by the idea of a cooperative economic society as the young men of 1776 and 1787 were motivated by the idea of a democratic political society." [33]

At the inaugural ceremonies for the beginning of his second term, Roosevelt and Chief Justice Charles Evans Hughes, both aware of the growing political tensions surrounding the Supreme Court, confronted each other as adversaries. In administering the oath, the Chief Justice emphasized the words "promise to support the Constitution of the United States." And Roosevelt in repeating the oath gave the words equal force. But he admitted later that he had wanted to exclaim, "Yes, but it's the Constitution as I understand it." [34]

In his Inaugural Address the President struck out at his critics. Democracy did not depend, he said, "upon the absence of power. . . . The Constitution of 1787 did not make our democracy impotent." Setting forth the continuing challenge of "one-third of a nation ill-housed, ill-clad, ill nourished . . . ," Roosevelt suggested a renewed program of positive New Deal legislation. "Government," he concluded, "is competent when all who compose it work as trustees for the whole people." [35]

Just before the start of the second administration, Rex Tugwell, Roosevelt's much criticized adviser and the most influential member of the original Brains Trust, retired from the political wars in Washington. At the farewell dinner given him by his fellow New Dealers, Harold Callender, a *New York Times* foreign correspondent recently returned to the United States from a long tour of duty in France, had a "good chance to see and hear them en masse, and an amazing crowd they are," he noted.

"They recall the mob of reformers and Leftists—to use a bad newspaper word—who flocked to Washington in the Wilson days. They were trying to remake the world, while the present lot are content to experiment with the United States." While in the capital, Callender also saw the President "and had a long talk with Secretary Wallace whom," he wrote, "I liked a great deal." Glad to be back home in the United States, he was nevertheless amazed at the changes that had taken place during his absence. "Washington is an interesting place, with many new buildings and such a lot more government than ever before!" [36]

It was with something of this same sense of awe and surprise that the country as a whole greeted the Roosevelt court plan for adding new justices. Friend and foe alike were disturbed by the trickery and secrecy involved in the idea. From the Court itself, where the liberal Brandeis joined the conservative Hughes in opposition, and in the Senate, where the old Progressives Hiram Johnson and Burton K. Wheeler led the fight against the Court bill, there was now a new and more unified criticism. In justifying his stand to Norman Thomas, Senator Wheeler recalled his own experiences in the Nonpartisan League in World War I. Had there not been then a Constitution and Bill of Rights backed up by the Supreme Court, Wheeler believed that he and his fellow liberals would all have been jailed. "It is an easy step," he warned, "from the control of a subservient Congress and the control of the Supreme Court to a modern democracy of a Hitler or a Mussolini." [37]

Like Wheeler, both Dorothy Thompson and Oswald Garrison Villard resented what they felt were the fascist-like implications of the court plan. At Town Hall in New York City, Miss Thompson, fresh from her experience as a newspaperwoman in Nazi Germany, contrasted traditional American liberal democracy to the concept of an unchecked democracy of pure majority rule. The latter was illustrated in the rise of popular tyrants like Mussolini and Hitler who claimed to be democratic because of overwhelming popular approval registered in their behalf by their own staged plebiscites. Villard, also no stranger to Germany, complained to William T. Evjue, the progressive editor of the Madison, Wisconsin, *Capital Times* that he opposed the Court bill because it might open the way for a dictator. "To me," he wrote, "the all-important issue today is the preservation of this country from Fascism. . . ." [38]

Villard's friend Frank Gannett, owner of a chain of independent conservative newspapers, widened the fight against the Court bill by organizing a National Committee to Uphold Constitutional Government. Supported mostly by conservatives, the roster of its members included, however, some liberal intellectuals. After the successful Court battle, the committee also worked to defeat the President's reorganization bill of 1938—a controversial measure designed to revamp the executive agencies which was widely dubbed "the dictator bill." Later, however, under the new revised and less revolutionary Reorganization Act of 1939, Roosevelt was able to establish the Executive Office of the President—the nucleus of the cluster of vital agencies gathered around the White House that are a part of the modern presidency. [39]

In respect to the Supreme Court bill, probably the most important and influential of the journalistic critics was Walter Lippmann. Back in 1935, after the Court declared the NRA unconstitutional, Lippmann had suggested to the President that he "have the New Deal legislation examined at once for doubtful points on delegated power and interstate commerce and that if necessary amendments be drafted and introduced at this session. What I have in mind," Lippmann added, "is not merely to protect the legislation against judicial destruction, but principally to seize the opportunity of putting Congress on record once again to reaffirm those measures. It seems to me that the moral, political and psychological effect of a series of big votes reaffirming the major policies would impress the country and the Court. . . .

It would be equivalent to asking and obtaining a new vote of confidence from Congress." [40]

Then, on the day before Roosevelt's court plan was announced, Lippmann wrote that anti–New Deal lawyers were putting too much burden on the Supreme Court. They encouraged the justices' attempts to control by judicial review what could be done more effectively, if the people so desired, by repealing the offending legislation. The catch, of course, was that the American people, in contrast to the Court, probably favored most of the New Deal laws—however improper they may have been in terms of constitutional precedents and procedures. In a democracy in which, as Lippmann admitted, the minority was bound by the decisions of the majority, an intransigent position on the part of the Supreme Court was almost inevitably open to popular attack. [41]

Lippmann's considerable sympathy for Roosevelt's problems vis-à-vis the Supreme Court was shattered, however, by the new turn of events in 1937. Under the heading "The Seizure of the Court," the columnist asserted: "No issue so great or so deep has been raised in America since secession. No blow has been struck, which if it is successful, would so deeply injure the moral foundations of the republic." Like Senator Wheeler, Lippmann recalled old World War I experiences in chiding those liberals who now supported the Court Plan.

> The so-called liberals who today think that federalism was invented by the Liberty League and is defended only by hirelings of the du Ponts, did not have the same appetite for centralized government when they ran afoul of it in war time and during the reign of the Anti-Saloon League. Nor will they have the same enthusiasm for it the next time they see a Congress which does not think as they do, a Congress, perhaps, which decides to regulate labor by imposing a compulsory service in labor camps as a measure of preparedness for war and as a way of teaching workingmen to take orders promptly. The current enthusiasm of the American liberals for a centralized government of unlimited pow-

ers arises from the happy idea that only liberals will run that government. They have forgotten that the landslide for Harding was as great a percentage of the popular vote as the recent landslide for Roosevelt, and if they think there will never be a reaction again, their optimism is far greater than their good sense. They will make the greatest mistake of their lives if, while they are in power, they destroy the defenses they will desperately need when in the course of human events the people turn once more the other way.[42]

Lippmann's ire was particularly stirred by the thinking of Robert H. Jackson, an Assistant Attorney General, who defended the court plan on the grounds that conservatives, if they controlled the presidency and congress, would have nothing to fear because the Court presumably would have no legislation to overrule. "Indeed," wrote Lippmann, "did Mr. Jackson ever hear of the espionage act, the anti-syndicalist laws, the teacher's oath, the expulsion of the Socialists from the New York Legislature? Has he ever heard of laws passed in other lands by very conservative administrations abolishing trade unions, conscripting labor, censoring the press, prohibiting assemblies, outlawing political parties?" [43]

Lippmann's fears over the Roosevelt court plan were part of his general concern for the fate of those traditional liberal values he associated with what he called "The Good Society." His *Inquiry into the Principles of the Good Society*, published in September 1937, he admitted was a product of his growing disillusionment over his old optimism about collectivism and part of his continuing search for a workable, meaningful philosophy. At the outset, Lippmann dissented from the widespread assumption, advanced most systematically by Lewis Mumford, that the progress of technology required a greater measure of political control. It was not machinery or the capitalist system, Lippmann insisted, that was responsible for the concentration of industrial power in society, but rather the legal benefits granted the modern limited liability corporation that were at fault. The collectivists, whether socialists or businessmen, despaired incorrectly of capitalism and turned to authoritarian conceptions of society. Governments, in turn, changed from the old theory of negative limitations on sovereignty to the enfranchisement of the masses and to the new meaning of freedom as a dictatorship of the majority. Meanwhile, all collectivisms, Lippmann argued, were basically operable only as war economies, even though they might be masked as social reforms. He noted, too, the paradox of the New Dealers and the publicists of planning who, though generally confirmed pacifists, nevertheless looked back upon the war experience of 1917 and 1918 as a tentative sketch of a rationally ordered society. "But who," he asked, "in a civilian society, is to decide what is to be the specific content of the abundant life? It cannot be the people deciding by referendum or through a majority of their elected representatives. . . . There is, in short, no way by which the objectives of a planned economy can be made to depend upon popular decision." [44]

Lippmann's book, written in the context of developing totalitarian movements abroad and from the background of his own increasing misgivings in regard to New Deal policies, was one of a number of works which pointed out that the loss of traditional liberties might be the price of the nationalism and statism growing in all countries. Everywhere, playwright Maxwell Anderson noted in *Knickerbocker Holiday*, "the gravest and most constant danger to a man's life, liberty and happiness is the government under which he lives." Even though the point of view of Lippmann's *Inquiry* was hardly welcomed by New Dealers, it reflected the concern of many moderate liberals. Allen Nevins, who thought it "capital," complained that "the nasty reception it has

had from much of the press is a sad reflection on the brainless-
ness of present-day radicalism in America. I refer to the press
of the intelligentsia, so-called," he added parenthetically.[45]

Speaking out as a representative of the radicals whom Nevins
deprecated, the left-wing newspaper columnist Max Lerner
agreed with Lippman in making a sharp distinction between
liberalism and democracy. "There is no greater confusion in the
layman's mind today," he wrote, "than the tendency to identify
the two." What Lippmann and other opponents of Roosevelt's
court plan really wanted, Lerner believed, was "minority-rights
liberalism" rather than democracy and majority rule. "This liberalism," he noted, "has three facets: a defense of individual civil
liberties against society, a defense of minority rights (including
both human and property rights) against the possible tyranny
of the government, and a belief in rationalism and in the final
triumph of the idea." What was disquieting to Lerner was the
readiness to identify majoritarian democracy with fascism on the
part of such intellectuals as Lippmann, Villard, and Dorothy
Thompson. "If that readiness spreads," he warned, "corporate
power will not lack those intellectual garments which it needs
to stave off a socialized democracy. . . ."[46]

Since the thirties, students of the Supreme Court have debated
the validity of Roosevelt's contention that in the Court fight he
lost the battle but won the war. Actually, most scholars have
concluded, it is more likely that, over the long run and as matters
turned out, "he lost the battle, won the campaign, but lost the
war." Moreover, "he had decimated his army. Never again would
he be able to rally his large majorities in Congress behind a
reform program with the same vibrant leadership of the past."
The bitter struggle not only alienated many of Roosevelt's followers, but it also split the ranks of the liberal intellectuals.
There was now more than ever, as Max Lerner pointed out, confusion over the meaning of democracy and its association with
New Deal reforms. And, for really the first interval since the

depression, progressives as well as conservatives began to look back again with real nostalgia to the older, traditional values of American life—values that seemed threatened at home as well as abroad.[47]

The Roosevelt Court, divided between the Holmesian negative canon of limited court action and the aggressive New Deal version of judicial positivism, had a curious double standard for judicial review. While not interferring generally with the states or Congress in cases involving regulation of the economy, the Court nevertheless interpreted the Constitution and the Bill of Rights broadly to defend certain individual rights and liberties. Yet even this progressive stand was strictly limited in time as the Court, despite the appointment of new liberal justices, adopted increasingly a more conservative, nationalistic point of view to meet the coming war emergency.[48]

In the national struggle to overcome the depression, the overriding goal of economic recovery had made the end justify the means. And, in some circles, the New Deal had become an end in itself. Now suddenly, in the aftermath of the Court fight, ends and means were important again. "If there is one conclusion to which human experience unmistakably points," wrote John Dewey, America's senior philosopher, "it is that democratic ends demand democratic methods for their realization." The most serious threat to American democracy was not the existence of foreign totalitarian states but the conditions and attitudes at home "similar to those which have given a victory to external authority, discipline, uniformity and dependence upon The Leader in foreign countries." The Marxist view that democracy was the mere creature of capitalism was countered, Dewey believed, by America's pluralistic, pragmatic, and empirical methods. Planning predicated on a set of final truths without freedom to change its goals was essentially totalitarian—the opposite of true social planning and pragmatism. Thus Dewey, in response to the alternate fears and demands that the New Deal move to the right or the left, called for planning on a continuing basis as a means to further extend democratic goals.[49]

The "landscape of freedom" in the United States, according to Mauritz Hallgren, author of a study of the history of American liberty and bigotry, was obscured by the paternalism of the New Deal. Making citizens virtually the wards of the state, "it enormously accelerated the movement toward centralization and regimentation in every field of political and economic endeavor. To a degree unprecedented in the republic's history farmers, workers, bankers, manufacturers, and others were told by their government precisely what they could and could not do." The "itch to do good" had again "resolved itself into a multiplicity of restrictive laws. That various of these prohibitions promised some social good," however, Hallgren wrote, "in no way changed the fact that all of them encroached upon the individual liberty." Yet he concluded that "The most disturbing factor was the almost complete absence of healthy criticism from the nation at large." [50]

The problem was "the deflation of American ideals." Writing "an ethical guide for New Dealers," Edgar Kemler, recently graduated from Harvard's Littauer school of public administration, summed up much of the intellectual criticism of the Roosevelt years in these terms. Convinced generally of a decline of traditional progressivism in the United States, Kemler noted the growing impact of fascist ways of thinking. Many of those who, like Dorothy Thompson, deplored fascist tendencies abroad "have accepted the inevitability of the Fascist impact in a period of preparedness . . . ," he observed. But the decline of liberal and democratic values in the United States was not only a result of mobilization and nationalism under the shadow of impending war. The New Deal, with its use of the big-city machines, its contradictory attitude toward the trusts, and its spending policies, had been politically successful at the price of American ideals.

"We have reduced a rich heritage of hopes and dreams to the bare endeavor to make the system work." [51]

Kemler himself was willing to pay this price, but he explained that most liberals and progressives were not. When they lived on too long, they became essentially conservatives. Their idealism and moralism were outraged as radical changes in the society seemed to go too far and as they themselves became the unconscious victims or dupes of the new men of power. Thus old-fashioned liberals like Oswald Garrison Villard were confused by the New Deal. "We do not like to become deflated. We find it much easier to move upward from cynicism to high moral attitudes than to move downward in the opposite direction." Uncertain himself whether FDR with all his opportunism was a valid subject for hero worship, Kemler nevertheless concluded that he was a better idol for the young men of his own generation than any of the conservatives of the twenties. "For while he may be lacking in moral virtues, he surely makes up for it in *joie de vivre*, intellectual stimulus, and in contributions of relief milk." [52]

Kemler, like Dewey and those intellectuals concerned with the New Deal's philosophy and goals, realized only too well that ends and means were becoming hopelessly entangled with the question of approaching war. As the Roosevelt magic lost some of its appeal at home, and as the New Deal seemed to reach its ideological limits, Mars came to the rescue, transforming earlier visions of peaceful reform into a preparedness and war economy. Thus the New Deal and the intellectuals, in their troubled inter-relations, were confronted alike by the ultimate challenge—the coming of the Second World War.

SEVEN

War and the Intellectuals

"The most vital question before the American people is whether or not they can keep out of war." Ernest K. Lindley, FDR's campaign biographer in 1936, thus defined the issue of the greatest future importance to the country and the administration.[1] Coming to power in 1933, on the eve of a renewed surge of popular peace sentiment, the New Dealers finally saw their reform program overtaken by the approach of war. Although the domestic difficulties of the depression remained paramount until the late 1930's, problems of foreign policy and the threat of war became ever more compelling subjects of concern in the inner counsels of the New Deal. Staunch isolationists with respect to involvement in a second Great Crusade, the American people continued to be suspicious of what Ernest Hemingway called "the hell broth" of Europe. As a presidential candidate in 1932, Roosevelt had cautiously repudiated his old Wilsonian support of the League of Nations, and three years later the Senate rejected American membership in the World Court.

Among the conditions that influenced the shape and character of international relations in the 1930's, none was more important than the worldwide economic depression. Under the impact of this post–World War I financial disaster, the intricate structure of intergovernmental debts and loans, trade and tariffs, and stable monetary exchange all but collapsed. The same forces of business stagnation, widespread unemployment, and popular despair that contributed to Roosevelt's election in 1932 also helped to overturn foreign governments and establish new political regimes in Europe. The most significant of these changes undoubtedly was Adolf Hitler's assumption of full power as Chancellor of Germany.

At first, the impact of the economic debacle of the thirties served to postpone international tensions and to strengthen the cause of world peace. In the initial shock of the financial crisis after 1929, governments were forced to concentrate upon home affairs, while peoples everywhere looked upon armaments as an extravagance. Especially in the capitalist countries of the West, the depression pushed into the background any developing notions of another war. Instead, hard times encouraged the kind of conciliatory foreign policy and economizing illustrated in the Hoover administration's efforts in behalf of world disarmament. Thus even Hitler's aggressive demands for revision of the Treaty of Versailles were overshadowed temporarily by the Nazis' need to deal first with the economic distress and mass unemployment that was paralyzing the German state.[2]

For a brief moment in the early days of the New Deal, it seemed that the representatives of the great powers, meeting at the London Economic Conference and in the World Disarmament Conference at Geneva, might find the key to international peace and security. But on the major subjects of discussion—war debts, tariffs, monetary stabilization, and disarmament—there was little agreement. Already the specter of a German revanche menaced the status quo in Europe. And Roosevelt, facing his own crisis at home, was not ready to make major concessions in the broader realms of international economic affairs. Although the President was criticized in some liberal and peace circles for "torpedoing" the London Economic Conference, it was not certain that even full United States cooperation at London and Geneva could have reversed the worldwide trend toward economic nationalism and war. In any event, the failure at London "dealt a heavy blow to international cooperation, and markedly accelerated the drift toward isolation, big-navyism, and extreme nationalism." [3] A few months later, Hitler withdrew Germany from both the Geneva Conference and the League of Nations. Thus, in varying degrees by the mid-1930's, the major world powers were nationalizing their economies, increasing the range of governmental regulations and controls, and establishing the forms of centralized planning that were to become commonplace in wartime.

The New Deal's own essentially nationalistic reaction to events abroad was illustrated in its espousal of a new program of American military preparedness and naval rearmament. With the breakdown of the old order in Europe and in Asia, where the Japanese had moved into Manchuria in 1931, Roosevelt gained the opportunity to approve policies that were congenial to his own lifelong interest in naval affairs and grand military strategy. Although there was little reason to doubt the President's personal sympathy for a larger army and navy, his 1932 campaign promises of economy and the strong isolationist and pacifist sentiments of the country resulted at first in a program of rearmament by indirection. Through the use of funds allocated for public works and unemployment relief, a good deal of construction of deliberately strategic military importance was accomplished even after public opposition to the policy persuaded Congress to state the specific purpose for which its appropriations were made. At the same time, the Civilian Conservation Corps was given a type of instruction which, in the opinion of its director, prepared the young men for military life and which was accepted by the Army as "an admirable substitute for military training." [4]

Most important of all in terms of the future, President Roosevelt soon after his inauguration permitted the Secretary of the

Navy to announce the administration's intention to bring the American battle fleet to treaty strength and to station the bulk of its units in the Pacific. Though Americans gave Japan—unhappy over its inferior ratio in capital ships—the major blame for disturbing the existing naval arrangements among the great powers, apparently the President was already persuaded that a larger navy was vital to the security of the United States. Thus he was not receptive to the issues raised in a personal appeal by the veteran peace leader Mary E. Woolley, president of Mount Holyoke College. "The proposed building up of the navy to treaty strength alarms me," Miss Woolley commented, "because of its psychological effect upon possible disarmament. Is it not going to make the way more, rather than less difficult? Will it not weaken the effect of the good neighbor attitude which you have so splendidly endorsed?" [5]

Until the late 1930's, public concentration upon the problems of the depression served to mask the evident contradictions in the New Deal's policies toward peace and war. President Roosevelt's own interests and inclinations were, on the whole, far less pacifist than those of his immediate predecessors in the White House. And except as a concession to the political pressures of the times, it was unlikely that he was ever friendly to an isolationist philosophy. But, in the face of the strong feelings of the people, he was forced to offer not only cooperation but leadership in the cause of peace and neutrality for the United States. And it was true that the major economic policies of the early New Deal assumed the continuance of a generally isolationist and peace-minded foreign policy. The climax of the presidential support of peace was Roosevelt's famous "I-hate-war" speech at Chautauqua, New York, in August 1936. At the historic summer encampment where many of the past leaders in American life and thought had offered their remarks in behalf of popular culture and adult education, the President made a major pronouncement on foreign policy.

Frankly admitting at the outset that he was less cheerful over world conditions than over the domestic prospects of the New Deal, Roosevelt nevertheless recalled his own longtime belief that "the United States could best serve the cause of a peaceful humanity by setting an example." As practical instances of his administration's vital interest in world peace, he cited the Good Neighbor policy, efforts at Geneva for disarmament, bilateral trade and tariff agreements, and the legislation approved by Congress to safeguard American neutrality in case of war. Although the country had continued to shun political commitments and entangling alliances, it was also true, the President asserted, that "We are not isolationists, except in so far as we seek to isolate ourselves completely from war." Yet there was always "some danger that even the Nation which most ardently desires peace may be drawn into war." Thus "the effective maintenance of American neutrality depends today, as in the past," he noted, "on the wisdom and determination of whoever at the moment occupy the offices of the President and Secretary of State." One special threat to neutrality that he chose to emphasize was the lure of wartime profits. "To resist the clamor of that greed, if war should come," he warned, "would require the unswerving support of all Americans who love peace. If we face the choice of profits or peace, the Nation will answer— must answer—'We choose peace.'" Adverting again to the particular responsibility of every occupant of the White House for the day-to-day decisions on which peace depended, Roosevelt concluded:

> We can keep out of war if those who watch and decide have a sufficiently detailed understanding of international affairs to make certain that the small decisions of each day do not lead toward war, and if, at the same time, they possess the courage to say "no" to those who selfishly or unwisely would let us go to war.[6]

The President's attention to the issue of peace in the midst of the political controversies that swirled about the domestic policies of the New Deal, and at a time when there was seemingly no immediate prospect of United States involvement in a foreign war, reflected the deep emotional commitment of the American people. "Permit me to make one suggestion," Senator Hugo Black wrote to Roosevelt in the final month before the 1936 elections. "Millions of people are anxious to vote for peace. You recall the spontaneous and extended applause given to your incidental reference to this subject in your remarks on reciprocal trade at Omaha. The fear of our possible embroilment in another European War is more widespread than I dreamed before starting on this campaign tour." Convinced, like the Senator, of the need to stress peace, the President spoke out again, with apparently even greater conviction, at Madison Square Garden in New York City. After summarizing once more the domestic accomplishments of his administration, he declared:

> All this—all these objectives—spell peace at home. All our actions, all our ideals, spell also peace with other nations.
> Today there is war and rumor of war. We want none of it. . . . You know well that those who stand to profit by war are not on our side in this campaign.
> "Peace on earth, good will toward men"—democracy must cling to that message. . . .
> That is the road to peace.[7]

The pacifist sentiment of the thirties was a heritage of bitter American disillusionment over the First World War. During the previous decade many Americans had hoped that disarmament and the outlawry of war would establish a new era of world peace. But the failure of the nations to disarm, the rise of Hitler, and the success of the Japanese in their conflict with China all indicated the approaching violent disruption of the international arrangements that had been preserved so precariously since 1918. Alarmed by the political instability and rising militarism in

Europe and Asia, the American people were more convinced than ever that isolation from war, rather than collective efforts to prevent war, was now the most realistic policy for the United States.

In behalf of some one hundred college presidents and out of concern "for the well-being of the tens of thousands of young men and women to whom we stand *in loco parentis*," Ernest H. Wilkins of Oberlin College transmitted an open letter to President Roosevelt in 1934, urging his support for "the passage of legislation intended to keep this country clear, so far as is humanly possible, of all circumstances and forces that draw nations into war. . . . We believe," the educators wrote, "the time for action against war is the immediate present, before the obvious world trend toward war reaches its end in the actual outbreak of hostilities, and while we and other major countries of the world are still at peace." [8]

The widespread and recurring demands—from veterans organizations to peace groups—for legislation to insure American neutrality and to take the profits out of military preparedness and war were tremendously strengthened, midway in Roosevelt's first administration, by a series of sensational revelations about the munitions industry. While a number of popular articles and best-selling books gave detailed accounts of the international traffic in arms carried on by the so-called "merchants of death," the United States Senate Special Committee on Investigation of the Munitions Industry, under the chairmanship of Gerald P. Nye of North Dakota, conducted with some interruptions extensive public hearings from the fall of 1934 until early in 1936. Though the Nye Committee was not able to prove to the satisfaction of scholars that American bankers and munitions makers had been responsible for drawing the United States into the First World War, its findings documented popular suspicions of profiteering and unneutrality on the part of business and financial leaders. At the same time, the depression mood of hostility to business leadership and the continuing publication of critical historical works, revising official accounts of the origins of the World War, added further weight to general demands for congressional legislation to protect the peace and neutrality of the United States.[9]

The Neutrality Acts, beginning with the temporary measure of 1935 and culminating in the modifications affected by the "cash-and-carry" provisions of the law of 1937, provided that whenever the President should proclaim the existence of a state of war in the world, the sale of arms and munitions, travel on belligerent ships, and loans to belligerents should be prohibited or restricted. The laws were hardly satisfactory to either the interventionist or noninterventionist forces in the United States. While the President and the State Department wanted legislation that would permit them to invoke a discriminatory embargo upon those nations deemed aggressors in time of war, the strict isolationists wanted a mandatory embargo to be applied to any and all belligerents. This embargo was also to be without the compromise implicit in permitting trade in raw materials on a cash-and-carry basis at the discretion of the President. With regard to this important feature of the 1937 Neutrality Act, John Bassett Moore, an American expert on international law, commented darkly:

> No one who wished unlimited power to make war could ask for more than the authority, in his own discretion, to impose and revoke, and to modify and adjust, embargoes on our foreign commerce. . . . To commit to the executive the power in his discretion to adopt and prosecute measures that naturally lead to war, is virtually to transfer to him the power to make war, so that the formal declaration by Congress of the existence of a state of war would be an essentially perfunctory act.[10]

The various neutrality laws were the subject of conflicting motivations, so it was not surprising that they were never really administered in the impartial sense intended by the more rigid isolationists. Fearful that this would indeed be the case, Raymond Moley, in a personal letter to Roosevelt late in 1935, protested that, while most of the New Deal's original supporters were staunch isolationists, the enforcement of neutrality through the State Department was to be entrusted to those who "are, almost without exception, of that school of thought that believes that participation in international coercive movements can save us from war. . . . They tell us now, in one form or another, that we can stop wars by engaging in wars to stop wars." [11] The product of a strong emotional opposition to war, rather than of a reasoned devotion to neutrality, the Neutrality Acts bespoke American desires to enjoy the profits and relative safety of peace without its costs and risks.

On through the 1930's the public opinion polls continued to show an overwhelming popular majority against war. The clergy and college students especially were clearcut in avowing their personal commitment to oppose all types of war and to refuse military service if war came. This pacifism in the colleges demonstrated the genuine apprehensiveness of the generation that would be called upon to do the fighting in any future war. But it also suggested the kind of intellectual ferment and youthful idealism to which the issues involved in the rise of fascism in Europe likewise made a strong emotional appeal. Thus there was apparent a conflict of loyalties which, as some of those who remembered the First World War predicted, could easily lead again to America's involvement in a new crusade overseas.[12]

As in 1812 or 1917, for example, hostility to war in time of peace was poor insurance of American neutrality as war spread over large portions of the globe. "The feeling today is obviously sincere. From surface indications it promises to be lasting," wrote Allen Dulles and Hamilton Fish Armstrong, the authors of *Can We Be Neutral?* In their book published for the Council on Foreign Relations in 1936, they warned: "Not more than any other people are we immune to a war fever." In any protracted foreign conflict, American sentiments were likely to become engaged. "Any serious incident which seemed to involve our national honor would find us again ready to fight. . . . What we should plan to do," they concluded, "if our principal desire is to avoid war, is to keep our national honor at home—not let it get tied up with the exercise abroad, in war zones, of any preconceived rights which are not in fact essential to our national existence." [13]

The American people surely wanted the United States to keep out of war, but the Neutrality Acts did not resolve the basic conflict—illustrated in the contrasting views of the State Department and Congress—between peace by collective security and peace by isolation. The resulting dilemma, which was particularly distressing to many intellectuals of the liberal left, was most clearly outlined after the outbreak of the Spanish Civil War in the summer of 1936. Earlier, Mussolini's invasion of Ethiopia had aroused considerable American hostility toward Italy. But despite the administration's basically unneutral effort to extend its arms embargo by adding an unofficial and discriminatory ban on raw materials, there was no concerted attempt to abandon the general principles of the neutrality legislation in order to help Emperor Haile Selassie's beleaguered African nation.

In the case of Spain, America's initial isolationist reaction resulted in hasty and overwhelming approval of a resolution applying the Neutrality Act specifically to any civil war deemed a threat to the peace of the United States. Although President Roosevelt quickly invoked the act, thereby forbidding the export of munitions "for the use of either of the opposing forces," many of the isolationists, even, expressed misgivings over this measure for which they had voted and which later they, including Senator Nye, were willing to modify or repeal. Similarly, the administration in supporting the embargo—belatedly called a mistake by President Roosevelt in 1941—seems at the outset to have believed that neutrality would help the Loyalists more than the Rebels. Prevailing American opinion also appeared confident that General Francisco Franco would be defeated in his attempt to overthrow the Spanish Republic. This was the view, for example, of the *Nation* and the *New Republic*, both staunchly Loyalist.[14]

Once they had approved the extension of the embargo legislation to the Spanish Civil War, it proved virtually impossible for Congress and the administration to reverse their position. This was particularly true because of strong Catholic Church and conservative anticommunist sympathies, if not directly with fascism, at least for the Spanish rebels under General Franco. On the other hand, it was also true that the American denial of arms to the existing legal government in Spain was in itself, if not an unneutral act, at least a departure from time-honored diplomatic procedures. To Charles Beard, the increasingly isolationist-minded historian, "it was a slap straight in the face of the Madrid government. The Loyalist government," he pointed out, "had been and continued to be officially accepted in Washington as the lawful government of Spain. The belligerency of the insurgents had not been recognized. Under American theory and practice hitherto prevailing, the Madrid regime was entitled to buy munitions and supplies in the United States on the same terms as other foreign governments." In Spain, therefore, Beard asserted, President Roosevelt in effect "threw the support of the United States on the side of dictators and the professional warmongers of Europe. Even if the Madrid government had no merits whatsoever in his eyes, his action was a gratuitous favor to the Spanish rebels, to Hitler, and to Mussolini. . . ."[15]

To a much greater extent than the relatively limited Italo-Ethiopian War, the Spanish civil conflict affected the United States. Despite the efforts of the English and French governments to limit outside intervention, the expanding civil war soon became a menace to the peace and stability of Europe. Direct foreign help for Franco from Italy and Germany, plus the less official and, on the whole, less valuable aid for the Loyalists from Soviet Russia and communist sympathizers, turned what had been a civil war into a military and ideological battleground between the forces of communism and fascism. In the United States popular sentiment was divided among uncompromising isolationists favoring complete neutrality, conservative defenders of General Franco's Nationalist forces, and radical partisans of the increasingly leftist Spanish Republic.

Although American thought and opinion ranged emotionally from the extremes of the communist left-wing to the Catholic right-wing position, intellectually the Spanish War aroused more complex and subtle reactions. To an extraordinary degree, Americans saw in Spain issues related to their own history and ideals. Liberals viewed the Loyalist government as a vital bastion against fascism and world reaction, while conservatives, in their denunciation of the radical Spanish Republic, accepted Franco's Nationalist forces as fighters for freedom against communism. Neither liberals nor conservatives, however, were properly cautious or critical in evaluating propaganda and atrocity stories. At the same time, numbers of well-meaning Americans found themselves denounced as fascists or communists as soon as they took any stand with respect to Spain. For many liberals, the war forced a hard choice between their desire for peace and neutrality and their hatred of fascism. A particularly complicated trouble-spot for President Roosevelt was the fact that the liberal and Catholic supporters of the New Deal held generally opposite views of the Spanish struggle. All in all, it was an indication of the strength of American feelings that the Spanish Civil War lingered on so uncomfortably in American memory.[16]

As a result of the struggle in Spain, many Americans found themselves confronted for perhaps the first time in the thirties with a direct and sharp conflict of loyalties. Late in 1935, for example, it was Ernest Hemingway, symbol of the Lost Generation, who had written that "in modern war there is nothing sweet nor fitting in your dying. You will die like a dog for no good reason." Two years later the novelist was in Spain, duly reporting the war as a devoted disciple and propagandist of the Loyalist cause. That wars were rackets foisted by demagogues and dictators, Hemingway may well have continued to believe. But much less certain now for himself and his fellow writers was his old 1935 argument that "of the hell broth that is brewing in Europe we have no need to drink. Europe has always fought; the intervals of peace are only armistices. We were fools to be sucked in once on a European war, and we should never be sucked in again." Significantly, late in 1937, the American League against War and Fascism, one of the most influential of the Popular Fronts, changed its name to the League for Peace and Democracy. As its more perceptive pacifist critics were able to point out, it had become in reality a League for War against Fascism. This truth was further demonstrated when in August 1938 the prominent revisionist historian Harry Elmer Barnes was ousted as the League's principal invited speaker because his strong antiwar views now proved embarrassing to the sponsors.[17]

More indicative perhaps of liberal thinking than the volatile emotions of a Hemingway or the extreme left was the troubled conscience of Norman Thomas, who tried to find some plausible rationale to bridge the growing gulf between his pacifism and his antifascism. Long a critic of what he believed were the militaristic tendencies of the New Deal, Thomas nevertheless took an early stand in favor of American aid to the Spanish Loyalist Government. Upbraided by old pacifist friends of the First World War for approving the organization of a socialist battalion to fight for Loyalist Spain, Thomas agreed that on the practical side the whole situation was "a mess." But in regard to his lifelong principles of peace and socialism, he avowed: "I am compelled to try to decide . . . what is the best way to minimize war

and to advance our cause in connection with the Spanish crisis."
"You speak of putting out the fire," Thomas wrote in reply
to John Haynes Holmes, who had recalled their common allegiance to the cause of peace. "The fire will never be put out in
our time, I am afraid, if Franco wins. It may be put out if his
aggressive attack is defeated." [18]

In repeated appeals to President Roosevelt, the Socialist leader
took the view that a true and impartial American neutrality
would require an embargo to be applied also to Germany and
Italy, the chief fascist suppliers of arms and men to Franco in
Spain. "If we are not prepared to do that we should scarcely
apply neutrality against Loyalist Spain. . . . Most emphatically,"
Thomas added, "I am not interested in involving the United
States government as such in European war. . . . I do, however,
think," he concluded, "that in its practical effect our neutral
policy thus far in the Spanish situation has tended not toward
genuine non-intervention but toward a kind of left-handed aid
to Franco, the Fascists, and the dictators who are supporting
him." [19]

Perhaps the most important measure of the degree to which
the Spanish Civil War stirred the conscience and feelings of
American liberals and intellectuals was their willingness to let
themselves be drawn into close alliance with the communist
policy of a common Popular Front against fascism. Not only
did several thousand idealistic Americans join the international
brigades organized largely by the communists to fight in Spain,
but with minor exceptions like the isolationist *Common Sense*,
the various liberal magazines headed by the *Nation* became increasingly and militantly pro-Loyalist and pro-interventionist.
Both the *Nation* and the *New Republic*, for example, followed
faithfully the communist *New Masses*' general interpretation of
the Spanish struggle.[20]

In New York in the summer of 1937, the second American
Writers' Congress "expressed the Popular Front ethos of col-

laboration with Communists, idealization of the Soviet Union, and solidarity with liberals everywhere in support of the Spanish Republicans." Archibald MacLeish, who presided over the first session addressed by Earl Browder, Ernest Hemingway, and Donald Ogden Stewart, sounded the keynote with his speech entitled "The War Is Ours." From Spain, George Seldes reported to the Congress that "for the first time in our history . . . all the intellectuals of the world are united. They are on our side—the side of the Spanish Republic today, the side of the people's front in France tomorrow, and eventually for us, in our war against fascism in America." To climax the proceedings of the Congress, there was a showing of parts of the Loyalist propaganda film, *The Spanish Earth*, for which Hemingway, MacLeish, and Lillian Hellman later composed and spoke portions of the dialogue. And prominent American poets also gave readings from their translations of Spanish Loyalist verse.[21]

Although the Spanish Civil War helped to build the Popular Front against fascism, persuading writers like Hemingway to abandon their sense of disillusioned detachment, it did not break the isolationist mood of the country. Public opinion polls continued to show that heavy majorities still believed the United States should not have entered World War I, and that it should not abandon its policies of peace and neutrality. Nevertheless, the struggle in Spain and its repercussions across the Atlantic marked the first serious questioning of isolationism and of the renunciation of war as instruments of American foreign policy.[22]

As the fortunes of the Spanish Republic continued to decline, and as the Japanese resumed large-scale military operations in China, President Roosevelt in his famous "quarantine speech" at Chicago in October 1937 launched a trial balloon in which he, in effect, "broke with isolationism, discarded the policy of strict neutrality, and stepped forward as an advocate of collective security." Making an appeal for "a concerted effort in opposition to those violations of treaties and those ignorings of humane instincts which today are creating a state of international anarchy . . . ," Roosevelt likened "the epidemic of world lawlessness" to a kind of plague in which "the community approves and joins in a quarantine. . . . America hates war. America hopes for peace. Therefore, America actively engages in the search for peace," the President concluded.[23]

What Roosevelt implied by the term "quarantine," or what he hoped to accomplish by his speech was not clear. Popular reaction was uncertain and confused, and generally favorable newspaper comment was qualified by the doubts of most editorial writers as to what the President's speech really meant. One result of it, however, was further division of the peace movement between its isolationist and internationalist wings. The clash between their longing for peace and hatred of war and their opposition, at the same time, to European fascism and Japan's pretensions in Asia forced upon American liberals and intellectuals a difficult moral choice. Peace leaders especially suffered an increasing ambivalence and uncertainty in their mixed attitudes toward an isolationist neutrality versus an interventionist collective security policy.[24]

Illustrative of the confusion in the top echelons of the peace ranks was the temporary concurrence of Nicholas Murray Butler and Oswald Garrison Villard in support of the President. From the differing vantage points of a conservative and a liberal, each managed equally to congratulate President Roosevelt on both his "I-hate-war" address at Chautauqua and his quarantine speech at Chicago. "The great mass of the people of every civilized state will respond with their hearts and with their heads to the doctrine which you preach," Butler, president of Columbia University and the Carnegie Endowment for World Peace, wrote in 1936. "What the governments of some of these nations may do is quite another matter." he added. "Your speech at Chicago yesterday morning," Butler again wrote enthusiastically a year later, "comes like a breath of fresh air to a world which is choking to death. . . . World leadership is now in our hands, and the greatest enemies of peace are those among us who are constantly preaching isolation and neutrality under circumstances in which those words mean absolutely nothing." [25]

In the afterglow of the President's Chautauqua speech and his overwhelming victory in the 1936 campaign, Villard, who had refused to vote for Roosevelt because of the militarism of his administration, now sent a fervent letter of congratulations to the White House. "Never was there a greater triumph of democracy. . . . Never was there a more discriminating voting. . . ." Spelling out the great opportunities for progressive reform that awaited the President, Villard concluded: "I am hoping with all my heart that you will stem and reduce our military and naval expenditures. . . . That you will lead us in the direction of peace I feel certain. . . . " More amazing, however, than Villard's curious idea that the New Deal's militarism and navalism was somehow consonant with his own pacifism was his enthusiastic reaction to both the Chautauqua and quarantine speeches. Of the former he wrote to Roosevelt: "It will do an enormous amount of good, and I am particularly grateful to you for the slap at Hitler and Mussolini. Also for what you say as to neutrality. . . ." Noting FDR's assertion of the ultimate responsibility of the President, Villard observed: "I think you prove my contention that Woodrow Wilson could have kept us out of war in 1917 had he had the backbone, the courage and the desire." [26]

On the eve of the quarantine speech, Villard telegraphed the President urging upon him the contradictory policies of enforcement of the neutrality laws and denunciation of Japan's undeclared war upon China. Certain that Roosevelt had now regained the moral leadership of the world which Wilson had lost at Paris, Villard, in a message for transmission to the President the day after his speech at Chicago, declared: "I think it is the greatest speech that he has made and if followed up it may easily become a great turning point in the world's history." Villard was immediately called to task by his pacifist and liberal friends for his laudatory public comments on Roosevelt's foreign policy in the *Nation*, but he explained that he had wanted to see someone protest against the dictators. "One reason why I welcomed particularly the President's statement at Chicago was just this fact, that we seem to have lost our old American capacity for indignation at wrong and the ill-treatment of others. . . . Of course I am still a complete pacifist. . . ." [27]

Between the lines of the liberal rhetoric in Villard's letters and Roosevelt's speeches was an underlying note of anxiety and qualification. The campaign of 1936 actually marked the high tide of the peace movement in the United States, and Villard accordingly was seeking to hold the President to commitments which Roosevelt was already in a sense disclaiming. FDR's references to the President's ultimate responsibility in diplomacy portended a conflict with the popular desire for peace and implied strongly the changing nature of the New Deal's foreign policy. Despite his brave words at Chautauqua, and his salute to leaders who "possess the courage to say 'no' to those who selfishly or unwisely would let us go to war," it was clear that President Roosevelt believed he had to re-educate American opinion to support policies that he himself had seemed to deplore and reject prior to 1937.[28]

What the isolationists generally refused to accept was the President's view that the deteriorating world situation justified drastic changes in American foreign policy. And what the President's interventionist supporters, in turn, failed to understand was the deep commitment to peace of the many disillusioned Americans who continued to believe that the United States had been tricked and seduced into entering the First World War.

"Truly a new age of faith is upon us," wrote Norman Thomas, "when men and women old enough to remember how we proposed to make the world safe for democracy in one war and got Hitler . . . can believe in a crusade for democracy led by Stalin, Roosevelt, Chamberlain and the French General Staff. . . . The first and perhaps the greatest of the enormous casualties of our next war," Thomas added, "will be liberty and democracy at home." [29]

Disillusioned by the direction of the New Deal's foreign policy, especially after the President's espousal of collective security and calls for a larger navy, the more pacifist liberals returned to isolationism as the only hope of averting American participation in another world war. Thus Villard, after the Japanese sinking of the American gunboat *Panay* in Chinese waters, urged isolationist Senators to speak out against the idea of war with Japan. "With things going from bad to worse domestically, is it not inevitable," asked the prominent Unitarian clergyman and Socialist John Haynes Holmes, "that the President, in the good old dictatorial fashion, will take us into war to cover up the mess at home?" "Everywhere we are being told and taught," Holmes complained, "that the end justifies the means, if the end is surely on the side of the worker in America, the Loyalist in Spain, and the Communist in Russia." "I see that Franklin is playing what is usually the jobholder's last card—'National defence,'" wrote Albert Jay Nock. For *Harper's Magazine* John T. Flynn asserted "The War Boom Begins," while Elmer Davis predicted "We Lose the Next War," and Norman Thomas argued "We Needn't Go To War." If its leaders persuaded America to embark on another holy crusade, "we might as well be prepared to bid good-bye to American civilization. For the 'next war,'" Mauritz Hallgren declared, "will undoubtedly usher in a period, more or less enduring, of military or semi-Fascist dictatorship." "As for Europe, I have lost hope of it," Allan Nevins confided to a friend early in 1938. "I doubt if we shall see a really decent world again in our time." [30]

Within the New Deal itself, as distinct from its varied critics, Jerome Frank, member and later chairman of the Securities and Exchange Commission, wrote an urgent plea to *Save America First*. In the face of the nation's obvious disunity, it was hopeless, he believed, for the United States to undertake *"the task of helping Europe or of promoting world order*. In the kind of a world we regrettably live in today, relative self-sufficiency for America is a profoundly sound ideal." Convinced that American prosperity required the continued relative isolation current under the early New Deal, Frank concluded:

> We have before us a magnificent opportunity, through wise statesmanship, to make in America a unique civilization—an economic-political democracy every citizen of which will have a full life. . . .
> We need to fix our full attention on the basic American problem today: how to make actual the vast increase in production which can be made possible by the maximum use of power and mass production in an integrated, well-supplied continent, and thus to provide for our people the enjoyment of an ever-increasing quantity of consumer goods, with adequate leisure and education.[31]

For many New Dealers, *Save America First* must have seemed a valedictory statement of their own early dreams. Confronted by war clouds in Europe and the storm over Asia, and puzzled by the President's mixed pleas for collective security overseas and national defense at home, American opinion was badly divided. Still generally isolationist and strongly antiwar, the American people were nevertheless becoming less and less neutral in their attitude toward world events. Never indifferent to the rise of totalitarian movements abroad, United States national sentiment was particularly hostile to Hitler and the Nazi state. Hitler's expansionist hopes, his determination to break the bonds of the Treaty of Versailles, and, most of all, his persecution of the Jews offended the American public conscience.

As Hitler moved first against Austria in March 1938, and then into Czechoslovakia a year later despite the Munich Agreement with Britain and France in September, Americans realized that, short of a major effort to reach a complete international understanding, war was the most likely outcome for Europe. The Munich Agreement itself provoked varied opinions. For example, Oswald Garrison Villard wrote the President, hopeful that "you will make it clear how horrifying this dismemberment of Czechoslovakia is. . . ." Yet Villard added that, given British Prime Minister Neville Chamberlain's situation, "I presume there was nothing else he could do." "I think he has done about as well as could be expected in all the circumstances," wrote James Truslow Adams. "I may be wrong, but I think, in view of what has happened, that Europe is now in for a number of years of peace, even if it be very uneasy peace. I think there is little question," Adams added, "but what we have got to undo much that was done at the Paris Conference in 1918–19." In a letter to Adams, Worthington C. Ford expressed the opposite view that for Munich "the price paid was much too high and that the 'peace' is only a breathing spell. . . . Germany," he contended, "is hopelessly barbarian and in giving Hitler more than he demanded his appetite will change the face of Europe for the worse. The terrible outbreak against the Jews of the last two days is a measure of the present rulers of Germany. They are worse than the Russians. . . ." [32]

In the United States, one result of Nazi discrimination and persecution of the Jews was that a stream of refugees was able to make an important contribution to American cultural and intellectual life. Of the estimated total of less than 250,000 refugees who fled to America in the decade after 1933, approximately half came originally from Germany. A relatively small minority there of some half-million persons, the Jews had enriched their society and country in a proportion beyond their numbers. They had been engaged mostly in trade and business, but a rather large percentage practiced law and medicine. In America, most of the Jewish refugees had higher skills and professional abilities than the normal immigrant, and many had some familiarity with English. Language was, of course, a vital tool for the intellectual, and lack of skill was a barrier to becoming licensed as doctors or dentists, or in establishing good classroom communication as teachers. Ultimately, however, most of those who had been university instructors in Europe found opportunities to teach in the United States, while others were able to engage in research.[33]

Albert Einstein, probably the most famous of all the Jewish refugees who came to the United States, took little part in American political questions. Other notables, non-Jewish as well as Jewish, entered more actively into the debate over foreign policy. Imbued naturally with a strong desire to encourage American action against Hitler, they tried to relate their own feelings to the larger framework of the history of democratic government. Prominent political refugees like Eduard Beneš, the exiled President of Czechoslovakia, made sobering analyses of the future of democracy. More hopeful than Beneš of what he called "The Coming Victory of Democracy," Thomas Mann, the distinguished German novelist, in a coast-to-coast American lecture tour early in 1938 pleaded for a pragmatic conception of democracy commensurate with its historic optimism over human nature and its desire to elevate mankind.[34]

The violent anti-Jewish pogroms in Germany a month after Munich especially stirred American feelings, reinforcing the country's increasing sense of outrage against all Nazi policy and drawing the particular condemnation of American scientists and professors. At their annual meetings in December 1938, a number of learned societies approved strong resolutions of protest. Voicing sympathy with its colleagues abroad in their difficult quest for truth, the American Association of University Professors expressed "its abhorrence at the action of totalitarian regimes which prevent the accomplishment of this duty by persecuting teachers on account of their race, religion, or political ideals. . . ." "Anthropology provides no scientific basis for discrimination against any people on the ground of racial inferiority, religious affiliation or linguistic heritage," declared the American Anthropological Association in decrying the misuse of the terms Aryan and Semitic. A group of psychologists at their annual meeting condemned the familiar political turn to scapegoats to explain national adversity—and hence the Nazis' heaping of all blame upon the Jews—and affirmed that the "Nazi theory that people must be related by blood in order to participate in the same cultural or intellectual heritage has absolutely no support from scientific findings." [35]

In calling race "a modern superstition," historian Jacques Barzun quoted the comment of John Stuart Mill that "Of all vulgar modes of escaping from the consideration of the effect of social and moral influences on the human mind, the most vulgar is that of attributing the diversities of conduct and character to inherent natural differences." What was really invidious, however, the anthropologist Ruth Benedict pointed out, was racism, not race. The latter was a fact of life, while the former "is the dogma that the hope of civilization depends upon eliminating some races and keeping others pure." [36]

The unfavorable American reaction, not only to Munich, but even more importantly to its aftermath in Czechoslovakia, plus the mounting intensity of Hitler's anti-Jewish propaganda and actions, strengthened the cause of collective security against fascism at a crucial time. Liberal support of collective security via Popular Front politics was already suffering from the uncertainty and suspicion that was substantiated dramatically with the announcement on August 23, 1939, of the Russo-German nonaggression pact. Munich itself had been much criticized by the left in 1938 on the grounds that it forecast a coalition of the West against Russia. But now, for most Americans, the outbreak of the European war, as the Nazis invaded Poland on September 1, 1939, was less of a shock than the agreement between Stalin and Hitler the week before. The news of the pact was difficult to believe, David E. Lilienthal, chairman of the TVA, noted in his *Journal*. "I recalled what Harry Elmer Barnes had said at Knoxville only a few weeks ago—that Fascism and Communism were essentially the same; that they are both social revolutions putting an end to capitalism as well as democracy." Ignored also by most American liberals were the guarded forecasts—like that of Bruce Bliven in the *New Republic* following Munich—that Germany and Russia had been friends in the 1920's and might well unite again to dismember Poland.[37]

Plainly, the accord reached by the Nazis and Soviets contradicted a decade of mutual public recriminations and hostility between fascists and communists around the world. For American liberals, and especially for dedicated fellow travelers and sympathizers with the Communist party line—some four hundred of whom had reaffirmed publicly their full support of the Soviet Union on the eve of the pact—this latest historical example of the sacrifice of ideology to diplomatic expediency was a sobering experience. Resented by the faithful were the warnings of those rebels and renegades like Max Eastman, who complained that the failure of Russia to realize the socialist ideal was "perhaps the greatest tragedy in human history. . . . " Calling the Communist policy of the Popular Front "the most significant though not the prettiest political romance of our time," Lillian Symes predicted in 1938:

The Communist Party, in the United States as elsewhere, exists to rally support behind the *realpolitik* of the Russian regime. If the interests of that regime can best be served by throwing Karl Marx overboard, cultivating the accents of Ed Howe, involving the United States in a war with one of Russia's probable enemies, and reviving the passions, prejudices, and slogans of the World War, it will go about the job with the utmost sincerity.[38]

While the Moscow trials of the mid-thirties, purging the Old Bolsheviks and leaving the Stalinists in supreme power, had been disillusioning to many American liberals, others had been able to condone violations of civil liberties in Russia that they would have protested in the United States. Thus, despite increasing disenchantment over the Soviet experiment by former American enthusiasts, and despite the collapse of the Popular Front in Spain, the idea of a united stand against fascism remained strong until the final denouement in August 1939.[39]

Divorced of its communist support, collective security became even more attractive for former left-wing liberals with internationalist or interventionist leanings. Converted originally to collective security by the Communist party's stand against fascism, these liberals in their post-Munich disillusionment refused to follow the new Communist line of nonintervention in the European war. For more and more Americans, stopping Hitler and his fellow dictators was of greater importance now than the maintenance of peace and neutrality by the United States. And the presence of the Nazi-Soviet pact opened the way for a "holy war" of democracy against totalitarianism. At the same time, the communists' newfound interest in peace, after a decade of calling for a common struggle to resist fascism, also had the effect of discrediting the old leftist and liberal assumption that modern war was merely a selfish struggle between rival imperialisms.

The economic interpretation of history, widely accepted by American opinion in the days of the Nye Committee, had been steadily losing favor since the Spanish Civil War. Charles Beard, Nestor of the liberal isolationists, complained that with the new liberals it was now all morals and no economics. No longer acceptable, it seemed, was the Beardian view that "foreign policy is a phase of domestic policy, an inseparable phase." Even more pessimistic than Beard, H. L. Mencken, who had condemned Stalin along with Hitler and Mussolini in the 1930's, was convinced that the "idealists of Washington are determined to get us into a war." "I am planning to become a spy hunter," he told Theodore Dreiser early in 1939. And to Ezra Pound he confided his belief that "Roosevelt will horn into the war at the first chance. He is, to be sure, still bellowing about keeping the United States out of it, but no rational man takes such talk seriously." [40]

Speaking for the Marxists of the independent left, Dwight Macdonald on the eve of the Nazi-Soviet pact had noted that once again the "war intellectuals," who idealized imperialistic wars when they broke out and debunked them only when they were over, were "off again on a moral spree." Already democracy was growing feebler at home while the intellectuals, committing themselves to the idea of war, forsook their role as critics of society. Thus, some twenty years after Randolph Bourne's famous indictment of the World War I intellectuals, Macdonald lamented, "All sections of the intelligentsia are swinging in behind the New Deal in its drive towards a second world war to save democracy." [41]

"Anti-Fascism," Alfred M. Bingham pointed out, "has now become a cult. It is almost as fanatical as fascism itself." One of the liberals who feared the effect of hostilities upon the New Deal's domestic program, Bingham had urged before the war began in Europe the granting of trade concessions to Hitler and the gradual absorption of all Germany's Jews. "What we have most to fear," he wrote, "is war. It is the final triumph of absolutist faith in one's own righteousness. . . . Yet," he urged, "what may seem to many of us no better than a lesser evil—a bold American initiative in the organization of peace—entails tremendous stakes for gain as well as loss." [42]

"What we need," Ferdinand Lundberg wrote to fellow Socialist Norman Thomas, "is a big 'united front' for peace, minus, of course, the neo-isolationist Stalinists. . . . Many intellectuals now zigzagging around without a rudder would be glad to work in such a united front. . . ." Thomas, in turn, advised President Roosevelt to apply the neutrality laws to Russia in September 1939 for the same reasons, as he continued to believe, they should have been applied earlier in the Far East. Modern total war, he pointed out to FDR, merely defeated its own ends. "Each particular war begets its more deadly successors. Intolerance, dictatorship, brutality, are its inevitable accompaniments and they live on even when exhaustion temporarily stills the guns." Stalin, in Thomas' opinion, was more likely than Hitler to be heir to Europe. "He has only to keep out of the vortex of war and wait for his rivals to destroy themselves." Continually urging upon the President in personal correspondence a policy of tolerating dissent and keeping out of war, Thomas privately confessed his lack of confidence in Roosevelt's devotion to peace. "Is there nothing at all that you folks in Washington can do to some degree," he wrote to Senator Burton K. Wheeler, "to take the play out of his hands?" [43]

Like Thomas, Oswald Garrison Villard, yielding reluctantly his old hopes for international peace by collective security, now devoted his efforts to keeping the United States out of the war that he feared the Roosevelt administration was eager to join. Differing with his old magazine's views on foreign policy, Villard wrote his last column in the *Nation* in June 1940. John Haynes Holmes congratulated the longtime editor for thus still standing fast for peace, and wrote that he was "heartsick to see our liberal friends whooping it up for war. As for their admiration of the President," he added, "it simply passes my comprehension."

Though Villard had to admit that he was still a New Dealer in domestic affairs, he feared more than ever the drift toward militarism and war. "As for the Russian situation," he wrote after Hitler's attack broke the 1939 pact, "I very much doubt that I can see any difference between Stalin and Hitler. . . ." Lincoln Colcord, Villard's journalistic colleague of World War I days, summed up the old liberals' disenchantment with Roosevelt. "Let us keep our sense of humor," he advised less than a month before Pearl Harbor, "and watch the unfolding of a splendid spectacle of idealism and sentimentality. It's going to be something super-colossal. For this, in sober truth, is a Hollywood foreign policy." [44]

Once actual fighting broke out in Europe, the United States moved steadily away from the isolationism and neutrality of the thirties to a position of increasing interventionism and eventual belligerency—just short of war itself. "What a majority of the American people want," wrote Freda Kirchwey in the *Nation*, "is to be as unneutral as possible without getting into war." The argument implicit in the growing war propaganda in the United States was that 1939 was not like 1914. This tack apparently won the early acceptance of President Roosevelt who, in contrast to President Wilson, pointed out in a radio address following the formal proclamation of neutrality required by law, that he could not ask that "every American remain neutral in thought as well." [45]

Repeal of the arms embargo in the fall of 1939 was followed a year later, after the collapse of France and the threatened Nazi invasion of England, by the passage of the first peacetime conscription law in American history, and by the destroyer-for-bases deal with Great Britain. In an Executive agreement, President Roosevelt promised to exchange fifty over-age American naval vessels for ninety-nine-year grants of land for military bases on Newfoundland and Bermuda. Then, after Roosevelt's re-election to an unprecedented third term, the Lend-Lease Act was voted in the spring of 1941. Lend-lease, and the ensuing United States convoying of war materiel more than halfway across the Atlantic, carried the country as far as it was possible to go and still remain technically a nonbelligerent. "Peace through war by proxy," was Senator Arthur H. Vandenberg's sarcastic description of the measure which "drove the final nail into the coffin of neutrality." Most astonishing, perhaps, was the comment of TRB, the Washington correspondent of the formerly isolationist *New Republic*. According to TRB's exalted view of lend-lease, FDR, whom he hailed as President of the World, "has not been taken unawares by his new assignment. . . . But as a kind of order emerged from the chaos of depression at home, and as his own hold on the electorate became secure, Mr. Roosevelt began preparing for the day when his domestic policies would become exportable, when they would have world relevancy." [46]

Previously, in the summer of 1940, the interventionist and noninterventionist forces, organized respectively into the Committee to Defend America by Aiding the Allies and the America First Committee, had carried on the great debate over foreign policy that was shirked in the main by the presidential candidates. William Allen White, chairman of the Committee to Defend America, who had already done yeoman service for the administration in working to repeal the embargo, became a national spokesman for the growing American desire to help Britain without actually entering the war. Personally opposed to the pro-war Eastern wing of the organization he headed, White did not believe the committee should be a propaganda front for American intervention and convoying. Earlier he had also become indignant over the administration's subterfuge of transferring the registry of United States ships to the Republic of Panama so that they could enter the European war zones. These ideological difficulties of the White Committee, which contributed to his own resignation late in 1940, were equally a problem for the isolationists of the America First Committee. Besides pacifists, America First included militant nationalists dedicated to the concept of a "fortress America" and the preservation of isolation and neutrality by armed might. Because of its conservative nationalistic leanings, the more liberal pacifists and isolationists therefore never fully accepted America First.[47]

Over much of the great debate of 1940 there hung a heavy air of unreality, compounded by the lack of any significant divergence in the foreign policy views of President Roosevelt and Wendell Willkie, the Republican party candidate. Although the two major party platforms promised that American boys would not be sent overseas to fight in foreign wars, neither candidate committed himself to the kind of defensive foreign policy that might have minimized the danger of an attack upon the continental United States. Moreover, it was apparent that the American people and their spokesmen were alike afraid to face frankly the costs of either an avowedly interventionist or a strictly noninterventionist diplomacy. Peace, it was clear, would entail a price in economic isolation and intellectual neutrality that most Americans were probably unwilling to pay—hence the compromise of repealing the embargo and the ensuing sale of war goods on a cash-and-carry basis to England and France. On the other hand, administration measures, such as lend-lease, that pointed obviously to direct American involvement in Europe were described as efforts to keep America out of war.

In the course of the political debate in 1940, American intellectuals were themselves profoundly agitated by charges that they had been irresponsible and unpatriotic in their alleged indifference to the rise of fascism and the likelihood of war. For many Americans the sense of uncertainty and confusion over the nature of the European "isms" was finally resolved only by their own essentially nationalistic reactions as the threat of war came closer to the United States. Communism's appeal to left-wing liberals had suffered drastic revision after the Nazi-Soviet pact, while fascism, in turn, lost most of its appeal to American right-wing groups after the outbreak of the European war. Whether fascism was a degenerate form of capitalism or a middle-class revolt against Marxism seemed of lesser importance than the fear, chiefly among isolationist liberals, that American entrance into the war might impose fascist-like controls over the country's economy and thought.[48]

A major concern, therefore, to liberals was the possibility suggested in the comments of James Burnham that "a 100% American totalitarianism would not be objectionable," and of Lawrence Dennis that all the "isms" were basically socialist. "In the United States," Dennis wrote in 1940, "it is obvious that we shall not have a Russian, Italian or German, but an American brand of national socialism." Pointing out that "what we call it is of little importance," he predicted:

> The first requisite of the new revolution in America will be a shift from success to sacrifice—for America. America as a big opportunity to write a personal success story is over. America as a unified great nation is about to be born—in war, travail, disillusionment and grim determination. Let the elite catch now, in advance of events, the vision of a new America the keystone of which will be the people and not the person. One will hear less about the rights of man and more about the duties of men and the rights of the American people.[49]

Fears of the extension of fascism and the European war stimulated several American authors to re-examine democracy and defend traditional American values. In reply to the communist left and to the general threat of totalitarianism, Sidney Hook, John Dewey, and a group of like-minded socialists and liberals formed in the spring of 1939 the Committee for Cultural Freedom. Dewey in his own book *Freedom and Culture* warned that, though democratic conditions did not automatically maintain themselves, neither was totalitarianism merely the result of foreign principles, so strange to America that "It can't happen here." "Resort to military force," he added, "is a first sure sign that we are giving up the struggle for the democratic way of life, and that the Old World has conquered morally as well as geographically—succeeding in imposing upon us its ideals and methods." [50]

Meanwhile, a variety of former critics of American civilization began to strike a more positive note in their new works of affirmation. "Between 1914 and 1929," Gilbert Seldes claimed, "the dominant tone in American literature was dislike of America." The critics had looked upon the United States "as if it had been created in one magnificent (probably malevolent) act by a rather incompetent, rather vulgar, and totally unidealistic God. . . ." By the late thirties, however, more authors were inspired to offer an optimistic evaluation of the prospects of democracy. In *America Now* Harold Stearns, the disillusioned literary expatriate of the twenties, edited a symposium which reflected a point of view markedly different from that of his similar book published back in 1922. "At whatever point you touch the complex American life of today," Stearns wrote in his own personal reappraisal in 1937, "you get a sense of new confidence, new pride, and even new hope. It is something deeper than mere economic recovery. . . . In a word, we do not believe that democracy has failed us, but that we have not yet fully explored the democratic way of life." [51]

Like the literary critics, American educators and college professors moved to encourage the concept of education for democracy and American values. Hopeful, in the face of war and possible dictatorship, that "the schools can teach democracy," George S. Counts, an influential professor of education at Teachers College, Columbia University, proposed that "we frankly reject the conception of social and moral neutrality and direct the energies of organized education without reservation to the defense and strengthening of the democratic tradition and way of life." William C. Bagley, a colleague of Counts at Teachers College, in his editorial introduction to the book *Indoctrination for American Democracy*, took the view that there were two ideals in American education: "One is the ideal of truth; the other, the ideal of democracy." In concluding his work, the author made a plea for teachers to sacrifice themselves in order to inculcate the democratic ideal in their pupils. On the level of adult education, the Department of Agriculture early in 1941 proposed, through the use of the land-grant colleges and the farm organizations, a nationwide, grass-roots series of popular discussions on the defense of democracy and its application in the local community.[52]

Assaying the place of the social sciences in American culture, Robert Lynd, co-author of the famous Middletown studies, deplored the decline of the sense of community and common purpose in American life. Short of war and a totalitarian society, this kind of unity was difficult to achieve in America's individualistic society. Yet the modern national state, Lynd wrote, must no longer be regarded as a neutral umpire confined to arbitrating the problems of a nineteenth-century laissez-faire economy. "We are today living," he noted, "through the end of that phase of our cultural history which was dominated by the quest for the conditions of individual liberty. Heavily laden with institutions developed to that end, we are reluctantly moving into a new phase in which we must somehow manage to rewrite our institutions in terms of organized community of purpose."[53]

The question stated in the title of Lynd's book—*Knowledge for What?*—was also behind Archibald MacLeish's bitter attack upon his fellow intellectuals in 1940. One of America's most distinguished poets, MacLeish early in life abandoned his training in law for the craft of writing. Back home in America after a postwar sojourn in Europe, the young poet participated actively in the left-wing and antiwar causes favored by his literary companions of the thirties. Meanwhile, in his own poetry he continued to stress the importance of the individual's private integrity and intellectual freedom. *The Fall of the City* and *Land of the Free,* published in 1937 and 1938, reflected his increasing personal concern over fascism and the totalitarian menace to democracy. Then after Munich, MacLeish, convinced that the Nazis threatened all the values he prized in life, became more impatient with those of his fellows who remained wary of new crusades for peace and democracy. As Hitler's armies began their invasion of France and the Low Countries in May 1940, MacLeish published in the *Nation* his famous essay castigating American intellectuals as "The Irresponsibles." A month later, Secretary of the Interior Harold Ickes noted in his diary that at luncheon, "To my utter astonishment, Archie MacLeish said that he was in favor of declaring war. MacLeish," Ickes added in explanation, "was one of the young intellectuals who, after the last war, wrote and preached about the futility of all war and helped educate the younger generation that in no circumstances should we ever go to war again." [54]

Why, MacLeish asked, did American intellectuals, witnessing the destruction of writing and scholarship in Europe, "fail to oppose those forces while they could—while there was still time and still place to oppose them with the arms of scholarship and writing?" Indicting the scholar for his detachment in a time of crisis, he wrote that "Nothing is more characteristic of the intellectuals of our generation than their failure to understand what it is that is happening to their world." In the past century the scholar and the writer had been united in support of the intellectual tradition; now, in modern fragmented society, neither accepted "responsibility for the common culture or its defense." [55] MacLeish quickly made his vague literary jeremiad, with its implications of a call to arms, more specific. In an address before the American Association for Adult Education, he complained that the effect of such antiwar novels as John Dos Passos' *Three Soldiers* and Ernest Hemingway's *A Farewell to Arms* was to inoculate American youth "against any attempt in its own country by its own leaders to foment a war by shouting rhetorical phrases or waving moral flags. . . . If the young generation in America is distrustful of all words, distrustful of all moral judgments of better and worse, then," MacLeish commented, "it is incapable of using the only weapon with which fascism can be fought—the moral conviction that fascism is evil and that a free society of free men is good and is worth fighting for." [56]

In the paper war touched off by MacLeish, whose own status as an administration spokesman had been enhanced by his appointment as Librarian of Congress, American intellectuals vigorously debated their proper role in the larger world struggle. Lewis Mumford, author of the premature 1939 call to arms *Men Must Act*, now published a year later in *Faith for Living* a passionate denunciation of the pragmatic liberalism and pacifism of the thirties. Reinhold Niebuhr, also growing steadily more critical of the peace principles he had once espoused, joined other militant clergymen in founding in 1941 a new Protestant journal, *Christianity and Crisis*, in order to combat pacifism in the churches and win support for the fight against Nazi Germany.[57]

"What we call treason now," wrote Max Lerner, "is not the political activity of the intellectuals but their withdrawal from politics and the fact that they were not realistic enough fighters." Yet Lerner could not blame his own generation or its sons for their inherent doubts about the war. After all, he explained, "I can understand its sources. How can we expect them to be anything but cynical considering the mess we have made of the world. . . ." Like Lerner, Harold Laski did not believe the scholar could be impartial in the face of Hitler. But the skepticism of youth, he suggested, was due to a suspicion that the intellectuals' enthusiasm for war would not be matched by an equal concern for the creation of a decent postwar world.[58]

Among MacLeish's critics none was more severe than his colleague in the world of letters, Edmund Wilson. In a personal commentary, Wilson intimated that MacLeish, remembering the company he had kept in the thirties, now wished to disassociate himself from the past. "Mr. MacLeish," Wilson added, "is at pains to tell us that he does not want to burn any books or regiment people's minds; but it does not create reassurance, at this moment of strain and excitement, to hear the Librarian of Congress talking about 'dangerous' books." [59]

It remained, however, for one of the original New Dealers to offer the most striking defense of his generation. Recent intellectual history, Rex Tugwell noted on the eve of Pearl Harbor, "has been enlivened if not enriched by certain loud affirmations of guilt. The *mea culpas* have resounded throughout the land. Sackcloth has been used; ashes have filled the air. Men of my age: Mumford, MacLeish, Millis, Lerner, Counts, Niebuhr, have been treading on each others' heels as they hurried to recant. I have felt the wind of their reversal," Tugwell admitted, "but no impulse to follow: indeed I have felt a slight embarrassment for them rather than for myself. For I have been unrepentant. I feel now as I have always felt that American institutions are far less than perfect although on the whole they seem to me better than any others." American youth, Tugwell was sure, were not Nazis or communists, but the younger generation was rightly skeptical. As a professor himself, he recalled that the essence of good teaching and of the scientific method was this skepticism and the realization that the world had to be understood as a competition of ideas. "Was it wrong for me, for instance," he asked, "in all the years when I was a teacher to insist that my students' minds should be open to facts and possibilities, especially damaging ones, and that they should develop ingenuity in projecting betterments?" The alternative, as in Germany, to teach "some phoney myth," Tugwell refused to accept. "To cast some American professor in the role of Goebbels is an outlandish suggestion, perhaps, but that is what some of our contemporaries, in the heat of sudden patriotism, now suggest." [60]

Confident almost to the last hour that the United States could call Japan's "bluff" in the Pacific and that the Japanese strategists would not dare to fight a major war, America's militant intellectuals concentrated most of their attention on Europe. For the American people all the important issues of the decade appeared to come to a focus in the fight against Hitler. Thus there was considerable irony in the fact that the war finally came to America from Asia—the area seemingly of the least direct concern to the United States.

The Japanese attack on Pearl Harbor closed a decade of bitter debate over foreign policy among American intellectuals. Yet in reacting to what seemed at the time an entirely unprovoked assault, the American people went to war for what were essentially conventional, defensive reasons. The Roosevelt rhetoric of Four Freedoms, after all, was never as inspiring an ideal as Wilson's Fourteen Points, and the United Nations at first was merely a wartime alliance and goal for the future. By uniting the country, Pearl Harbor overcame much of the ideological confusion and division of the preceding years. The mixed fears of fascism or communism and the antagonisms of right and left, of isolationists and interventionists, were sublimated in the process of winning the war and building a new patriotic consensus. Whether these heightened nationalistic goals of wartime could be translated later into a brave new world remained, of course, the overriding question for the future postwar and post–New Deal generation. Meanwhile, American intellectuals, like Americans generally, accepted with only a few dissenting voices the judgment implied in the *New Republic's* first post–Pearl Harbor editorial, "Our War." [61]

EIGHT

🔖

The Wave of the Future

IN THAT INTERVAL in the Second World War between its outbreak in Europe and the Japanese attack on Pearl Harbor, Anne
Morrow Lindbergh published a short and poignant essay entitled
The Wave of the Future. Daughter of the eminent financier and
diplomat Dwight Morrow, and wife of the celebrated aviator
Charles Lindbergh, Mrs. Lindbergh was also distinguished in her
own right. She had seen the rise of totalitarianism and militarism
in Europe in her travels abroad, and she feared their extension
to the United States. Also nostalgic about the individualistic
ideals and values of a treasured American past which was now
beyond recall, she tried to analyze the reasons for her distress
and the possibilities for the future. Like many Americans who
held aloof from the political activities in which her husband, for
example, was engaged via the America First Committee and who,
at the same time, did not look upon the European conflict as a
holy crusade calling for American involvement, Mrs. Lindbergh
sought some semblance of a rational faith or understanding to
explain a war-torn, war-mad world. What, in particular, she
asked, was America's role in such a world?

Because the United States enjoyed a rich heritage of reform,
Mrs. Lindbergh "hoped that in America, if nowhere else in the

world, it should be possible to meet the wave of the future in comparative harmony and peace. It should be possible," she suggested, "to change an old life to a new without such terrible bloodshed as we see today in the process in Europe." Yet, more significant than Mrs. Lindbergh's underlying note of isolationism or heartfelt desire for peace was her belief that the war and fascism in Europe were merely the most malign forms—the "scum on the wave of the future"—of what was, in reality, a vast worldwide revolution. Thus she spoke for the millions of Americans who, in their mixed hopes and fears for the future, nevertheless understood, however vaguely, that the years of the depression, the New Deal, and finally the war were all part of what was indeed the revolution of our time and the wave of the future.[1]

Free of the sense of foreboding with which Anne Lindbergh contemplated this wave of the future, a group of her contemporaries—including such important figures as Henry Luce, Henry Wallace, and Wendell Willkie—saw somewhat different portents outlined against the darkening background of the war. Thus, shortly after President Roosevelt urged popular support of his lend-lease program of aid to the Allies, on the grounds that "We must be the great arsenal of democracy,"[2] Henry Luce, founding father of the journalistic empire of the *Time*, *Life*, and *Fortune* magazines, called for the creation of what he described as "The American Century."

In language as vague as that of Mrs. Lindbergh, but with the more strident, polemical tones of a practiced and controversial journalist, Luce argued the interventionist cause. Convinced that America was already in the war, and that American goals transcended the mere defense of its shores or a restricted conception of its national interests, he depicted the world struggle in terms of the opportunities offered to the United States for global leadership. Luce was therefore critical of President Roosevelt for what, he believed, were his efforts to make the New Deal work on a narrowly nationalistic basis. "Our only chance now to make it work," he wrote, "is in terms of a vital international economy and in terms of an international moral order." The twentieth century "is ours," he declared, "because it is America's first century as a dominant power in the world." It was, moreover, a revolutionary century because the world was, "for the first time in history, one world, fundamentally indivisible, . . . capable of producing all the material needs of the entire human family." [3]

Buttressed by its system of free economic enterprise, its technical and artistic skills, its missionary zeal, and its passionate devotion to its own high ideals, America "must undertake now," Luce asserted, "to be the Good Samaritan of the entire world. . . . America as the dynamic center of ever-widening spheres of enterprise, America as the training center of the skillful servants of mankind, America as the Good Samaritan, really believing again that it is more blessed to give than to receive, and America as the powerhouse of the ideals of Freedom and Justice—out of these elements surely can be fashioned a vision of the 20th Century to which we can and will devote ourselves in joy and gladness and vigor and enthusiasm." [4]

The goal of an American Century which Luce invoked to justify his interventionist brand of internationalism was also used by others to sustain such a position after the United States formally entered the war. But while Luce stirred the imagination of American conservatives, liberals and progressives were more impressed by Henry Wallace's "Century of the Common Man" and Wendell Willkie's "One World."

Wallace particularly urged that the political democracy long traditional in the United States be broadened to include a new and wider sort of economic democracy for the masses of the people, not only at home but abroad. Derided by critics for his contention, "half in fun and half seriously," that the point of the war was to insure that "everybody in the world has the privilege of drinking a quart of milk a day," Wallace was nevertheless determined in his belief that the war and eventual peace "must mean a better standard of living for the common man, not merely in the United States and England, but also in India, Russia, China and Latin America—not merely in the United Nations, but also in Germany and Italy and Japan. Some have spoken of the 'American Century,' " Wallace observed, but "I say that the century on which we are entering—the century which will come out of this war—can be and must be the century of the common man." [5]

Exceeding the hopes of even Wallace and Luce, Wendell Willkie was able to bring to an enormous popular audience his tract for the times entitled *One World*. To help make this possible, President Roosevelt, laying aside the bitterness of the 1940 campaign, encouraged his former political opponent to undertake an extended world tour in 1942 and report his conclusions. For Willkie, not burdened with the responsibilities of high political office, it was easy to see the war as an intense ideological struggle for men's minds. In respect to North Africa and the Middle East, Soviet Russia and Nationalist China, he urged the United States to espouse a liberal position, accepting thereby the new revolutionary forces on the rise in the world, and refraining from support of all vestiges of imperialism and colonialism. In the same way, he complained strongly that the American attitude toward the Negro was characteristic of a domestic kind of imperialism which reflected seriously on the sincerity of the nation's foreign policy.[6]

Thus both at home and abroad, Willkie called for a new and more generous equality of opportunity to realize America's wartime ideals and aspirations. "Our Western world and our presumed supremacy are now on trial," he wrote. "Our boasting and our big talk leave Asia cold. Men and women in Russia and China and in the Middle East are conscious now of their own potential strength. They are coming to know that many of the decisions about the future of the world lie in their hands. And they intend that these decisions shall leave the peoples of each nation free from foreign domination, free for economic, social, and spiritual growth." [7]

In their appeals to American idealism, Wallace and Willkie helped to prepare the way for a New Deal abroad, and each contributed much to the missionary work which President Roosevelt himself had begun even before America's full participation in the war. Thus, early in 1941, in his annual message to Congress, the President asserted that "we look forward to a world founded upon four essential freedoms."

> The first is freedom of speech and expression—everywhere in the world.
> The second is freedom of every person to worship God in his own way—everywhere in the world.
> The third is freedom from want—which, translated into world terms, means economic understanding which will secure to every nation a healthy peacetime life for its inhabitants—everywhere in the world.
> The fourth is freedom from fear—which, translated into world terms, means a world-wide reduction of armaments to such a point and in such a thorough fashion that no nation will be in a position to commit an act of physical aggression against any neighbor —anywhere in the world.[8]

Later that year, after a secret summer meeting off the coast of Newfoundland with British Prime Minister Winston Churchill, Roosevelt issued a joint communiqué in which the two statesmen declared the common aims of the United States and the United Kingdom in the Atlantic Charter. Like the Fourteen Points of President Wilson in the First World War, the charter stressed the importance of world cooperation and unity in achieving the goals of true international peace and security. Soon after America's formal entrance into the war, these blueprints for the future were given official sanction in the declaration and organization of the United Nations.[9]

The proclamation of the Four Freedoms and the Atlantic Charter were the most conspicuous instances of Roosevelt's attempt to formulate America's wartime ideals and aspirations. Alive to the criticism that this idealistic rhetoric could not be translated into the realities of foreign policy, the President subsequently expressed his annoyance with "those who assert vociferously that the four freedoms and the Atlantic Charter are nonsense because they are unattainable. If those people had lived a century and a half ago they would have sneered and said that the Declaration of Independence was utter piffle. If they had lived nearly a thousand years ago," the President continued, "they would have laughed uproariously at the ideals of the Magna Charta. And if they had lived several thousand years ago they would have derided Moses when he came from the Mountain with the Ten Commandments." [10]

Despite the aggressive manner in which Roosevelt thus chided his critics, it is easy to see in retrospect that the crisis of the war was likely to interfere, as much as help, with the realization of many of the old New Deal goals. More significant, therefore, as a portent of the shape of the future than the ecstatic visions of some of America's most prominent wartime leaders was the actual status of the New Deal's progressivism and reforms as they were modified, or even abandoned, to suit the needs of the 1940's. One clue to the contours of change was provided in the books of Carl Becker, a respected cultural historian who had once analyzed with much perception the intellectual currents underlying the American and French revolutions. Among Becker's many volumes, his collection of essays, *New Liberties for Old*, published at the beginning of the war, answered, at least in part, the question which he raised again toward its close in his book *How New Will the Better World Be?* The postwar world, Becker expected, would continue to be an evolution based on the historical past, and not nearly so new as customarily imagined. For example, war and unemployment, which he saw as the two chief faults of modern civilization, were not likely to be eliminated by World War II. And the world would also find it difficult to avoid nationalism, imperialism, and power politics.[11]

As Becker indicated, the war almost inevitably would transform the character of traditional American rights and liberties. Familiar himself with the fate of civil liberties in wartime, and sensitive to the charges of his political opponents that the violation of individual rights would again be the price of American belligerency, President Roosevelt, as the war came, tried to minimize the possibility of widespread dissent by placing an increasing emphasis on the theme of national unity. To the White House correspondents at their annual dinner in March 1941, the President pointed out that the enemies of democracy had been wrong in their predictions that the United States could not mobilize its arms and still remain a democracy. In carrying out the task of production "the Nation is calling for the sacrifice of some privileges, not for the sacrifice of fundamental rights," Roosevelt told the members of the press.[12]

During the first months of the war, Archibald MacLeish, alternately poet laureate and public information officer of the administration, reiterated the need for national unity. Annoyed by the "defeatists and divisionists in the United States," whom he called "also our chief enemies," MacLeish insisted that "if American opinion is not determined, if the American people are not committed entirely and irrevocably to a complete and final victory, this war can be lost." In explaining to the press the duties of the Committee on War Information, of which he was the head, MacLeish took the opportunity to urge the newspapers to police themselves in order to distinguish between loyal criticism and defeatist propaganda. MacLeish was convinced that a negotiated peace was not possible: "nothing but an absolute and final victory will suffice." [13]

Actually MacLeish's concern was unnecessary. Although there was a minimum of flag waving and much public apathy, the circumstances of the coming of the war to the United States, through the attack on Pearl Harbor, eliminated most of the opposition that might have been expected as a residue of the bitter debates of 1940 and 1941. Also important, though not always so well remembered, was the extent to which the possibility of significant dissent had already been muffled in the United States before the war became a fact. While the Supreme Court, for example, in its protection of civil liberties in the thirties seemed determined to give the country more individual freedom, some of the state legislatures and Congress were giving it less. Fears of communism resulted in state laws interfering with freedom of speech, press, and teaching. At the same time, the depression dissipated the distrust of the state and weakened old liberal suspicions of governmental restraints upon traditional civil liberties. Then in 1938, the Dies Committee of the House of Representatives began the formal congressional investigation of what it called "un-American activities." Although concerned mostly with communist and Nazi propaganda in America, the Dies Committee's work also intimidated left-wing and radical sentiment in New Deal circles and within the labor movement.[14]

Meanwhile, the post–World War I interest of Congress in the idea of a peacetime sedition law revived again and resulted in the passage in June 1940 of the Alien Registration or Smith Act. Despite its misleading title and its final approval at a time when Nazi armies were moving across Western Europe, the

Smith Act was as much an antiradical as a war or preparedness measure. The widespread impression that it was merely a statute for the registration and fingerprinting of aliens resident in the United States obscured the fact that it was also an unprecedented restriction upon American citizens. Conceived at first by Congress in an angry mood of antiforeign feeling, the bill was then amended and broadened to prohibit not only subversive activities involving the armed forces, but to forbid anyone from teaching or advocating the "overthrow or destruction of any government in the United States by force or violence; or to be or become a member of, or affiliate with, any such society, group, or assembly of persons. . . ." [15]

Just as the Smith Act was passed in advance of American entry into the war, so Congress also approved in the fall of 1940 the nation's first peacetime conscription law. In reality a war measure, looking toward an American expeditionary force in Europe or Asia as soon as the United States became an actual belligerent, the new Selective Service legislation was denounced by its opponents as a sure path to war and as a measure that would go far to transform the traditional antimilitaristic pattern of American life. Accepted reluctantly by such media of pro-war liberal thinking as the *Nation* and the *New Republic*, the conscription law drew from some conservative as well as radical spokesmen the suggestion that it was a typical New Deal measure. For example, the *Commercial and Financial Chronicle*, which had greeted the introduction of the Selective Service bill with the warning: "Involuntary servitude must not be restored," asked upon its passage: "Does not this defense program in some of its aspects take on the appearance of another New Deal project tainted with the philosophy of totalitarianism and heavy with risk of further infringement of individual liberty?" [16]

After Pearl Harbor the most serious violation of individual rights as well as a glaring example of wartime hysteria and hate was the forced evacuation of Americans of Japanese ancestry and Japanese aliens living along the Pacific coast. Although there was no record of espionage or sabotage by a Japanese-American, all those on the coast were compelled to move from their homes, and military government was imposed upon the Hawaiian Islands. Later, after the close of the war, the Supreme Court declared the army rule of Hawaii to have been an illegal invasion of the rights of the inhabitants. But in the case of the West Coast Japanese-Americans, the Court refused to intervene or interfere in a policy that had been carried out under the authority of the Secretary of War and the President.[17]

Apart from the harsh treatment of the Japanese-Americans, there was no concerted official or mass violation of civil liberties during the war. This improved record, compared with that of the First World War, owed much to the Roosevelt administration and its Attorney General Francis Biddle. But the New Deal's generally liberal stand could also be explained, at least in part, by the lack of any organized opposition. Except for six thousand conscientious objectors and Jehovah's Witnesses who went to prison rather than accept some form of alternate or noncombatant service, there was little overt hostility to either conscription or the war.[18] In contrast to the radical labor and socialist attacks upon World War I, both the communist and non-communist left in the United States supported enthusiastically a conflict in which Russia was a vital member of the Grand Alliance against the Nazis. Assured of general backing for its war policies, the Roosevelt administration could afford to be tolerant of its few academic and intellectual critics. The sensational raids and vindictive prosecutions of World War I were, on the whole, avoided, and the attempt to prosecute a group of American pro-Nazi sympathizers resulted in a mistrial.

The Smith Act, virtually unused and unworkable during hostilities, did not come into its own until after the war, when its doctrine of guilt by association proved useful against left-wing and radical groups. Military conscription, with its control over the lives and careers of the nation's youth, was also carried over into the postwar period, and only the belated intervention of the Supreme Court after 1945 corrected in a small way the wartime injustice meted out to Japanese-Americans. Such violations of traditional American liberties, as well as the earlier progressive measures of the New Deal, became a part of the wave of the future carried along on the tide of the war.

It is self-evident, of course, that modern total war, even when fought by a democratic government committed to the defense of free institutions, involves a tremendous regulation and control of the lives of individuals and of the nation's economy. Faced with some of the same problems that had confronted Lincoln and Wilson in wartime, President Roosevelt, though he avoided the worst excesses of his predecessors, like them assumed many of the prerogatives of a dictator. Emergency powers granted to the New Deal with little question in the crisis of the depression were expanded even more readily in the course of the war.[19]

Although Congress continued to function and although normal democratic processes were maintained, both conservative and liberal critics of the administration were alarmed over trends which, however to be expected in wartime, could also extend far beyond the period of actual hostilities. This was particularly true in the matter of the increasing concentration and control of the nation's economic life by the joint forces of big business and big government. When the Temporary National Economic Committee, created in 1938 to investigate just this problem, submitted its final report in 1941, it was embarrassed to find on every side fresh evidence of the concentration of economic power. Later during the war, a special committee appointed by the Senate to study the status of the smaller business and industrial plants, reported an alarming rate of wartime casualties so that there were one-half million fewer enterprises in 1943 than in 1941. Other figures showed that a high proportion of government contracts were being awarded to the largest corporations, which naturally were thereby placed in a close relationship with the Army and Navy. Even allowing for considerable sub-contracting to smaller firms, an important feature of the war economy was the strengthening of big business and the rise of a new group of practical men—many of them former corporation executives on loan to the government—to power in Washington.[20]

As the wartime expansion of military needs dominated the civilian economy, and as the power of the military extended to more and more areas of American life, the classic differences between a civil and a military society were obscured. With virtually an entire people caught up in total war, the sense of distinction of a civil society was in danger of being lost. Although the Army and certain business leaders who favored closer ties between industry and the military were thwarted in their efforts to secure a labor draft during the war, the technological imperatives of modern warfare made possible a new kind of militarism and conscription even for those not in uniform. As Harold Laski later was to point out, in looking back at the great war effort of the Allies, "Anyone who thinks for one moment of the effort involved in building the atomic bomb will not find it difficult to realize that, in the new warfare, the engineering factory is a unit of the army, and the worker may be in uniform without being aware of it. The new militarism may clothe itself in civilian uniforms; and, if the present relations of production are maintained, it may be imposed upon a people who see in its development no more than a way to full employment." [21]

In the midst of the wartime regimentation of the national economy, the argument intensified that centralized economic planning would result in some sort of permanent, totalitarian, collectivist order. This thesis attracted the attention of a wide variety of economists, publicists, and scholars who depicted the United States as marching toward fascism or returning to serfdom. Of all this wartime literature, the work that had the greatest impact was probably the former Austrian economist Friedrich Hayek's *The Road to Serfdom*, published in 1944. In essence it contended that the United States, though not resembling the Germany of Hitler and World War II, did bear a close analogy to the Germany of World War I and after. The progressive abandonment of freedom in economic affairs, Hayek feared, was leading to a similar destruction of political and personal freedom. Political democracy in itself was no guarantee against arbitrary power, and in the advance of economic collectivism under centralized state planning, Hayek saw a new despotism and reversion to a feudal type of social order.[22]

In reply to its detractors on both the left and right, President Roosevelt defended the long-range goals of the New Deal— at home as well as abroad. Already the conservative resurgence in the mid-term congressional elections in 1942 indicated that at least the domestic program of the administration had lost considerable popular backing. Thus by 1943 some of the most characteristic New Deal agencies, especially the ones responsible for economic reforms and social welfare activities, and including the remnants of the WPA, were being terminated by Congress. And even the President, in a famous press conference at the end of the year, seemed to agree that the New Deal might well be postponed for the duration of hostilities. Dr. Win-the-War, he suggested, had been called in to take over the patient, already largely cured by Dr. New Deal, but now suffering from the new pains of the war.[23]

A week before this press conference, the President in a fireside chat on Christmas Eve had rendered his report to the

country after his return from the Teheran and Cairo conferences. There the representatives of the wartime alliances had
devoted themselves "to consideration of the future—to plans
for the kind of world which alone can justify all the sacrifices
of this war." Although international relationships were discussed
"from the point of view of big, broad objectives, rather than
details," Roosevelt did not "think any insoluble differences will
arise among Russia, Great Britain, and the United States. In
these conferences," the President reiterated, "we were concerned
with basic principles—principles which involve the security and
the welfare and the standard of living of human beings in countries large and small." [24]

What these basic principles, to be extended eventually to the
whole world, might include was implied in the list which the
President spelled out in calling attention to the accomplishments
of the administration under Dr. New Deal: banking and financial
reforms, farm legislation and conservation, slum clearance and
decent housing, reduction of farm tenancy, social security measures, public works, the end of child labor, consumer protection,
TVA, and agricultural resettlement. "But at the present time,"
Roosevelt cautioned, in reverting again to his role as commander-
in-chief, "obviously the principal emphasis, the overwhelming
first emphasis, should be on winning the war." Later the general
outlines of a coming New Deal abroad could be made more
specific, but the President warned: "We don't want to confuse
people by talking about it now." Still, in his annual message to
Congress in January 1944, he took the opportunity to offer a
catalogue of "a second Bill of Rights under which a new basis
of security and prosperity can be established for all—regardless
of station, race or creed." Political freedom and true individual
rights, Roosevelt pointed out, "cannot exist without economic
security and independence." [25]

Unlike Churchill, Roosevelt believed that an early effort to
reach a more precise understanding with Stalin over future ar-

rangements in Europe would interfere with winning the war, as well as increasing his own political problems in the United States. Wendell Willkie's contention that "a war won without a purpose is a war won without victory" Roosevelt could answer by pointing to the principles of the Four Freedoms and the Atlantic Charter—principles to which Russia had also acceded in the working coalition fashioned at Teheran. In his 1944 campaign for a fourth presidential term, Roosevelt, though stressing the war, also defended the record of the New Deal and the new Economic Bill of Rights which he had urged upon Congress. Then at the Yalta Conference after the elections, plans were made for the first meeting of the United Nations scheduled to convene at San Francisco in April 1945.[26]

In terms of planning the end of the war and of organizing the United Nations, Yalta was a success. Even its most spectacular failure—the inability to guarantee a Free Poland—was not immediately apparent. But despite the disagreements at Yalta and the face-saving nature of the U.N. Charter for all three of the war-time leaders—Churchill, Stalin, and Roosevelt—it seemed true that in the United States, as Harry Hopkins later recalled:

> We really believed in our hearts that this was the dawn of the new day we had all been praying for and talking about for so many years. We were absolutely certain that we had won the first great victory of the peace—and by "we," I mean *all* of us, the whole civilized human race. The Russians had proved that they could be reasonable and farseeing and there wasn't any doubt in the minds of the President or any of us that we could live with them and get along with them peacefully for so far into the future as any of us could imagine.[27]

Unfortunately, in spite of the presidential and popular optimism of the war years, it was soon apparent that the task of achieving not only peace but worldwide reforms would not be an easy one. Vague speeches and official pronouncements by the Big Three were likely to be difficult to translate into definite commitments even if the coalition of the great powers survived the close of the war. Neither the crusading spirit of a Wallace or a Willkie, nor the confidence of Roosevelt provided, after all, a realistic insight into the troubled nature of the wartime alliance of the United States, Great Britain, and the Soviet Union. Certainly it was naive to expect that the principles of the Four Freedoms and the Atlantic Charter could be satisfactorily applied to the rest of the world merely as a result of the war. Total war by its very nature was at odds with the healing processes so necessary to peace and reconstruction. And, at the same time, the kind of popular unity enforced by an awareness of a common enemy was unlikely to prevail once the fighting stopped.[28]

In the fervor of their recent conversion from isolationism to internationalism, it was also true that the American public were all too frequently blind to the fact that their new views projected older nationalistic prejudices upon a world stage. "The trouble with America," Chester Bowles had observed on the eve of Pearl Harbor, "is her belief in Isolationism in time of peace and her fascination for Intervention in time of war." [29] Thus, despite the enthusiasm of a Wendell Willkie for the idea of One World, it was probable that most Americans thought of the future more in the essentially nationalistic terms of Henry Luce's American Century.

Whatever the shape and force of the wave of the future, it seemed clear, as Anne Morrow Lindbergh feared, that new and revolutionary changes were being accelerated, even if they had not always been created, by the war. Tragically, President Roosevelt, like Lincoln, failed to live to see the aftermath of the terrible carnage of the years of fighting, but his death on April 12, 1945, did not prevent the United Nations from convening as scheduled less than two weeks later. Whether, if Roosevelt had lived, American diplomacy could have averted the Cold War, as his son Elliott and others have maintained, no one knows. Actually, however, United States foreign policy was never as internationally minded as Roosevelt's wartime speeches tried to indicate. And the Grand Alliance against the Axis was, in itself, despite the rhetoric of collective security, sometimes "hard to distinguish from the timeworn statecraft of alliances designed to achieve for their adherents some kind of 'balance,' which usually meant predominance." [30]

The "reservoir of good will" which America had enjoyed in history, and which Willkie and others hoped would become the basis for One World, was endangered almost immediately by the fear and resentment with which other countries regarded the tremendous postwar wealth and military power of the United States. Thus America, despite its undoubted economic and military influence, was in danger of being isolated by its sheer affluence, as well as by its lingering race prejudices and practices. Earlier gains under the New Deal, and the partial breakdown of patterns of racial segregation and discrimination in the armed forces and defense industries, indicated a sure redefinition of the Negroes' status after the war. In decrying Nazi racist doctrines, America also committed itself before the whole world to racial tolerance and equality, and Negroes themselves were better prepared than ever before in their history to secure the rights that Americans had fought for during the war.[31]

Though the precise nature and degree of the New Deal's influence on American foreign policy remained uncertain, there was abundant evidence of its continuing impact on domestic affairs. World War II, of course, curtailed many New Deal reforms, and other administration measures died from want of popular and congressional support. But the war years made possible not only Roosevelt's third and abbreviated fourth terms but the steady growth of the federal bureaucracy. New governmental agencies and specially created federal corporations became involved in all kinds of novel economic activities. Under swollen wartime budgets, the New Deal was able to expand its spending policies, while conservative businessmen, though hostile to appropriations for domestic reforms, eagerly accepted governmental outlays for military purposes. They wanted the war contracts that piled up mounting federal deficits, and especially after Pearl Harbor the government needed their cooperation and support. But later, with the war over, business found that it could not enforce any such widespread reaction against government controls and peacetime spending as had occurred in the 1920's.

Despite the change of pace and direction in the New Deal occasioned by the war, little of the basic legislation of the thirties, not declared unconstitutional by the Supreme Court, was subsequently altered or repealed. As a recent study of that era points out, the New Deal stopped growing, but it did not disappear. "A subsidized, regulated welfare capitalism still stands, thirty years later, as the core of American domestic policy." [32]

Although the New Deal, like other major movements in history, drew certain of its ideas from the past, it was nevertheless truly revolutionary in the broader terms of its implications for the future. This was, perhaps, not always readily apparent because its first task was the emergency effort to lift the country from the slough of the depression. But in this process of its redemption, capitalism was also set on the road of its modern transformation into an adjunct of a welfare-warfare state. If President Roosevelt frequently disguised radical New Deal legislation in the more conservative language of the American reform tradition, it was also true, as Harold Laski pointed out, that he "brought into being a positive federal state in America." [33] Thus the wave of the future was not so much the fascism or communism of Europe as it was a new Americanized form of state capitalism, increasingly dependent on the tensions aggravated by the Cold War and upon the ever-mounting defense budgets of the postwar policies of international containment.

Forced into many of its policies by the depression, the Roosevelt administration happily tried to humanize the degree of regimentation entailed by the new economic and social revolution. Roosevelt, who exemplified the government as a protector, was able to communicate a sense of individual warmth to the paternalism of the modern bureaucratic state. Concern for the underprivileged and minority groups was reflected in the feeling of security imparted by the social welfare measures of the thirties. And the combination of depression and New Deal reforms, together with lowered immigration, minimized social distinctions and encouraged the assimilation of all classes into the matrix of American life. Yet, even as the spirit and events of the thirties encouraged social and economic equality, there emerged again in the years after World War II a new affluent society characterized still by a significant gap between the comfortably rich and the hopelessly poor.[34] Moreover, like its successor administrations, the New Deal proved unable to reduce significantly the numbers of the unemployed except through continued heavy expenditures on arms and national security measures. Thus, against the restoration of public confidence in the economy, there had to be assessed the overarching fear of war and possible nuclear destruction. Science could no longer be counted on to provide a never-ending frontier or automatic guarantee of unlimited future progress.

Little concerned, at least until the Supreme Court fight, with reforms in the structure of American government, the New Deal was eminently practical in its manipulation of the political process and in its appeals to the electorate. Roosevelt was the first President to make frequent use of the radio, and he remained a master in the arts of mass political persuasion. By sharing its favors among all major groups and sections of the nation, the New Deal was able to win the support of the lower economic classes, rehabilitate the middle class, and safeguard capitalism. FDR preferred a conception of the state as an honest broker among competing economic interests, so he avoided both the rigid class alignment and the new radical party ever in the minds of many intellectuals. Instead, the New Deal represented a popular consensus, achieved first through its program of recovery and reform, then maintained by the rising nationalistic and patriotic temper of the war years.

Most alarming perhaps, at least in terms of older liberal ideals, was the increasingly official tone of American intellectual life. As a result of the depression and the war, the government's needs and rules became paramount. Much of the thinking in education, science, and even religion became ever more influenced by the criteria of national security and national loyalty. At the same time, public opinion, confused by the new military technology and global diplomacy, was less able to contribute meaningfully to political debate on important issues confronting the nation. Democracy by the 1940's frequently seemed, therefore, a matter of dogmatic faith or patriotic exhortation, rather than a political process based on popular education and understanding. Yet President Roosevelt, though he served in an age of dictators and new Caesars, was able to maintain a leadership in keeping with the broad outlines and tenets of the American democratic tradition. And to many peoples and lands his name was a symbol of enduring hope for a better future.[35]

Never a single ideology and never a complete utopia, the New Deal was nonetheless the most significant political and intellectual movement in twentieth-century America. To an extent unique in the nation's history, it influenced and inspired an entire generation, transmitting its goals to the far corners of the globe. Coming into power in the most disastrous depression the country had ever experienced, the New Deal was able to reverse the pessimistic psychology of the American people and restore to the millions who had despaired of all progress a renewed feeling of security and hope. Singularly modern in its nationalistic concepts of planning and collective social action, the New Deal carried the country further away from the individualistic heritage of its past. Similarly, the administration's determination to resist the challenge of fascism and totalitarianism abroad endangered, as well as safeguarded, fundamental liberties at home. This turn from peace to war, whether forced from the outside or accepted as conscious national policy, marked an interruption and shift in the New Deal's program of reconstruction and reform. Revolutionary in its more lasting implications without being always revolutionary in its methods, the New Deal became under Franklin D. Roosevelt the driving force behind that powerful wave of social change which still hovers uncertainly over America and the rest of the world.

A Note on Sources

THE SPECIFIC SOURCES of my study in the intellectual history of the New Deal are indicated in the following Notes. To avoid undue distraction to the reader and excessive clutter in the text, the references for an entire paragraph have generally been gathered into a single citation. In addition to the biographies, memoirs, and general works dealing with the period of the thirties, there is an ever-increasing number of scholarly monographs exploring in depth particular New Deal agencies and ideas. The interested reader may also wish to examine some of the contemporary literature of the thirties now conveniently gathered in the many excellent anthologies which cover the politics and economics as well as *belles lettres* of the decade. FDR's own contribution is documented in *The Public Papers and Addresses of Franklin D. Roosevelt*, edited by Samuel Rosenman (13 vols., New York: Random House; Macmillan; Harper, 1938–1950), and is cited in the notes as *PPAFDR*.

Standard secondary works of particular merit for this study include the later chapters of Merle Curti's *The Growth of American Thought* (3rd ed., New York: Harper and Row, 1964); Charles and Mary Beard's broad cultural history of the thirties, *America in Midpassage* (2 vols., New York: Macmillan,

1939); Dixon Wecter's excellent social history, *The Age of the Great Depression, 1929–1941* (New York: Macmillan, 1948); and William E. Leuchtenburg's essentially political account, *Franklin D. Roosevelt and the New Deal, 1932–1940* (New York: Harper and Row, 1963). The three volumes of Arthur M. Schlesinger, Jr.'s, as yet incomplete *The Age of Roosevelt* (Boston: Houghton Mifflin, 1957–1960) are the most useful and full of the biographical studies of FDR that cover the presidency, but James Mac-Gregor Burns's biography, *Roosevelt: The Lion and the Fox* (New York: Harcourt, Brace, 1956), should not be overlooked.

In addition to the published materials, I consulted pertinent manuscript records and private correspondence in a number of important collections:

The Franklin D. Roosevelt Library at Hyde Park, New York, is, of course, a prime repository for the history of the New Deal. The President's Personal Files (cited as PPF in the notes) were most useful for my purposes and include a surprisingly frank and wide range of correspondence with the intellectuals of the thirties. Some materials were also found in the President's Official Files (POF) and in certain of the subject area files.

Of the vast storehouse of historical records in the National Archives, the richest and most valuable for my research were the Records of the Works Progress Administration, Record Group 69 (WPA, RG 69), including the Central Correspondence Files and, more especially, the various files of the so-called Four Arts Projects of the WPA; and the Records of the Public Building Service (RG 121), including the correspondence and files of the Public Works of Art Project (PWAP), and the Treasury Relief Art Project (TRAP). For each of these Record Groups there are excellent inventories and checklists available at the National Archives.

At the Library of Congress, Manuscripts Division, correspondence was used from the papers of Frederick Lewis Allen, Newton

D. Baker, Felix Frankfurter, Amos Pinchot, and William Allen White.

In the New York Public Library, the best collection bearing on the New Deal is in the Norman Thomas Papers, even though the greater part of the material is confined to routine Socialist party matters. Also of some use were the Victor F. Calverton and the Lillian Wald Papers.

In the Butler Library of Columbia University, an excellent collection with a wide range of correspondence for the thirties is in the James Truslow Adams Papers. I also consulted the Lincoln Steffens Papers and the Oral History Collection at Columbia.

The Houghton Library at Harvard University has the Oswald Garrison Villard Papers, which I examined originally in my study of American antimilitarism. This valuable collection covers almost all facets of twentieth-century intellectual history.

Notes

CHAPTER ONE: *The Crisis in the American Dream*

1. Joel Barlow, *The Vision of Columbus* (Hartford: Hudson and Goodwin, 1787), pp. 240–241.
2. R. S. Baker and W. E. Dodd, ed., *The Public Papers of Woodrow Wilson* (New York: Harper, 1925–1927), V, 12; VI, 515.
3. December 6, 1825, in J. D. Richardson, ed., *A Compilation of the Messages and Papers of the Presidents* (Washington: Government Printing Office, 1896–1899), II, 311.
4. James Truslow Adams, *The Epic of America* (Boston: Little, Brown, 1931), p. 174.
5. *Ibid.*, pp. 198, 403–404.
6. *Ibid.*, p. 391.
7. *Ibid.*, pp. 393, 398; Adams to Mark A. DeW. Howe, July 12, 1929, James Truslow Adams Papers.
8. Adams, *Epic of America*, pp. 395–396, 405–406; Adams, *The Tempo of Modern Life* (New York: Boni, 1931), p. 42; Adams, *Our Business Civilization* (New York: Boni, 1929), Chap. 2.
9. Adams to Wilbur L. Cross, July 19, 1932; Adams to Mark A. De W. Howe, November 1, 1929, Adams Papers; Adams, *Epic of America*, p. 400.
10. Adams, *Epic of America*, pp. 410–411, 415–416.
11. Adams, *Tempo of Modern Life*, pp. 277, 295. See also the statements of Republican leaders compiled in Edward Angly, *Oh Yeah?* (New York: Viking, 1931), *passim*.
12. See Henry F. May, *The End of American Innocence: A Study of the First Years of Our Own Time, 1912–1917* (New York: Knopf, 1959), Introduction and *passim*.
13. Harold Stearns, *Civilization in the United States* (New York: Harcourt, Brace, 1922).

14. Stearns, *Liberalism in America* (New York: Boni and Liveright, 1919), pp. 5, 102–103, 143.
15. Lippmann to Fosdick, August 15, 1919, in *Letters on the League of Nations, From the Files of Raymond B. Fosdick* (Princeton: Princeton University Press, 1966), pp. 10–12.
16. Lippmann to Baker, January 17, July 23, 1920, Newton D. Baker Papers, Box 12.
17. Baker to Lippmann, January 20, 1920, Baker Papers, Box 12.
18. Walter Lippmann, *Public Opinion* (New York: Penguin, 1946; c1922), pp. 34–35, 203; Lippmann, *The Phantom Public* (New York: Harcourt, Brace, 1925), pp. 61–62, 185. See also the analysis in Stow Persons, *American Minds* (New York: Holt, 1958), pp. 374ff.
19. Lippmann, *A Preface to Morals* (New York: Macmillan, 1929), pp. 3–4, 9–10, 314. See also Joseph Wood Krutch, *The Modern Temper* (New York: Harcourt, Brace, 1929), Chaps. 2, 8.
20. Lippmann, *Men of Destiny* (New York: Macmillan, 1927), p. 61.
21. H. L. Mencken, *Notes on Democracy* (New York: Knopf, 1926), pp. 22ff., 38, 181ff.
22. Mencken, *Prejudices, Second Series* (New York: Knopf, 1920), pp. 102, 111–112; *Prejudices, Third Series* (New York: Knopf, 1922), p. 314.
23. Frederic C. Howe, *The Confessions of a Reformer* (New York: Scribner's, 1925), p. 282. See also Howe, *Revolution and Democracy* (New York: Huebsch, 1921), *passim*.
24. J. Allen Smith, *The Growth and Decadence of Constitutional Government* (New York: Holt, 1930), p. 197.
25. Parrington to Professor Ross L. Finney, January 23, 1929, quoted in Eric F. Goldman, "J. Allen Smith," *Pacific Northwest Quarterly*, xxxv (July 1944), 209.
26. Charles and Mary Beard, *The Rise of American Civilization* (New York: Macmillan, 1927), I, 737.
27. Beard, *Whither Mankind: A Panorama of Modern Civilization* (New York: Longmans, Green, 1928), pp. 3, 19.
28. *Ibid.*, p. 78.
29. John Dewey, "The Ethics of Democracy," *University of Michigan Philosophical Papers* (Ann Arbor: Andrews, 1888), p. 28; Dewey, *Democracy and Education* (New York: Macmillan, 1916), pp. 100–101; Dewey, *The Public and Its Problems* (New York: Holt, 1927), pp. 109, 168–169.
30. Dewey, *Public and Its Problems*, pp. 212–213; Dewey, *Individualism Old and New* (New York: Minton, Balch, 1930), pp. 28, 35ff.
31. T. C. Cochran, *The American Business System* (Cambridge, Mass.: Harvard University Press, 1957), p. 140; Lippmann, *Men of Destiny*, pp. 23–26. See also Henry F. May, "Shifting Perspectives on the 1920's," *Mississippi Valley Historical Review*, xliii (December 1956), 405–427.
32. Arthur M. Schlesinger, Jr., *The Crisis of the Old Order* (Boston: Houghton Mifflin, 1957), p. 142; *The Autobiography of Lincoln Steffens* (New York: Harcourt, Brace, 1931), pp. 851ff., 865ff.; Steffens to Jo Davidson, February 18, 1929, in Ella Winter and Granville Hicks, ed.,

The Letters of Lincoln Steffens (New York: Harcourt, Brace, 1938), II, 829–830.

33. Beard and Beard, *Rise of American Civilization*, II, 719–720, 800.
34. Zechariah Chafee, Jr., "Prosperity," *Nation*, CXXIX (July 24, 1929), 84–85.
35. *Nation*, CXXIX (October 23, 1929), 460–462, and seqq.
36. *Nation*, CXXIX (November 6, 13, 27, 1929), 511, 539–540, 614.
37. *New Republic*, LXI (November 27, 1929), 4–6; *ibid.*, LXI (January 29, 1930), 263–264; *ibid.*, LXIII (May 21, 1930), 4–5.
38. Lewis Corey, "Wall Street and Hard Times," *New Republic*, LXII (March 26, 1930), 145–148.
39. Frankfurter to Bliven, June 13, 19, 1931; January 8, 1932; Bliven to Frankfurter, June 17, 1931, General Correspondence Box 5, Felix Frankfurter Papers.
40. Quoted in Don Congdon, ed., *The Thirties: A Time to Remember* (New York: Simon and Schuster, 1962), p. 24.
41. Douglas Waples, *People and Print: Social Aspects of Reading in the Depression* (Chicago: University of Chicago Press, 1937), pp. 10, 59ff.; Alfred R. McIntyre to Adams, January 10, 1933, Adams Papers.
42. R. L. Duffus, *Books: Their Place in a Democracy* (Boston: Houghton Mifflin, 1930), pp. 1–3; Dixon Wecter, *The Age of the Great Depression* (New York: Macmillan, 1948), p. 244.
43. R. L. Duffus, *Our Starving Libraries* (Boston: Houghton Mifflin, 1933), pp. 1–2, 27ff.
44. C. J. Enzler, *Some Social Aspects of the Depression* (Washington: Catholic University of America Press, 1939), Chap. 5.
45. W. H. Hale, "A Dirge for College Liberalism," *New Republic*, LXVI (May 13, 1931), 348–350; Harold J. Laski, "Why Don't Your Young Men Care?", *Harper's Magazine*, CLXIII (July 1931), 130–136; William Allen White, *Emporia Gazette*, April 8, 1932, in R. H. Fitzgibbon, ed., *Forty Years on Main Street* (New York: Farrar and Rinehart, 1937), p. 331.
46. Quoted in R. L. Duffus, *Lillian Wald* (New York: Macmillan, 1938), pp. 287, 349; *Nation*, CXXXIV (January 6, 1932), 4. See also Clarke Chambers, *Seedtime of Reform: American Social Service and Social Action, 1918–1933* (Minneapolis: University of Minnesota Press, 1963), Chap. 8.
47. Claude Bowers to Adams, November 27, 1929, Adams Papers.
48. Allan Nevins to Adams, November 27, 1930; January 31, 1931, Adams Papers.
49. Adams, "Wanted Perspective," *Harper's Magazine*, CLXIII (August 1931), 261ff.; "The Responsibility of Bankers," *Forum*, LXXXVI (August 1931), 80–86; "Shadow of the Man on Horseback," *Atlantic Monthly*, CLXIX (January 1932), 1–10; Edward C. Aswell to Adams, May 4, 1931; Adams to Henry Hazlitt, January 8, 1932, Adams Papers.
50. See Christopher Lasch, *The New Radicalism in America* (New York: Knopf, 1965), Chap. 8.
51. Steffens to Alfred Harcourt, April 24, 1930, *Letters*, II, 870.

52. Steffens to Sam Darcy, April 28, 1934; Steffens to Jo Davidson, June 3, 1932, *Letters*, II, 982–983, 923; Steffens to Dreiser, December 16, 1932, Lincoln Steffens Papers.

53. Gilbert Seldes, *The Years of the Locust* (Boston: Little, Brown, 1933), p. 331; Edmund Wilson, "The Literary Consequences of the Crash" (1932), in *The Shores of Light: A Literary Chronicle of the Twenties and Thirties* (New York: Farrar, Straus and Young, 1952), p. 498. See also Matthew Josephson, *Infidel in the Temple: A Memoir of the Nineteen-Thirties* (New York: Knopf, 1967), pp. xi, 155ff.

Chapter Two: *The Search for Solutions*

1. Schlesinger, *Crisis of the Old Order*, p. 184.

2. John Maynard Keynes, *The Economic Consequences of the Peace* (New York: Harcourt, Brace, 1920), p. 274fn.

3. Quoted in Charles Beard, "The Constitution and States' Rights," *Virginia Quarterly Review*, XI (October 1935), 493.

4. Quoted in R. L. Wilbur and A. M. Hyde, *The Hoover Policies* (New York: Scribner's, 1937), pp. 2–3; W. S. Myers, ed., *The State Papers and Other Public Writings of Herbert Hoover* (Garden City: Doubleday, Doran, 1934), I, 6–7, 12.

5. See the summary of Hoover's political philosophy in Albert U. Romasco, *The Poverty of Abundance: Hoover, the Nation, the Depression* (New York: Oxford, 1965), Chap. 2.

6. John T. Flynn, "Inside the R. F. C.," *Harper's Magazine*, CLXVI (January 1933), 161–169. See also H. G. Warren, *Herbert Hoover and the Great Depression* (New York: Oxford, 1959), pp. 146–147.

7. Adams to Wilbur L. Cross, July 19, 1932, Adams Papers; Leffingwell to Alexander Sachs, January 4, 1935, Roosevelt Papers, quoted in Schlesinger, *Crisis of the Old Order*, p. 237.

8. Murray N. Rothbard, *America's Great Depression* (Princeton: Van Nostrand, 1963), pp. 167, 294–295.

9. Walter Lippmann, "The Permanent New Deal," *Yale Review*, XXIV (June 1935), 652; Charles and Mary Beard, *America in Midpassage* (New York: Macmillan, 1939), I, 90.

10. Romasco, *Poverty of Abundance*, pp. 231–232, 234.

11. *State Papers of Herbert Hoover*, II, 249–250.

12. Romasco, *Poverty of Abundance*, p. 230.

13. U.S. Department of Commerce, Bureau of the Census, *Historical Statistics of the United States* (Washington: Government Printing Office, 1960), Sections E and F. See also the added data and analysis in Beard and Beard, *America in Midpassage*, I, 61–65; John Kenneth Galbraith, *The Great Crash: 1929* (Boston: Houghton Mifflin, 1955), p. 173; Arthur S. Link, *American Epoch* (New York: Knopf, 1955), pp. 357–361; David Shannon, *Between the Wars: America, 1919–1941* (Boston: Houghton Mifflin, 1965), pp. 109–111.

14. Daniel Willard, "The Challenge to Capitalism," *Review of Reviews*, LXXXIII (May 1931), 61.
15. Seldes, *The Years of the Locust*, p. 258fn.
16. Romasco, *Poverty of Abundance*, p. 200.
17. W. B. Donham, *Business Adrift* (New York: McGraw-Hill, 1931), p. 118; William E. Leuchtenburg, "The New Deal and the Analogue of War," in John Braeman, *et al.*, *Change and Continuity in Twentieth-Century America* (New York: Harper and Row, 1966), pp. 93–94; Joseph Dorfman, *The Economic Mind in American Civilization* (New York: Viking, 1946–1959), v, 671–672.
18. Stuart Chase, "A Ten Year Plan for America," *Harper's Magazine*, CLXIII (June 1931), 1–10; George Soule, *A Planned Society* (New York: Macmillan, 1932), pp. 184, 187; W. T. Foster, "When a Horse Balks," *North American Review*, CCXXXIV (July 1932), 10.
19. Charles Beard, "A 'Five-Year Plan' for America," *Forum*, LXXXVI (July 1931), 5–6; "The Reminiscences of Gerard Swope" (Oral History Research Office, Columbia University, 1959), p. 112, and *passim*.
20. J. G. Frederick, ed., *The Swope Plan: Details, Criticisms, Analysis* (New York: Business Bourse, 1931), Chap. 2.
21. Quoted in Charles Beard, *America Faces the Future* (Boston: Houghton Mifflin, 1932), pp. 189–190.
22. *Ibid.*, pp. 191, 203, 217. See also Frederick, *Swope Plan*, Chap. 3.
23. H. I. Harriman, "American Business Turns a Page," *New York Times Magazine* (December 3, 1933), pp. 1–2.
24. *Business Week* (June 24, 1931), p. 44.
25. Quoted in Beard and Beard, *America in Midpassage*, I, 100; and in Schlesinger, *Crisis of the Old Order*, p. 185.
26. Sidney Hillman, "Unemployment Reserves," *Atlantic Monthly*, CXLVIII (November 1931), 668; Hillman, "Labor Leads Toward Planning," *Survey Graphic*, LXVII (March 1, 1932), 588.
27. See the studies by Paul A. Carter, *The Decline and Revival of the Social Gospel* (Ithaca: Cornell University Press, 1956), pp. 129ff.; Robert M. Miller, *American Protestantism and Social Issues, 1919–1939* (Chapel Hill: University of North Carolina Press, 1958), pp. 63ff.
28. J. H. Nichols, *Democracy and the Churches* (Philadelphia: Westminster Press, 1951), p. 226; Beard, *America Faces the Future*, p. 28.
29. Quoted in Donald B. Meyer, *The Protestant Search for Political Realism, 1919–1941* (Berkeley: University of California Press, 1960), p. 169. See also Federal Council of the Churches of Christ in America, *Our Economic Life in the Light of Christian Ideals* (New York: Association Press, 1932), *passim*.
30. H. E. Fosdick, "Religion Without God?", *Harper's Magazine*, CLX (December 1929), 50–60; H. F. Ward, *Our Economic Morality and the Ethic of Jesus* (New York: Macmillan, 1930), pp. 9–10; Ward, *Which Way Religion?* (New York: Macmillan, 1931), pp. 216ff. See also F. Ernest Johnson, *The Church and Society* (Nashville: Abingdon-Cokesbury, 1935), *passim*.

31. Reinhold Niebuhr, *Moral Man and Immoral Society* (New York: Scribner's, 1932), Introduction and Chap. 1.

32. Reinhold Niebuhr, *Reflections on the End of an Era* (New York: Scribner's, 1934), pp. ix, 28, 104.

33. Lewis S. Feuer, "American Travelers to the Soviet Union 1917–32: The Formation of a Component of New Deal Ideology," *American Quarterly*, XIV (Summer 1962), 119–149; Peter G. Filene, *Americans and the Soviet Experiment, 1917–1933* (Cambridge, Mass.: Harvard University Press, 1967), *passim*.

34. W. W. Brickman, ed., *John Dewey's Impressions of Soviet Russia* (New York: Teachers College, 1964), pp. 45, 93.

35. Feuer, "American Travelers to the Soviet Union," pp. 123–124.

36. Quoted in *ibid.*, p. 125; Stuart Chase, *A New Deal* (New York: Macmillan, 1932), p. 252.

37. On the background of these works see Frank A. Warren, *Liberals and Communism* (Bloomington: Indiana University Press, 1966), Chap. 4 and *passim*.

38. William Henry Chamberlin, "Russia and the World Crisis," *New Republic*, LXVI (February 18, 1931), 8–10; Maurice Hindus, *The Great Offensive* (New York: Smith and Haas, 1933), p. viii; Steffens to Anna Louise Strong, October 1934, in Winter and Hicks, *Letters of Lincoln Steffens*, II, 1001.

39. Charles A. Beard, "The Myth of Rugged American Individualism," *Harper's Magazine*, CLXIV (December 1931), 22; Beard, *Toward Civilization* (New York: Longmans, Green, 1930), Chap. 16.

40. G. S. Ford, *Science and Civilization* (Minneapolis: University of Minnesota Press, 1933), pp. 14, 23; H. P. Fairchild, "The Great Economic Paradox," *Harper's Magazine*, CLXIV (May 1932), 652.

41. W. B. Donham, *Business Adrift*, pp. 33ff.; Donham, *Business Looks at the Unforeseen* (New York: McGraw-Hill, 1932), p. 207.

42. Quoted in Beard, *America Faces the Future*, p. 16.

43. Walter Lippmann, *Interpretations 1931–1932*, ed. Allan Nevins (New York: Macmillan, 1933), pp. 32, 334. See also Francis Neilson, *Control from the Top* (New York: Putnam, 1933), *passim*.

44. Lippmann, *Interpretations*, pp. 40, 71, 336.

45. John Strachey, *The Coming Struggle for Power* (New York: Covici, Friede, 1933), pp. 155, 356, 359.

46. John Chamberlain, *Farewell to Reform: Being a History of the Rise, Life and Decay of the Progressive Mind in America* (New York: Liveright, 1932), pp. 275, 323; Mauritz A. Hallgren, *Seeds of Revolt: A Study of American Life and the Temper of the American People During the Depression* (New York: Knopf, 1933), p. 348, Chap. 14.

47. Lawrence Dennis, *Is Capitalism Doomed?* (New York: Harper, 1932), p. 316.

48. See John P. Diggins, "Flirtation with Fascism: American Pragmatic Liberals and Mussolini's Italy," *American Historical Review*, LXXI (January 1966), 487–506.

49. Adolf A. Berle and Gardiner C. Means, *The Modern Corporation and Private Property* (New York: Macmillan, 1932), pp. 1–2, 357.

50. Rexford G. Tugwell, *The Industrial Discipline and the Governmental Arts* (New York: Columbia University Press, 1933), p. 186; Tugwell, "The Principle of Planning and the Institution of Laissez Faire," *American Economic Review*, XXII (March 1932), Supp., p. 92.

51. Howard Scott, *et al.*, *Introduction to Technocracy* (New York: John Day, 1933), pp. 39ff., 59–61; Scott, "Technology Smashes the Price System," *Harper's Magazine*, CLXVI (January 1933), 129–142; Harold Rugg, *The Great Technology* (New York: John Day, 1933), *passim*; Joseph Dorfman, *Thorstein Veblen and His America* (New York: Viking, 1934), pp. 510ff.; Frederick Lewis Allen, *Since Yesterday* (New York: Harper, 1940), pp. 89–92; Henry Elsner, *The Technocrats: Prophets of Automation* (Syracuse: Syracuse University Press, 1967), *passim*.

52. Lewis Mumford, *Technics and Civilization* (New York: Harcourt, Brace, 1934); Stuart Chase, *The Economy of Abundance* (New York: Macmillan, 1934), *passim*.

53. Donald R. McCoy, *Angry Voices: Left-of-Center Politics in the New Deal Era* (Lawrence: University of Kansas Press, 1958), pp. 5, 8.

54. *Ibid.*, p. 9; John Dewey, "Who Might Make a New Party?", *New Republic*, LXVI (April 1, 1931), 177.

CHAPTER THREE: *Roosevelt in a Word*

1. Heinz Eulau, "Neither Ideology Nor Utopia: The New Deal in Retrospect," *Antioch Review*, XIX (Winter 1959–60), 533. For a convenient compendium of personal appraisals, see William E. Leuchtenburg, ed., *Franklin D. Roosevelt: A Profile* (New York: Hill and Wang, 1967).

2. The fullest account of the early years is Frank Freidel, *Franklin D. Roosevelt: The Apprenticeship, The Ordeal*, and *The Triumph* (3 vols., Boston: Little, Brown, 1952, 1954, 1956).

3. James MacGregor Burns, *Roosevelt: The Lion and the Fox* (New York: Harcourt, Brace, 1956), p. 89; Paul Conkin, *The New Deal* (New York: Crowell, 1967), p. 7.

4. D. R. Fusfeld, *The Economic Thought of Franklin D. Roosevelt and the Origins of the New Deal* (New York: Columbia University Press, 1956), Introduction; Frankfurter to Stephen S. Wise, September 14, 1932, Subject File Box 65, Frankfurter Papers; H. B. Phillips, ed., *Felix Frankfurter Reminisces* (New York: Reynal, 1960), Chap. 23. Frankfurter's extraordinary continuing personal influence on FDR and the New Deal is thoroughly documented in Max Freedman, ed., *Roosevelt and Frankfurter: Their Correspondence, 1928–1945* (Boston: Little, Brown, 1967).

5. Frances Perkins, *The Roosevelt I Knew* (New York: Viking, 1946), pp. 153–154; Raymond Moley, *The First New Deal* (New York: Harcourt, Brace and World, 1966), p. 4.

6. Bernard Bellush, *Franklin D. Roosevelt as Governor of New York* (New York: Columbia University Press, 1955), pp. xi–xii, 282–285.

7. Samuel Rosenman, *Working with Roosevelt* (New York: Harper, 1952), Chap. 5; Rexford G. Tugwell, *The Brains Trust* (New York: Viking, 1968), pp. 5–11 and *passim.*

8. Raymond Moley, *After Seven Years* (New York: Harper, 1939), pp. 23–24.

9. Samuel Rosenman, ed., *The Public Papers and Addresses of Franklin D. Roosevelt* (New York: Random House; Macmillan; Harper, 1938–1950), I, 288–302, 486, 495. Hereafter cited as *PPAFDR.*

10. *Ibid.,* I, 624–627.

11. *Ibid.,* I, 631–632.

12. *Ibid.,* I, 645–646.

13. Stanley High, *Roosevelt—And Then?* (New York: Harper, 1937), pp. 5ff.; Rosenman, *Working with Roosevelt*, Chap. 1; Ernest K. Lindley, *The Roosevelt Revolution: First Phase* (New York: Viking, 1933), p. 7.

14. Schlesinger, *Crisis of the Old Order*, p. 416.

15. *Ibid.,* p. 420.

16. *PPAFDR*, I, 658; cf. *The Memoirs of Herbert Hoover: The Great Depression, 1929–1941* (New York: Macmillan, 1952), p. 336.

17. Bernard Sternsher, *Rexford Tugwell and the New Deal* (New Brunswick: Rutgers University Press, 1964), pp. 45ff.

18. *PPAFDR*, I, 699–700.

19. *Ibid.,* I, 750ff.

20. Quoted in *Memoirs*, pp. 340–341.

21. *Ibid.,* p. 329; Lewis Lorwin, *Time for Planning* (New York: Harper, 1945), p. 137.

22. *New Republic*, LXVI (April 1, 1931), 165–166; *Nation*, CXXXIV (January 20, April 27, 1932), 58, 487–489.

23. Lippmann, *Interpretations 1931–1932*, pp. 261–262.

24. Perkins to Calverton, February 13, 1932, V. F. Calverton Papers; Sedgwick to Adams, February 23, 1932; Ford to Adams, April 8, 1932, Adams Papers; R. M. Lovett, "Hoover," *New Republic*, LXX (April 20, 1932), 277–278.

25. Elliott Roosevelt, ed., *F. D. R.: His Personal Letters, 1928–1945* (New York: Duell, Sloan and Pearce, 1950), I, 282–283.

26. *Nation*, CXXXV (July 13, 1932), 22; *New Republic*, LXXI (June 1, 1932), 62–64.

27. David Shannon, *The Socialist Party of America* (New York: Macmillan, 1955), p. 222.

28. August 17, 1932, Malcolm Cowley Papers, quoted in Daniel Aaron, *Writers on the Left* (New York: Harcourt, Brace and World, 1961), p. 258; "How I Shall Vote," *Forum*, LXXXVIII (November 1932), 257–258.

29. *Culture and the Crisis* (New York City, October 1932, pamphlet, Columbia University Library), pp. 5–6, 30, and *passim.* See also Aaron, *Writers on the Left*, pp. 196–197; Schlesinger, *Crisis of the Old Order*, p. 436; Josephson, *Infidel in the Temple*, pp. 149ff.

30. Ford to Adams, October 8, 1932; Adams to Wilbur L. Cross, August 30, 1932; Nevins to Adams, August 24, 1932, Adams Papers; White to Gutzon Borglum, October 13, 1932, in Walter Johnson, ed., *Selected Letters of William Allen White* (New York: Holt, 1947), pp. 327–328.

31. *Nation,* cxxxv (October 26, November 16, 1932), 390, 470; *New States-man and Nation,* n.s. v (May 13, 1933), 593; Mencken to Ezra Pound, November 26, 1932, in G. J. Forgue, ed., *Letters of H. L. Mencken* (New York: Knopf, 1961), p. 352; *Common Sense,* 1 (December 5, 1932), 5.

32. Walter Lippmann, *Interpretations 1933–1935,* ed. Allan Nevins (New York: Macmillan, 1936), pp. 17–18.

33. White to Ickes, May 23, 1933, Roosevelt Papers, PPF 1196; White to Howe, November 27, 1933, *Selected Letters of William Allen White,* p. 339.

34. *PPAFDR,* II, 11, 14–16.

35. Moley, *After Seven Years,* p. 191; Leuchtenburg, "The New Deal and the Analogue of War," pp. 105ff.

36. Charles Beard and George Smith, *The Future Comes* (New York: Macmillan, 1934), p. 165.

37. Anderson letter, October 8, 1933, quoted in William E. Leuchtenburg, *Franklin D. Roosevelt and the New Deal* (New York: Harper and Row, 1963), pp. 63–64. See also Mario Einaudi, *The Roosevelt Revolution* (New York: Harcourt, Brace, 1959), pp. 134ff.

38. John Hope Franklin, *From Slavery to Freedom* (New York: Knopf, 1947), pp. 519–522; Arthur M. Schlesinger, Jr., *The Politics of Upheaval* (Boston: Houghton Mifflin, 1960), pp. 425–438.

39. Arthur M. Schlesinger, Jr., *The Coming of the New Deal* (Boston: Houghton Mifflin, 1958), p. 19; Link, *American Epoch,* p. 440.

40. April 13, 1933, *The Secret Diary of Harold L. Ickes: The First Thousand Days, 1933–1936* (New York: Simon and Schuster, 1953), pp. 20–21.

41. Schlesinger, *Coming of the New Deal,* pp. 52–53; Earl Latham, *The Communist Controversy in Washington: From the New Deal to McCarthy* (Cambridge, Mass.: Harvard University Press, 1966), pp. 107ff.; Josephson, *Infidel in the Temple,* Chap. 13; Richard S. Kirkendall, *Social Scientists and Farm Politics in the Age of Roosevelt* (Columbia: University of Missouri Press, 1966), *passim.*

42. Lewis Coser, *Men of Ideas* (New York: Free Press, 1965), pp. 180ff.; Leo Gurko, *Heroes, Highbrows and the Popular Mind* (Indianapolis: Bobbs-Merrill, 1953), pp. 284–285.

43. *Vital Speeches,* II (July 1, 1936), 604.

44. FDR Press Conference no. 44, August 16, 1933, in T. H. Greer, *What Roosevelt Thought* (East Lansing: Michigan State University Press, 1958), p. 144; *PPAFDR,* IV, 282–287; v, 80–84.

45. American Association of University Professors, *Depression, Recovery and Higher Education* (New York: McGraw-Hill, 1937), Chap. 14; James Wechsler, *Revolt on the Campus* (New York: Covici, Friede, 1935), *passim;* Wechsler, *The Age of Suspicion* (New York: Random House, 1953), p. 20; "Youth in College," *Fortune Magazine,* XIII (June 1936), 99–102, 155ff.

46. *PPAFDR,* II, 139; Conkin, *New Deal,* p. 16; Allen to his sister, October 28, 1934, Frederick Lewis Allen Papers.

47. *PPAFDR,* II, 246, 301–302. See also Elisha Hanson, "Official Propaganda

and the New Deal," *Annals of the American Academy of Political and Social Science*, CLXXIX (May 1935), 176–186.

48. *PPAFDR*, II, 122. See also Arthur A. Ekirch, Jr., *The Civilian and the Military* (New York: Oxford, 1956), p. 239; Leuchtenburg, "The New Deal and the Analogue of War," p. 139; John A. Salmond, *The Civilian Conservation Corps, 1933–1942: A New Deal Case Study* (Durham: Duke University Press, 1967), pp. 84–87, 116–120, 221.

49. Leuchtenburg, "The New Deal and the Analogue of War," p. 124.

50. *PPAFDR*, III, 375; Burns, *Roosevelt: The Lion and the Fox*, p. 184.

51. See E. P. Herring, *Public Administration and the Public Interest* (New York: McGraw-Hill, 1936), Chap. 1 and *passim*; T. P. Jenkin, *Reactions of Major Groups to Positive Government in the United States, 1930–1940* (Berkeley: University of California Press, 1945), Chap. 2; Eric Goldman, *Rendezvous with Destiny* (New York: Knopf, 1952), pp. 328ff.

52. *PPAFDR*, III, 124, 198; IV, 405; V, 16.

53. Ford to Adams, August 6, 20, 1933, Adams Papers; White to Nevins, May 24, 1934, *Selected Letters of William Allen White*, pp. 344–345; Adams to FDR, October 31, 1934, Roosevelt Papers, PPF 2439. See also James Truslow Adams, "Rights Without Duties," *Yale Review*, XXIV (December 1934), 237–250.

54. Mauritz A. Hallgren, *The Gay Reformer: Profits before Plenty under Franklin D. Roosevelt* (New York: Knopf, 1935), p. 287; Steffens to Frederic C. Howe, September 16, 1934, in Winter and Hicks, *Letters of Lincoln Steffens*, II, 997; Mencken to Ben W. Huebsch, January 28, 1935, *Letters of H. L. Mencken*, p. 387.

55. Shannon, *Socialist Party of America*, pp. 229, 235.

CHAPTER FOUR: *Toward a New Public Philosophy*

1. Alfred Kazin, *On Native Grounds* (New York: Reynal and Hitchcock, 1942), p. 363.

2. Chase, *Economy of Abundance*, p. 261; and Chase, *Government in Business* (New York: Macmillan, 1935), p. 2; *Nation*, CXXXIX (October 31, 1934), 494–495. See also E. O. Golob, *The "Isms": A History and Evaluation* (New York: Harper, 1954), pp. 126ff.; Lloyd C. Gardner, *Economic Aspects of New Deal Diplomacy* (Madison: University of Wisconsin Press, 1964), pp. 98ff.

3. Richard Hofstadter, *The Age of Reform* (New York: Knopf, 1955), pp. 305–306.

4. Beard and Beard, *America in Midpassage*, I, 253.

5. See Russell Lord, *The Wallaces of Iowa* (Boston: Houghton Mifflin, 1947), *passim*.

6. *PPAFDR*, II, 74.

7. Henry A. Wallace, *New Frontiers* (New York: Reynal and Hitchcock, 1934), pp. 11, 134, 151.

8. *Ibid.*, pp. 21, 226.
9. *Ibid.*, pp. 21, 28–29, 32, 128.
10. Wallace, *America Must Choose* (New York: Foreign Policy Association; Boston: World Peace Foundation, 1934), pp. 15, 19, 31.
11. Wallace, *New Frontiers*, pp. 274, 286.
12. *Nation*, cxxiv (April 6, 1927), 364–367.
13. "After the New Deal," *New Republic*, xcix (July 26, 1939), 323–325.
14. Rexford G. Tugwell, *The Battle for Democracy* (New York: Columbia University Press, 1935), pp. 91–92, 95–96, 266–267.
15. Schlesinger, *Coming of the New Deal*, p. 369.
16. John Crowe Ransom, *et al.*, *I'll Take My Stand—The South and the Agrarian Tradition* (New York: Harper, 1930), p. xxi; Pieter W. Fosburgh, *The Natural Thing: The Land and Its Citizens* (New York: Macmillan, 1959), pp. 19–20; Paul Conkin, *Tomorrow a New World: The New Deal Community Program* (Ithaca: Cornell University Press, 1959), Chaps. 1–3.
17. Conkin, *Tomorrow a New World*, p. 6, Chap. 7. See also Grant McConnell, *The Decline of Agrarian Democracy* (Berkeley: University of California Press, 1953), *passim*.
18. See A. H. Dupree, *Science in the Federal Government* (Cambridge, Mass.: Harvard University Press, 1957), pp. 354ff.; Louis Brownlow, *A Passion for Anonymity* (Chicago: University of Chicago Press, 1958), pp. 284–285; Barry Karl, *Executive Reorganization and Reform in the New Deal* (Cambridge, Mass.: Harvard University Press, 1963), Chap. 2.
19. *PPAFDR*, ii, 122. See also Stuart Chase, *Rich Land Poor Land* (New York: McGraw-Hill, 1936), *passim*.
20. David E. Lilienthal, *TVA: Democracy on the March* (New York: Harper, 1944), pp. 6, 142, 146, 196. See also Lilienthal, *This I Do Believe* (New York: Harper, 1949), Chap. 8.
21. Rexford G. Tugwell and Edward C. Banfield, "Grass Roots Democracy —Myth or Reality," *Public Administration Review*, x (Winter 1950), 49.
22. A. M. Bingham, *Man's Estate: Adventures in Economic Discovery* (New York: Norton, 1939), pp. 31ff.
23. *Common Sense*, i (December 5, 1932; April 27, May 11, June 8, 1933), 2, 18, 8–9, 15.
24. *Ibid.*, i (March 30, 1933), 3–5; Bingham, *Insurgent America: Revolt of the Middle-Classes* (New York: Harper, 1935), p. 47.
25. *Ibid.*, pp. 73, 211, 226–227.
26. *Common Sense*, v (October 1936), 3.
27. John Dewey, *The Quest for Certainty: A Study of the Relation of Knowledge and Action* (New York: Minton, Balch, 1929), pp. 244, 282–283.
28. Dewey, *Individualism Old and New*, pp. 28, 35–36, 52, 54, 142.
29. Dewey in A. M. Bingham and Selden Rodman, *Challenge to the New Deal* (New York: Falcon, 1934), p. vi; Dewey, *Liberalism and Social Action* (New York: Putnam, 1935), pp. 54, 90.

30. Dewey, "The Future of Liberalism," *Journal of Philosophy*, XXXII (April 1935), 225–230.
31. Beard in J. B. Bury, *The Idea of Progress* (New York: Macmillan, 1932), pp. xxii–xxiii. See also Howard K. Beale, *et al.*, *Charles A. Beard: An Appraisal* (Lexington: University of Kentucky Press, 1954), p. 157; Cushing Strout, *The Pragmatic Revolt in American History* (New Haven: Yale University Press, 1958), Chap. 7.
32. Charles A. Beard, *The Open Door at Home: A Trial Philosophy of National Interest* (New York: Macmillan, 1934), pp. 131, 319. See also Bernard C. Borning, *The Political and Social Thought of Charles A. Beard* (Seattle: University of Washington Press, 1962), pp. 194–196.
33. Beard, *et al.*, *Conclusions and Recommendations of the American Historical Association Commission on the Social Studies in the Schools* (New York: Scribner's, 1934), pp. 16, 37. See also George S. Counts, *The Social Foundations of Education* (New York: Scribner's, 1934), pp. 531, 548; Harry D. Gideonse, "Nationalist Collectivism and Charles A. Beard," *Journal of Political Economy*, XLIII (December 1935), 778–799.
34. Beard, "America Must Stay Big," *Today* (September 14, 1935), pp. 3–4, 21; Beard, "National Politics and War," *Scribner's Magazine*, XCVII (February 1935), 66–70; Beard to Moley, May 18, 1935, Roosevelt Papers, PPF 743.
35. Beard and George H. E. Smith, *The Old Deal and the New* (New York: Macmillan, 1940), pp. 120–121, 150–151, 231, 282.
36. Thurman W. Arnold, *The Symbols of Government* (New Haven: Yale University Press, 1935), pp. 5, 21–22, 105, 125. See also Hofstadter, *Age of Reform*, p. 321.
37. Arnold, *Symbols of Government*, pp. 270–271.
38. Arnold, *The Folklore of Capitalism* (New Haven: Yale University Press, 1937), pp. iii, 90, 356, 387, 393.
39. *Ibid.*, pp. 81–82.
40. *Ibid.*, p. 211.
41. See A. T. Mason, *Brandeis: A Free Man's Life* (New York: Viking, 1946), Chap. 39; Alfred Lief, ed., *The Brandeis Guide to the Modern World* (Boston: Little, Brown, 1941), *passim;* and the comments, critical of bigness, by Marquis Childs in his book, much admired in New Deal circles, *Sweden: The Middle Way* (New Haven: Yale University Press, 1936), pp. xi–xii.
42. *PPAFDR*, VII, 305ff.
43. "Investigation of Concentration of Economic Power," *Senate Doc. No. 35*, 77th Cong., 1st Sess. (Washington: Government Printing Office, 1941), p. 7. See also David Lynch, *The Concentration of Economic Power* (New York: Columbia University Press, 1946), pp. 5, 362ff.; Ellis W. Hawley, *The New Deal and the Problem of Monopoly* (Princeton: Princeton University Press, 1966), *passim.*
44. Gene M. Gressley, "Thurman Arnold, Antitrust, and the New Deal," *Business History Review*, XXXVIII (Summer 1964), 230; Arnold, "How Far Should Government Control Business?," *Vital Speeches*, V (March

1, 1939), 290–292; Arnold, "Must 1929 Repeat Itself?", *Harvard Business Review*, xxvi (January 1948), 43; Arnold, *Fair Rights and Foul: A Dissenting Lawyer's Life* (New York: Harcourt, Brace and World, 1965), p. 138.

45. Richberg quoted in Gressley, "Thurman Arnold," p. 220; Schlesinger, *Politics of Upheaval*, p. 390; Sternsher, *Rexford Tugwell and the New Deal*, p. 133.

46. Burns, *Roosevelt: The Lion and the Fox*, p. 331.

47. Seymour Harris, *John Maynard Keynes: Economist and Policy Maker* (New York: Scribner's, 1955), pp. 106, 191–196; Robert Lekachman, *The Age of Keynes* (New York: Random House, 1966), Chap. 5. On Laski's influence see Schlesinger, *Politics of Upheaval*, pp. 170ff., and the many Laski letters to FDR from 1935 on in the Roosevelt Papers, PPF 3014, with copies of more Laski letters to FDR in the Felix Frankfurter Papers, General Correspondence Box 34.

48. *New Republic*, ciii (July 29, 1940), 158.

Chapter Five: *Life Can Be Beautiful*

1. George Biddle, *An American Artist's Story* (Boston: Little, Brown, 1939), p. 268 and *passim*.

2. Ray A. Billington, "Government and the Arts: The W.P.A. Experience," *American Quarterly*, xiii (Winter 1961), 468. See also Lillian B. Miller, *Patrons and Patriotism: The Encouragement of the Fine Arts in the United States, 1790–1860* (Chicago: University of Chicago Press, 1966), Part II and *passim*.

3. Transcript of press release, November 29, 1933, Entry 109, Folder A, Miscellaneous Central Office Files of the Public Works of Art Project (PWAP), National Archives (NA), Record Group (RG) 121. Hereafter cited in abbreviated form.

4. See B. R. Contreras, "The New Deal Treasury Department Art Programs and the American Artist: 1933 to 1943" (unpublished Ph.D. dissertation, American University, 1967), Chap. 1; "Preliminary Inventory of the Records of the Public Buildings Service," comp. W. L. Van Neste and V. E. Baugh (mimeographed, Washington: National Archives, 1958), pp. 28ff.

5. Kimball to the Secretary of the Treasury, February 23, 1934, Entry 108, Folder K, Central Office Correspondence with Artists, PWAP, NA, RG 121; newspaper clippings, March 1934, Entry 111, *ibid*.

6. *American Magazine of Art*, xxvii (January, March, 1934), 6–9, 113–115; Personal File of Forbes Watson, Entry 105, Central File of the Advisory Committee, PWAP, NA, RG 121; Edholm to President Roosevelt, April 12, 1934, Entry 109, Folder B, Miscellaneous Central Office Files, *ibid*. See also the artists' letters quoted in Contreras, "The New Deal Treasury Department Art Programs," pp. 26–28.

7. Grace Overmyer, *Government and the Arts* (New York: Norton,

1939), p. 95; John Morton Blum, *From the Morgenthau Diaries: Years of Crisis, 1928–1938* (Boston: Houghton Mifflin, 1959), pp. 91–93.

8. FDR Memo for M. McIntyre, May 15, 1934, Art and Artists Box 1, Roosevelt Papers, POF 954; George Biddle, "A Conversation with President Roosevelt," typescript of an informal interview in 1936, *ibid.*, POF 954; "Preliminary Inventory of the Records of the Public Building Service," pp. 32–33.

9. Biddle, *American Artist's Story*, pp. 276–278.

10. For the public notice in regard to FDR's reaction to an exhibition of the PWAP at the Corcoran Gallery in Washington in the spring of 1934, and in regard to the Cadmus painting at the show, see newspaper clippings, April 1934, Entry 110, Folder A, PWAP, NA, RG 121; Contreras, "The New Deal Treasury Department Art Programs," pp. 71ff.

11. Memo to the Secretary of the Treasury from the Section of Painting and Sculpture, December 19, 1935, Entry 119, Box 7, Central Office Correspondence, PWAP, NA, RG 121; Contreras, "The New Deal Treasury Department Art Programs," pp. 188ff; Benton to Bruce, April 24, 1939, Entry 124, Box 132, Correspondence of Edward Bruce, PWAP, NA, RG 121.

12. For commentaries with profuse illustrations see Edward Bruce and Forbes Watson, *Art in Federal Buildings* (Washington: Art in Federal Buildings, Inc., 1936); Contreras, "The New Deal Treasury Department Art Programs," Chap. 4.

13. Edward Bruce, "Art and Democracy," *Atlantic Monthly*, CLVI (August 1935), 149–152.

14. John Dewey, *Art as Experience* (New York: Minton, Balch, 1934), pp. 3, 8–9, 15–16, 105. See also Jacques Barzun, *Of Human Freedom* (Boston: Little, Brown, 1939), Chap. 5.

15. Overmyer, *Government and the Arts*, Chap. 8; WPA, "Work Projects Administration: Record of Program," Vol. I, Art (bound volume of typed and mimeographed reports in the Search Room of the Library, National Archives), *passim.*

16. Holger Cahill, *New Horizons in American Art* (New York: Museum of Modern Art, 1936), *passim;* WPA, "Record of Program," Vol. I, Art, Exhibit B; *New Yorker*, XII (September 26, 1936), 30–34; Untermeyer to Cahill, October 28, 1936, Central Files Box 442, WPA, NA, RG 69.

17. Memo and Report from Holger Cahill to Mrs. Ellen S. Woodward, September 21, 1938, Central Files Box 431, WPA, NA, RG 69; Sheldon Cheney, "Art in the United States, 1938," in Harold Stearns, *America Now* (New York: Scribner's, 1938), pp. 95ff.; Erica Beckh, "Government Art in the Roosevelt Era," *Art Journal*, XX (Fall 1960), 2–8.

18. E. O. Christensen, *The Index of American Design* (New York: Macmillan, 1950), *passim;* Mary Beard to T. C. Parker, July 29, 1937, Central Files Box 432, WPA, NA, RG 69; Constance Rourke to T. C. Parker, August 25, 1937, Central Files Box 441, *ibid.;* FDR to Florence Kerr, November 22, 1941, General Correspondence, WPA, NA, RG 69.

19. *New Republic*, LXXXIX (December 30, 1936), 265.
20. Cahill to Stuart Davis, April 13, 1937, Central Files Box 431, WPA, NA, RG 69; Arthur Emptage to FDR and Harry Hopkins, November 28, 1938, *ibid.*
21. House Committee on Patents, "Department of Science, Art and Literature," *Hearings*, 75th Cong., 3rd Sess. (Washington: Government Printing Office, 1938), pp. 76–77, 87ff; FDR to Claude Pepper, July 31, 1939, Roosevelt Papers, POF 1630.
22. *Magazine of Art*, XXXI (March 1938), 156–157, 186ff.; George Biddle, "Art Under Five Years of Federal Patronage," *American Scholar*, IX (Summer 1940), 327–338.
23. House Committee on Patents, "Department of Science, Art and Literature," pp. 71–73.
24. Bruce to Florence Kerr, June 11, 1940, Entry 124, Box 146, Correspondence of Edward Bruce, PWAP, NA, RG 121; Art Program Exhibitions, General Correspondence Box 450, WPA, NA, RG 69; Contreras, "The New Deal Treasury Department Art Programs," Chap. 9.
25. A recent thorough history is Jane D. Mathews, *The Federal Theatre, 1935–1939* (Princeton: Princeton University Press, 1967).
26. Willson Whitman, *Bread and Circuses* (New York: Oxford, 1937), p. 9; Hallie Flanagan, *Arena* (New York: Duell, Sloan and Pearce, 1940), pp. 3ff., 16.
27. *New York Times*, Drama Section (January 5, 1936), p. 1.
28. Flanagan to K. E. Lowe, October 3, 1935, General Correspondence Box 398, WPA, NA, RG 69; Flanagan to Harry Hopkins, December 23, 1935, General Correspondence Box 391, *ibid.*; "Letter to Regional Directors," December 24, 1935, General Correspondence Box 395, *ibid.*
29. Hallie Flanagan, "Summary of Federal Theatre Activities to September 1938," a Report to Harry Hopkins, mimeographed, September 9, 1938. See also C. J. Wittler, *Some Social Trends in WPA Drama* (Washington: Catholic University of America Press, 1939), Chap. 2.
30. Summaries of press opinion, General Correspondence Box 385, WPA, NA, RG 69.
31. Joan Peyser, "The Troubled Time of Marc Blitzstein," *Columbia University Forum*, IX (Winter 1966), 34; John O. Hunter, "Marc Blitzstein's 'The Cradle Will Rock' as a Document of America, 1937," *American Quarterly*, XVIII (Summer 1966), 227–233. See also MacLeish to Harry Hopkins, June 25, 1937, General Correspondence Box 398, WPA, NA, RG 69.
32. See the contemporary accounts by Irving Kolodin, "Footlights Federal Style: The Astonishing Story of the Federal Theater," *Harper's Magazine*, CLXXIII (November 1936), 621–631; and Lawrence Langner, "The Future of the Government in the Theatre," *Yale Review*, XXVII (September 1937), 64–76. O'Neill to Hallie Flanagan, April 26, 1937, General Correspondence Box 403, WPA, NA, RG 69.
33. *New York Times Magazine* (November 22, 1936), p. 6; *Fortune*, XV (May 1937), 109–117, 168ff.
34. Howard to Hallie Flanagan, October 25, 1935, General Correspondence

Box 394, WPA, NA, RG 69; *Stage,* xiv (December 1936), 78, in Max Lerner, *Ideas Are Weapons* (New York: Viking, 1939), p. 283.

35. *New York Times,* Drama Section (May 28, 1939), p. 1.
36. Wecter, *Age of the Great Depression,* p. 264; Mathews, *Federal Theatre,* Chaps. 5–6.
37. Flanagan to Vito Marcantonio, June 30, 1939, General Correspondence Box 398, WPA, NA, RG 69; Flanagan, *Arena,* pp. 334–335, 372.
38. See also the appraisal in Mathews, *Federal Theatre,* Chap. 7 and *passim.*
39. Deems Taylor, "Music," in Stearns, *America Now,* pp. 64–65.
40. Nikolai Sokoloff, *The Federal Music Project* (Washington: Government Printing Office, 1936), *passim.*
41. Lewis to Rowan, September 4, 1934, Entry 107, Correspondence of Edward P. Rowan, pwap, NA, RG 121; Wecter, *Age of the Great Depression,* p. 260.
42. MacLeish to Rowan [September 1934], Entry 107, Correspondence of Edward P. Rowan, pwap, NA, RG 121.
43. August to September 1934, *ibid.*
44. Notes and plans for the American Guide Series, General Correspondence File of the Writers' Program, Box 460, WPA, NA, RG 69; D. M. Fox, "The Achievement of the Federal Writers' Project," *American Quarterly,* xiii (Spring 1961), 3–19; C. I. Glicksberg, "The Federal Writers' Project," *South Atlantic Quarterly,* xxxvii (April 1938), 157–169.
45. Brooks to Henry G. Alsberg, September 18, 1938, General Correspondence File Box 461, WPA, NA, RG 69.
46. N. R. Yetman, "The Background of the Slave Narrative Collection," *American Quarterly,* xix (Fall 1967), 534–553; Charles Beard, Dixon Ryan Fox, *et al.,* in Endorsement Letters 1939, Historical Records Survey Box 266, WPA, NA, RG 69. See also file of correspondence from Henry Steele Commager to Luther Evans, Historical Records Survey, General Project Correspondence Box 78, WPA, NA, RG 69.
47. R. C. Binkley, "The Cultural Program of the W. P. A.," *Harvard Educational Review,* ix (March 1939), 156–174.
48. Billington, "Government and the Arts," p. 475; M. S. Ulrich, "Salvaging Culture for the WPA," *Harper's Magazine,* clxxviii (May 1939), 653–664.
49. Billington, "Government and the Arts," p. 479.
50. Biddle to FDR, December 11, 1933, Roosevelt Papers, POF 954.
51. Gilbert Seldes, *The Movies Come from America* (New York: Scribner's, 1937), p. 14. See also Edgar Dale, *The Content of Motion Pictures* (New York: Macmillan, 1935), *passim.*
52. *Magazine of Art,* xxxi (July 1938), 387.
53. See W. B. Rideout, *The Radical Novel in the United States* (Cambridge, Mass.: Harvard University Press, 1956); H. E. Luccock, *American Mirror: Social, Ethical and Religious Aspects of American Literature, 1930–1940* (New York: Macmillan, 1940).
54. Henry Hart, ed., *American Writers' Congress* (New York: International, 1935); V. F. Calverton, *The Liberation of American Literature* (New York: Scribner's, 1932); Alfred Kazin, *On Native Grounds*

(New York: Reynal and Hitchcock, 1942), Chap. 16; Gellhorn to Flanagan, November 14, 1936, General Correspondence Box 393, WPA, NA, RG 69.

55. See Malcolm Cowley, "A Farewell to the 1930's," *New Republic*, CI (November 8, 1939), 42–44; Harold Clurman, *The Fervent Years: The Story of the Group Theatre and the Thirties* (New York: Knopf, 1945), pp. 142ff.; William Phillips, "What Happened in the 30's," *Commentary*, XXXIV (September 1962), 204–212; Granville Hicks, "The Thirties: A Reappraisal," *Saturday Review*, XLVI (May 4, 1963), 27–28.

CHAPTER SIX: *A Chorus of Dissent*

1. Henry Steele Commager, *The American Mind* (New Haven: Yale University Press, 1950), p. 354. See also Edgar E. Robinson, *The Roosevelt Leadership, 1933–1945* (Philadelphia: Lippincott, 1955), p. 189.
2. See Otis L. Graham, Jr., *An Encore for Reform: The Old Progressives and the New Deal* (New York: Oxford, 1967), Chap. 2, Appendix I; Hofstadter, *Age of Reform*, p. 315; R. B. Nye, *Midwestern Progressive Politics* (East Lansing: Michigan State College Press, 1951), pp. 358, 382.
3. *Modern Monthly*, VII (February 1933), 5–6, 27–32; *ibid.*, VIII (March 1934), 87–92.
4. Lewis Corey, *The Crisis of the Middle Class* (New York: Covici, Friede, 1935), p. 365.
5. Jerome Davis, *Capitalism and Its Culture* (New York: Farrar and Rinehart, 1935), pp. 509, 513ff.
6. *Modern Monthly*, VII (June 1933), 261–265; *Harper's Magazine*, CLXVIII (January 1934), 121–133; *ibid.*, CLXX (December 1934), 3–13. See also Louis M. Hacker, *American Problems of Today* (New York: Crofts, 1939), pp. 277–278.
7. Harold J. Laski, *The State in Theory and Practice* (New York: Viking, 1935), pp. 110–111, 165; *New Republic*, LXXXIII (June 12, 1935), 116–118. See also Laski, *Democracy in Crisis* (Chapel Hill: University of North Carolina Press, 1933); and his "The Crisis in the Theory of the State," in *Law: A Century of Progress, 1835–1935* (New York: New York University Press, 1937), I, 1–31; Henry Pelling, *America and the British Left* (New York: New York University Press, 1957), Chap. 8.
8. Benjamin Stolberg and W. J. Vinton, *The Economic Consequences of the New Deal* (New York: Harcourt, Brace, 1935), pp. 7, 12, 80, 85.
9. H. W. Laidler, *Socializing Our Democracy* (New York: Harper, 1935), p. 115; Shannon, *Socialist Party of America*, pp. 228ff.; Fairchild to Thomas, February 28, 1933, Norman Thomas Papers.
10. Quoted in Shannon, *Socialist Party of America*, p. 229.
11. See M. S. Venkataramani, "Norman Thomas, Arkansas Sharecroppers, and the Roosevelt Agricultural Policies, 1933–1937," *Mississippi Valley Historical Review*, XLVII (September 1960), 225–246; D. E. Conrad, *The Forgotten Farmers: The Story of the Sharecroppers in the New Deal*

(Urbana: University of Illinois Press, 1965), Chap. 9; Gunnar Myrdal, *An American Dilemma* (New York: Harper, 1944), pp. 256–258, 343ff.; Franklin, *From Slavery to Freedom*, pp. 522ff.; F. L. Broderick and August Meier, *Negro Protest Thought in the Twentieth Century* (Indianapolis: Bobbs-Merrill, 1966), Part III.

12. Norman Thomas, *The Choice Before Us: Mankind at the Crossroads* (New York: Macmillan, 1934), pp. 83, 96, 127. See also Thomas, *After the New Deal, What?* (New York: Macmillan, 1936), p. 142.

13. Shannon, *Socialist Party of America*, p. 233; Willard M. Kiplinger to Thomas, June 14, 1933, and Thomas to Kiplinger, June 16, 1933, Thomas Papers.

14. Broadus Mitchell, *Depression Decade* (New York: Rinehart, 1947), Appendix pp. 438–453, has useful statistical data; Schlesinger, *Politics of Upheaval*, p. 3.

15. See Nye, *Midwestern Progressive Politics*, pp. 358–382; McCoy, *Angry Voices, passim;* and the retrospective reflections by some of the participants in these movements in R. J. Simon, ed., *As We Saw the Thirties* (Urbana: University of Illinois Press, 1967), *passim.*

16. Thomas to Upton Sinclair, September 27, 1933, Thomas Papers.

17. Charles E. Coughlin to Thomas, May 11, 1934; May 31, 1935, Thomas Papers.

18. *Current History*, XXXVIII (September 1933), 701–704; Mauritz A. Hallgren to Calverton, September 4, 1933, V. F. Calverton Papers.

19. Raymond Gram Swing, *Forerunners of American Fascism* (New York: Messner, 1935), pp. 14ff.

20. Lawrence Dennis, *The Coming American Fascism* (New York: Harper, 1936), pp. xi, 181.

21. See Frederick Rudolph, "The American Liberty League, 1934–1940," *American Historical Review*, LVI (October 1950), 19–33; R. E. Desvernine, *Democratic Despotism* (New York: Dodd, Mead, 1936), *passim.*

22. Quoted in George Wolfskill, *The Revolt of the Conservatives: A History of the American Liberty League, 1934–1940* (Boston: Houghton Mifflin, 1962), p. 30.

23. *Memoirs of Herbert Hoover: The Great Depression, 1929–1941*, pp. 454–455; *New York Times*, August 30, 1934, in Rudolph, "The American Liberty League," p. 26 fn. 22.

24. A. T. Mason, *Harlan Fiske Stone* (New York: Viking, 1956), pp. 370, 374.

25. Herbert Hoover, *The Challenge to Liberty* (New York: Scribner's, 1934), pp. 126ff. See also Hoover to White, September 12, 1934, Selected Correspondence, 1897–1942, William Allen White Papers; and Lewis W. Douglas, *The Liberal Tradition* (New York: Van Nostrand, 1935); Ogden L. Mills, *Liberalism Fights On* (New York: Macmillan, 1936).

26. Albert Jay Nock, *Journal of Forgotten Days* (Hinsdale: Regnery, 1948), p. 33; Nock, "Officialism and Lawlessness," *Harper's Magazine*, CLX (December 1929), 11–19; Nock, *A Journal of These Days* (New York: Morrow, 1934), pp. 111–112; *Letters from Albert Jay Nock, 1924–1945* (Caldwell: Caxton, 1949), p. 56.

27. Nock, *Our Enemy, the State* (New York: Morrow, 1935), pp. 205–206. See also R. M. Crunden, *The Mind and Art of Albert Jay Nock* (Chicago: Regnery, 1964), Chaps. 10–11.

28. Walter Lippmann, *The Method of Freedom* (New York: Macmillan, 1934), pp. 25ff.; Walter Johnson, *William Allen White's America* (New York: Holt, 1947), pp. 445–446; Pinchot to Roy Howard, May 21, 1936, General Correspondence Box 58, Amos Pinchot Papers; James Truslow Adams, "Planned Economy: Is It for Us?," *New York Times Magazine* (September 30, 1934), pp. 1–2, 16.

29. Holmes to Pinchot, October 20, 1936; December 30, 1937, General Correspondence Box 59, 61, Pinchot Papers; Jerold S. Auerbach, *Labor and Liberty: The La Follette Committee and the New Deal* (Indianapolis: Bobbs-Merrill, 1966), pp. 25, 215.

30. See, for example, H. M. Kallen, *A Free Society* (New York: Ballou, 1934); B. S. Morgan, *Individuality in a Collective World* (New York: Norton, 1935); T. V. Smith, *The Promise of American Politics* (Chicago: University of Chicago Press, 1936), *passim*.

31. Joseph Wood Krutch, *Was Europe A Success?* (New York: Farrar and Rinehart, 1934), p. 47.

32. Stephen Early Memo for FDR, April 23, 1936, Roosevelt Papers, PPF 41. See also Schlesinger, *Politics of Upheaval*, p. 575.

33. Richberg to FDR, December 28, 1936, Roosevelt Papers, PPF 2418; Henry A. Wallace, *Whose Constitution: An Inquiry into the General Welfare* (New York: Reynal and Hitchcock, 1936), pp. 323–324.

34. Burns, *Roosevelt: The Lion and the Fox*, p. 291.

35. *PPAFDR*, VI, 1–6.

36. Callender to Adams, January 16, 1937, Adams Papers.

37. Mason, *Brandeis: A Free Man's Life*, pp. 624ff.; Wheeler to Thomas, March 8, 1937, Thomas Papers.

38. Dorothy Thompson, *Essentials of Democracy* (New York: Town Hall, 1938), *passim*; Villard to William T. Evjue, August 8, 1937, Villard Papers.

39. "Report to All Financial Supporters by Frank E. Gannett," printed flier, 1938, in Adams Papers; Gannett to Adams, April 12, 1938, *ibid.*; Gannett to Villard, September 19, 1938, Villard Papers; S. T. Williamson, *Imprint of a Publisher: The Story of Frank Gannett* (New York: McBride, 1948), Chap. 22. See also Brownlow, *Passion for Anonymity*, Chaps. 31, 33; Karl, *Executive Reorganization and Reform in the New Deal*, Chaps. 5–6; Richard Polenberg, *Reorganizing Roosevelt's Government: The Controversy over Executive Reorganization, 1936–1939* (Cambridge, Mass.: Harvard University Press, 1966), *passim*; Clinton Rossiter, *The American Presidency* (New York: Harcourt, Brace, 1956), pp. 98ff.

40. Lippmann to FDR, June 4, 1935, Roosevelt Papers, PPF 2037.

41. Syndicated newspaper column, February 4, 1937, quoted in Walter Lippmann, *The Supreme Court: Independent or Controlled?* (New York: Harper, 1937), pp. 1–4.

42. *Ibid.*, pp. 5–9, 19.

43. *Ibid.*, pp. 55–56.
44. Walter Lippmann, *An Inquiry into the Principles of the Good Society* (Boston: Little, Brown, 1937), pp. ix–xiii, 8ff., 89, 103, 315fn. See also D. E. Weingast, *Walter Lippmann: A Study in Personal Journalism* (New Brunswick: Rutgers University Press, 1949), Chaps. 3–4; W. I. Giles, "The Contribution of Walter Lippmann to American Political Thought" (unpublished M.A. thesis, Georgetown University, 1945), pp. 36ff.
45. Maxwell Anderson, *Knickerbocker Holiday* (Washington: Anderson House, 1938), p. v; Allan Nevins to Adams, October 11, 1937, Adams Papers. See Rudolph Rocker, *Nationalism and Culture* (New York: Covici, Friede, 1937); S. McKee Rosen, *Modern Individualism* (New York: Harper, 1937); M. C. Swabey, *Theory of the Democratic State* (Cambridge, Mass.: Harvard University Press, 1937); Adolph Löwe, *The Price of Liberty* (London: Hogarth, 1937).
46. Max Lerner, *Ideas Are Weapons* (New York: Viking, 1939), pp. 469–470, 477. See also Edward S. Corwin, *Court over Constitution: A Study of Judicial Review as an Instrument of Popular Government* (Princeton: Princeton University Press, 1938).
47. Burns, *Roosevelt: The Lion and the Fox*, p. 315; E. David Cronon, *Twentieth Century America* (Homewood: Dorsey, 1965–1966), II, 184. See also James T. Patterson, *Congressional Conservatism and the New Deal* (Lexington: University of Kentucky Press, 1967), Chap. 3 and *passim*; Leonard Baker, *Back to Back: The Duel between FDR and the Supreme Court* (New York: Macmillan, 1967), *passim*.
48. See C. Herman Pritchett, *The Roosevelt Court: A Study in Judicial Politics and Values, 1937–1947* (New York: Macmillan, 1948), Chap. 4 and *passim*.
49. John Dewey, *Freedom and Culture* (New York: Putnam, 1939), pp. 34–35, 49, 175. See also Dewey, *Intelligence in the Modern World*, ed. Joseph Ratner (New York: Modern Library, 1939), pp. 416–433.
50. Mauritz A. Hallgren, *Landscape of Freedom* (New York: Howell, Soskin, 1941), p. 426.
51. Edgar Kemler, *The Deflation of American Ideals* (Washington: Public Affairs, 1941), pp. 6, 71.
52. *Ibid.*, pp. 74, 130.

CHAPTER SEVEN: *War and the Intellectuals*

1. Ernest K. Lindley, *Half Way with Roosevelt* (New York: Viking, 1936), p. 282.
2. Robert H. Ferrell, *American Diplomacy in the Great Depression* (New Haven: Yale University Press, 1957), Chap. 1.
3. Thomas A. Bailey, *A Diplomatic History of the American People* (3rd ed., New York: Crofts, 1947), p. 733.
4. See Ekirch, *Civilian and the Military*, pp. 238–239.

5. *Annual Report of the Secretary of the Navy . . . 1933* (Washington: Government Printing Office, 1933), p. 2; George T. Davis, *A Navy Second to None: The Development of Modern American Naval Policy* (New York: Harcourt, Brace, 1940), pp. 358ff.; M. E. Woolley to FDR, February 2, 1934, Roosevelt Papers, PPF 537.

6. *PPAFDR*, v, 285–292.

7. Black to FDR, October 18, 1936, Roosevelt Papers, PPF 607; *PPAFDR*, v, 572–573.

8. Wilkins to FDR, May 15, 1934, Roosevelt Papers, PPF 1616.

9. See Charles Beard, *The Devil Theory of War* (New York: Vanguard, 1936), *passim;* Wayne Cole, *Senator Gerald P. Nye and American Foreign Relations* (Minneapolis: University of Minnesota Press, 1962), Chap. 5, pp. 95–96; John Wiltz, *In Search of Peace: The Senate Munitions Inquiry, 1934–36* (Baton Rouge: Louisiana State University Press, 1963), *passim;* Warren Cohen, *The American Revisionists* (Chicago: University of Chicago Press, 1966), *passim.*

10. Quoted in Beard and Beard, *America in Midpassage*, I, 480–481. See also Robert A. Divine, *The Illusion of Neutrality* (Chicago: University of Chicago Press, 1962), *passim.*

11. Moley to FDR, November 30, 1935, Roosevelt Papers, PPF 743.

12. See Hadley Cantril, *Public Opinion, 1935–1946* (Princeton: Princeton University Press, 1951), pp. 966ff.; Reinhold Niebuhr, "Pacifism Against the Wall," *American Scholar*, v (Spring 1936), 133–141; Ekirch, *Civilian and the Military*, p. 235.

13. Allen Dulles and H. F. Armstrong, *Can We Be Neutral?* (New York: Harper, 1936), pp. 6–7, 34. See also Phillips Bradley, *Can We Stay Out of War?* (New York: Norton, 1936), *passim.*

14. Cole, *Senator Gerald P. Nye*, pp. 111ff.; Manfred Jonas, *Isolationism in America, 1935–1941* (Ithaca: Cornell University Press, 1966), pp. 189ff.

15. Beard and Beard, *America in Midpassage*, I, 478–479.

16. See Allen Guttmann, *The Wound in the Heart: America and the Spanish Civil War* (New York: Free Press, 1962), *passim.*

17. Ernest Hemingway, "Notes on the Next War" (September 1935), in W. H. Cordell and K. C. Cordell, ed., *American Points of View* (New York: Doubleday, 1936), pp. 5–6, 8; Hemingway, "The Malady of Power" (November 1935), *ibid.*, p. 191; James J. Martin, *American Liberalism and World Politics, 1931–1941* (New York: Devin-Adair, 1964), I, xxiv–xxvi; II, 729–730. See also Aaron, *Writers on the Left, passim;* Josephson, *Infidel in the Temple*, Chap. 20.

18. Thomas, *After the New Deal, What?*, pp. 43, 45; John Nevin Sayre to Thomas, December 29, 1936, and Thomas to Sayre, December 30, 1936; Thomas to Holmes, January 19, 1937, Thomas Papers. See also Murray Seidler, *Norman Thomas: Respectable Rebel* (Syracuse: Syracuse University Press, 1961), pp. 203ff.

19. Thomas to FDR, June 9, 1937, Roosevelt Papers, PPF 4840. See also Jonas, *Isolationism in America*, pp. 186ff.

20. See Martin, *American Liberalism*, I, Chap. 17; Warren, *Liberals and Communism*, Chap. 7.

21. See Henry Hart, ed., *The Writer in a Changing World* (New York: Equinox, 1937), pp. 56ff., 69ff.; Cushing Strout, *The American Image of the Old World* (New York: Harper, 1963), pp. 201–202; Granville Hicks, *Part of the Truth* (New York: Harcourt, Brace and World, 1965), pp. 147–148.
22. See Cantril, *Public Opinion*, pp. 201, 966.
23. William L. Langer and S. Everett Gleason, *The Challenge to Isolation, 1937–1940* (New York: Harper, 1952), p. 18; *PPAFDR*, VI, 410–411.
24. See Martin, *American Liberalism*, II, Chap. 24.
25. Butler to FDR, August 15, 1936; October 6, 1937, Roosevelt Papers, PPF 445.
26. *Nation*, CXLIII (October 10, 1936), 420; Villard to FDR, August 18, November 14, 1936, Roosevelt Papers, PPF 2178.
27. Villard to FDR, August 31, October 6, 1937, Roosevelt Papers, PPF 2178; Villard to Frederick H. Allen, October 17, 1937, Villard Papers.
28. *PPAFDR*, V, 292; Charles Beard, *American Foreign Policy in the Making, 1932–1940* (New Haven: Yale University Press, 1946), Chap. 8 and *passim*.
29. Norman Thomas, "How Can We Escape War? Neutrality Plus Socialism," *Nation*, CXLV (December 25, 1937), 708.
30. *Nation*, CXLVI (February 12, 1938), 184; Villard to Senators La Follette, Nye, Wheeler, December 15, 1937, Villard Papers; Holmes to Pinchot, December 10, 30, 1937, General Correspondence Box 61, 65, Pinchot Papers; Nock to Ellen Winsor, March 24, 1938, *Letters from Albert Jay Nock, 1924–1945*, p. 103. *Harper's Magazine*, CLXXV–CLXXVII (July 1937; March, November, 1938), 113, 337, 657; Mauritz A. Hallgren, "War," in Stearns, *America Now*, p. 293; Nevins to Adams, March 20, 1938, Adams Papers.
31. Jerome Frank, *Save America First* (New York: Harper, 1938), pp. 89, 416.
32. Villard to FDR, October 5, 1938, Roosevelt Papers, PPF 2178; Adams to Charles Kingsley, October 4, 1938; Ford to Adams, November 11, 1938, Adams Papers.
33. See Harold Fields, *The Refugee in the United States* (New York: Oxford, 1938); M. R. Davie, *Refugees in America* (New York: Harper, 1947); Stephen Duggan and Betty Drury, *The Rescue of Science and Learning* (New York: Macmillan, 1948); D. P. Kent, *The Refugee Intellectual* (New York: Columbia University Press, 1953); Laura Fermi, *Illustrious Immigrants: The Intellectual Migration from Europe, 1930–41* (Chicago: University of Chicago Press, 1968), *passim*.
34. Eduard Beneš, *Democracy Today and Tomorrow* (New York: Macmillan, 1939), pp. 214ff.; Thomas Mann, *The Coming Victory of Democracy* (New York: Knopf, 1938), pp. 25–28.
35. Quoted in Ruth Benedict, *Race: Science and Politics* (New York: Modern Age, 1940), Appendix pp. 259–266.
36. Jacques Barzun, *Race: A Study in Modern Superstition* (New York: Harcourt, Brace, 1937), p. 299; Benedict, *Race*, pp. 152–153.
37. *The Journals of David E. Lilienthal* (New York: Harper and Row, 1964), I, 121; *New Republic*, XCVI (October 19, 1938), 294.

38. "To All Active Supporters of Democracy and Peace," letter to the editors, dated August 10, *Nation*, CXLIX (August 26, 1939), 228; Max Eastman, "Russia and the Socialist Ideal," *Harper's Magazine*, CLXXVI (March 1938), 374; Lillian Symes, "Communism Twenty Years After," *ibid.*, CLXXVII (June 1938), 86.

39. See Irving Howe and Lewis Coser, *The American Communist Party* (Boston: Beacon, 1957), Chaps. 7–8; Eugene Lyons, *The Red Decade* (Indianapolis: Bobbs-Merrill, 1941), Chaps. 18, 28.

40. Goldman, *Rendezvous with Destiny*, pp. 382–384; Charles A. Beard, *A Foreign Policy for America* (New York: Knopf, 1940), p. 9; Beard, "We're Blundering into War," *American Mercury*, XLVI (April 1939), 388–399; Mencken to Theodore Dreiser, April 8, 1939; Mencken to Ezra Pound, October 4, 1939, in Forgue, *Letters of H. L. Mencken*, pp. 431–432, 438.

41. *Partisan Review*, VI (Spring 1939), 3ff., 20.

42. A. M. Bingham, *Man's Estate* (New York: Norton, 1939), pp. 436–437; Bingham, *The United States of Europe* (New York: Duell, Sloan and Pearce, 1940), p. 323. See also D. C. Coyle, *The American Way* (New York: Harper, 1938); George Soule, *An Economic Constitution for Democracy* (New Haven: Yale University Press, 1939), *passim*.

43. Ferdinand Lundberg to Thomas, September 18, 1939, Thomas Papers; Thomas to FDR, September 23, October 8, 1939, Roosevelt Papers, PPF 4840; Thomas to FDR, June 24, 1940, *ibid.*, POF 133; Seidler, *Norman Thomas*, pp. 208–209.

44. *Nation*, CL (June 29, 1940), 782; Holmes to Villard, October 3, 1940; Villard to E. P. Adler, August 2, 1939; Villard to D. A. Bailey, June 23, 1941, Villard Papers; Colcord to Pinchot, November 15, 1941, General Correspondence Box 71, Pinchot Papers. See also Villard, *Fighting Years: Memoirs of a Liberal Editor* (New York: Harcourt, Brace, 1939), pp. 526ff.; Michael Wreszin, *Oswald Garrison Villard: Pacifist at War* (Bloomington: Indiana University Press, 1965), Chap. 15.

45. *Nation*, CXLIX (September 23, 1939), 307. *PPAFDR*, VIII, 518. See also Harold Lavine and James Wechsler, *War Propaganda and the United States* (New Haven: Yale University Press, 1940), *passim*.

46. Arthur H. Vandenberg, Jr., ed., *The Private Papers of Senator Vandenberg* (Boston: Houghton Mifflin, 1952), p. 8; Richard W. Leopold, *The Growth of American Foreign Policy* (New York: Knopf, 1962), p. 570; *New Republic*, CIV (March 31, 1941), 434.

47. White to Cordell Hull, November 9, 1939, Roosevelt Papers, PPF 1196; Josephus Daniels to White, November 17, 1939, Selected Correspondence Box 324, William Allen White Papers; Walter Johnson, *The Battle Against Isolation* (Chicago: University of Chicago Press, 1944), pp. 61, 87, 195ff.; Wayne Cole, *America First: The Battle Against Intervention, 1940–1941* (Madison: University of Wisconsin Press, 1953), pp. 89ff.; J. L. Morrison, *Josephus Daniels* (Chapel Hill: University of North Carolina Press, 1966), p. 217.

48. See Stephen Raushenbush, *The March of Fascism* (New Haven: Yale University Press, 1939), Chap. 1; H. B. Parkes, *Marxism: An Autopsy* (Boston: Houghton Mifflin, 1939), pp. 212–213; Peter Drucker, *The*

End of Economic Man (New York: John Day, 1939), pp. 22–23, 42ff., 129ff.; E. P. Herring, *The Impact of War* (New York: Farrar and Rinehart, 1941), *passim*.

49. James Burnham, *The Managerial Revolution* (New York: John Day, 1941), p. 153; Lawrence Dennis, *The Dynamics of War and Revolution* (New York: Weekly Foreign Letter, 1940), pp. xxvi, 250.

50. Dewey, *Freedom and Culture*, pp. 34–35, 175. See also Charles E. Merriam, *The New Democracy and the New Despotism* (New York: McGraw-Hill, 1939); James Feibleman, *Positive Democracy* (Chapel Hill: University of North Carolina Press, 1940); John Chamberlain, *The American Stakes* (New York: Carrick and Evans, 1940); T. V. Smith, *The Democratic Tradition in America* (New York: Farrar and Rinehart, 1941), *passim*.

51. Gilbert Seldes, *Mainland* (New York: Scribner's, 1936), pp. 13, 122; Harold Stearns, *America: A Re-appraisal* (New York: Hillman-Curl, 1937), p. 11.

52. G. S. Counts, *The Schools Can Teach Democracy* (New York: John Day, 1939), pp. 15–16; Counts, *The Prospects of American Democracy* (New York: John Day, 1938), Chap. 11; W. C. Bagley in B. F. Pittenger, *Indoctrination for American Democracy* (New York: Macmillan, 1941), pp. ix–xi, 110; Claude Wickard to Reinhold Niebuhr, *et al.*, January 18, 1941, General Files, Office of the Secretary, Department of Agriculture, NA, RG 16.

53. Robert S. Lynd, *Knowledge for What?* (Princeton: Princeton University Press, 1939), p. 87.

54. *Nation*, CL (May 18, 1940), 618–623; *The Secret Diary of Harold L. Ickes: The Lowering Clouds, 1939–1941* (New York: Simon and Schuster, 1954), p. 209.

55. Archibald MacLeish, *The Irresponsibles: A Declaration* (New York: Duell, Sloan and Pearce, 1940), pp. 3–4, 9, 20–21.

56. *New Republic*, CII (June 10, 1940), 789–790.

57. See W. G. Carleton, "American Intellectuals and American Democracy," *Antioch Review*, XIX (Summer 1959), 185–204; C. E. Eisinger, *Fiction of the Forties* (Chicago: University of Chicago Press, 1963), pp. 8ff.

58. Max Lerner, *Ideas for the Ice Age* (New York: Viking, 1941), pp. 10–11, 15; Harold J. Laski, "The Duty of the Intellectual Now," *Harper's Magazine*, CLXXX (December 1939), 70–79; and Laski, "Letter to MacLeish," *New Republic*, CIII (September 2, 1940), 299–300. See also Frankfurter to Laski, June 20, 1940, General Correspondence Box 22, Frankfurter Papers.

59. Edmund Wilson, "Archibald MacLeish and 'the Word,'" *New Republic*, CIII (July 1, 1940), 30–32.

60. Rexford G. Tugwell, "The Crisis of Freedom," *Common Sense*, X (October 1941), 291–295.

61. *New Republic*, CV (December 15, 1941), 811.

CHAPTER EIGHT: *The Wave of the Future*

1. Anne Morrow Lindbergh, *The Wave of the Future: A Confession of Faith* (New York: Harcourt, Brace, 1940), pp. 39 and *passim*.
2. *PPAFDR*, IX, 643.
3. Henry R. Luce, *The American Century* (New York: Farrar and Rinehart, 1941), pp. 25ff.
4. *Ibid.*, p. 39.
5. Henry A. Wallace, "The Price of a Free World Victory" (1942), in Russell Lord, ed., *Democracy Reborn* (New York: Reynal and Hitchcock, 1944), p. 193.
6. Wendell L. Willkie, *One World* (New York: Simon and Schuster, 1943), p. 190.
7. *Ibid.*, p. 204.
8. *PPAFDR*, IX, 672.
9. *Ibid.*, X, 314–315.
10. *Ibid.*, XII, 368.
11. Carl Becker, *How New Will the Better World Be?* (New York: Knopf, 1944), Chaps. 1–2, pp. 63ff.
12. *PPAFDR*, X, 65.
13. Archibald MacLeish, "Defeatists and Divisionists in U.S. Also Our Chief Enemies" (Address . . . Freedom House, March 19, 1942), p. 1; MacLeish, "Address . . . American Society of Newspaper Editors in NYC, April 17, 1942," pp. 3, 5, 7–8; MacLeish, "Address . . . Associated Press Annual Luncheon, April 20, 1942," p. 12. Printed or mimeographed text of above speeches on file in the Rare Book Room of the Library of Congress.
14. See Robert Sherwood, *Roosevelt and Hopkins* (New York: Harper, 1948), p. 438; Roosevelt to Russell C. Leffingwell, March 16, 1942, in Elliott Roosevelt, ed., *F.D.R.: His Personal Letters, 1928–1945* (New York: Duell, Sloan and Pearce, 1950), II, 1298–1299; A. R. Ogden, *The Dies Committee* (Washington: Catholic University of America Press, 1945), Chap. 1, p. 152.
15. *U.S. Statutes at Large*, LIV, 670–671. See also Zechariah Chafee, Jr., *Free Speech in the United States* (Cambridge, Mass.: Harvard University Press, 1948), pp. 440ff.
16. *Commercial and Financial Chronicle*, CL (June 29, 1940), 4027–4029; CLI (August 3, 1940), 591–593. See also Ekirch, *Civilian and the Military*, pp. 256ff.
17. See Morton Grodzins, *Americans Betrayed* (Chicago: University of Chicago Press, 1949), *passim*.
18. See Mulford Sibley and Philip Jacob, *Conscription of Conscience* (Ithaca: Cornell University Press, 1952), pp. 332ff.
19. See Burns, *Roosevelt: The Lion and the Fox*, p. 463; Rossiter, *American Presidency*, pp. 115–116.

20. "Economic Concentration and World War II: Report of the Smaller War Plants Corporation," *Senate Doc. No. 206*, 79th Cong., 2nd Sess. (Washington: Government Printing Office, 1946), pp. vii–viii and *passim*.

21. Harold Laski, *Liberty in the Modern State* (rev. ed., New York: Viking, 1949), p. 20.

22. Friedrich Hayek, *The Road to Serfdom* (Chicago: University of Chicago Press, 1944), pp. 2, 13, 71, 206, 215. See also Elliott V. Bell, "Planned Economy—and/or Democracy," *New York Times Magazine* (November 23, 1941), pp. 5, 19, 21; Malcolm Cowley, "The End of the New Deal," *New Republic*, cviii (May 31, 1943), 729–732; John T. Flynn, *As We Go Marching* (Garden City: Doubleday Doran, 1944), *passim*.

23. *PPAFDR*, xii, 569–575.

24. *Ibid.*, xii, 555, 558.

25. *Ibid.*, xii, 572–573; xiii, 41.

26. *Ibid.*, xiii, 291.

27. Sherwood, *Roosevelt and Hopkins*, p. 870.

28. See William L. Neumann, *After Victory: Churchill, Roosevelt, Stalin and the Making of the Peace* (New York: Harper and Row, 1967); Willard Range, *Franklin D. Roosevelt's World Order* (Athens: University of Georgia Press, 1959), *passim*.

29. Chester Bowles, "What's Wrong with the Isolationists," *Common Sense*, x (December 1941), 377.

30. Elliott Roosevelt, *As He Saw It* (New York: Duell, Sloan and Pearce, 1946), pp. 247–259. D. F. Fleming, *The Cold War and Its Origins* (Garden City: Doubleday, 1961), i, 265ff.; Richard N. Current, "The United States and 'Collective Security,'" in Alexander DeConde, ed., *Isolation and Security* (Durham: Duke University Press, 1957), p. 55.

31. See Myrdal, *American Dilemma*, Chaps. 19, 45.

32. Conkin, *New Deal*, p. 103.

33. Harold Laski, *The American Democracy* (New York: Viking, 1948), p. 81; Laski, *The American Presidency* (New York: Harper, 1940), p. 251.

34. See the respective analyses in Herman P. Miller, *Rich Man, Poor Man* (New York: Crowell, 1964); Gabriel Kolko, *Wealth and Power in America* (New York: Praeger, 1962), *passim*.

35. See the varying estimates in Robinson, *The Roosevelt Leadership, 1933–1945*, p. 376; Amaury de Riencourt, *The Coming Caesars* (New York: Coward-McCann, 1957), Chap. 17; Carl Degler, *Out of Our Past: The Forces That Shaped Modern America* (New York: Harper, 1959), pp. 412ff.

Index

Index

Index

Index

Index

Ford, James W., 89
Ford, Worthington C., 86, 89, 102, 228
Foreign Policy Association, 112
Fortune, 246
Forum, 33
Fosdick, Harry Emerson, 57
Foster, William Trufant, 52
Foster, William Z., 62, 88–89
Four Arts Projects, WPA, 151–172. *See also* Federal Art, Music, Theatre, Writers' Projects.
Four Freedoms, 244, 249–250, 259–260
Fourteen Points, 244, 249
Franco, Francisco, 218–221
Frank, Jerome, 95, 227
Frank, Waldo, 62, 89
Frankenstein, Alfred, 174
Frankfurter, Felix, 27–28, 75, 81, 95, 135
Freedom and Culture (Dewey), 239
Freeman, 193
Freeman, Joseph, 62
Frontier concept, 83–84
Future Comes, The (Beard), 132

Gannett, Frank, 200
Gannett, Lewis, 88
Garner, John Nance, 81, 89
Gay Reformer, The (Hallgren), 103
Gellhorn, Martha, 175
General Electric Company, 53
General Theory of Employment, Interest and Money, The (Keynes), 139
Geneva Disarmament Conference, 209–210, 212
George, Henry, 193
German-American Bund, 187
Gershwin, George, 88
Gifford, Walter S., 42
Glass, Carter, 81
Godkin Lectures, 195
Goebbels, Joseph Paul, 205
Golden Boy (Odets), 175
Good Neighbor policy, 211–212
Grapes of Wrath (Steinbeck), 175

Great Society, 10, 22
Green, William, 55
Greenwich Village, 12
Growth and Decadence of Constitutional Government, The (Smith), 18

Hacker, Louis M., 180
Hallgren, Mauritz A., 66, 103, 188–189, 206, 226
Harding, Warren G., 8, 39, 60, 109, 111
Harper's Magazine, 32, 44, 64, 98, 226
Harriman, Henry I., 54–55
Harvard *Crimson*, 75
Harvard University, 12–13, 51, 64, 73, 75, 95, 195, 206
Hawley-Smoot tariff, 42
Hayek, Friedrich, 257
Hays, Arthur Garfield, 191
Hazlitt, Henry, 33, 88
Hegel, G. W. F., 194
Hellman, Lillian, 222
Hemingway, Ernest, 208, 219–220, 222
Henry Street settlement house, 31
Hicks, Granville, 89
Hillman, Sidney, 56
Hindus, Maurice, 62
Historical Records Survey, WPA, 169–171
History of the American People (Wilson), 5
Hitler, Adolf, 63, 102, 106, 180, 194, 199, 209–210, 218, 224–228, 230, 233–235, 241, 244
Hofstadter, Richard, 107
Holmes, John Haynes, 88, 195–196, 221, 226, 234
Holmes, Oliver Wendell, Jr., 205
Holy Alliance, 13
Hook, Sidney, 89, 238
Hoover, Herbert Clark: early career and presidency, 8, 11, 24, 26, 32, 35, 38–50, 53, 65; and Liberty League, 191–193; and New Deal, 72–76, 81–90, 111, 119, 129

Index

Index

Index

Index

Index

A NOTE ON THE AUTHOR

ARTHUR A. EKIRCH, JR., was born in New York City and studied at Dartmouth College and Columbia University. His other books include *The Idea of Progress in America, The Decline of American Liberalism, The Civilian and the Military, Man and Nature in America, The American Democratic Tradition*, and *Ideas, Ideals, and American Diplomacy.* For many years Mr. Ekirch taught history at the American University in Washington, D.C. He is now Professor of History at the State University of New York at Albany, and lives with his wife, Dorothy, in Delmar, New York.